FOWL LANGUAGE
WELCOME TO PARENTING

BRIAN GORDON

Andrews McMeel
Publishing®
a division of Andrews McMeel Universal

For my ducklings, Max and Phoebe

INTRODUCTION

My wife and I were beside ourselves with excitement in the weeks leading up to the birth of our first child. We had read all the parenting books, taken all the classes, and we were ready!

Or so we thought.

Months later, as I paced my son's room, bouncing an incon-solable bundle of screaming joy at 4 a.m., I remember thinking that this crap was WAY less magical than I had been promised.

For all we had learned about burping and breastfeeding, there were no classes to help us deal with all the sleeplessness, tedium, and crushing self-doubt that also came home with us from the nursery.

As I started to trade notes with other parents, my deepest fears were soon realized. We were the only parents with a hard baby. We were the only ones who really sucked at this. Everyone else seemed to be having a grand time with their perfect little ones.

It was only after I started posting cartoons about my fears and frustrations that I realized I in fact wasn't alone. Turns out, a lot of people are big fat liars. No one wants to admit their kid isn't perfect or that they don't always love being a parent. No one wants to admit they're falling apart.

Once you cut through the bullshit, you soon realize that every parent is a little scared. No one really knows what they're doing. Turns out, all of us (yes, even you, big fat liars) are just kind of making it up as we go along.

My hope is that this little collection of cartoons will give a little comfort to any parent out there who feels a little frazzled at times. Hang in there, guys. You're not alone.

Seriously. You're *never* alone. Just try using the bathroom by yourself. I dare you.

— Brian Gordon, December 2015

BABIES

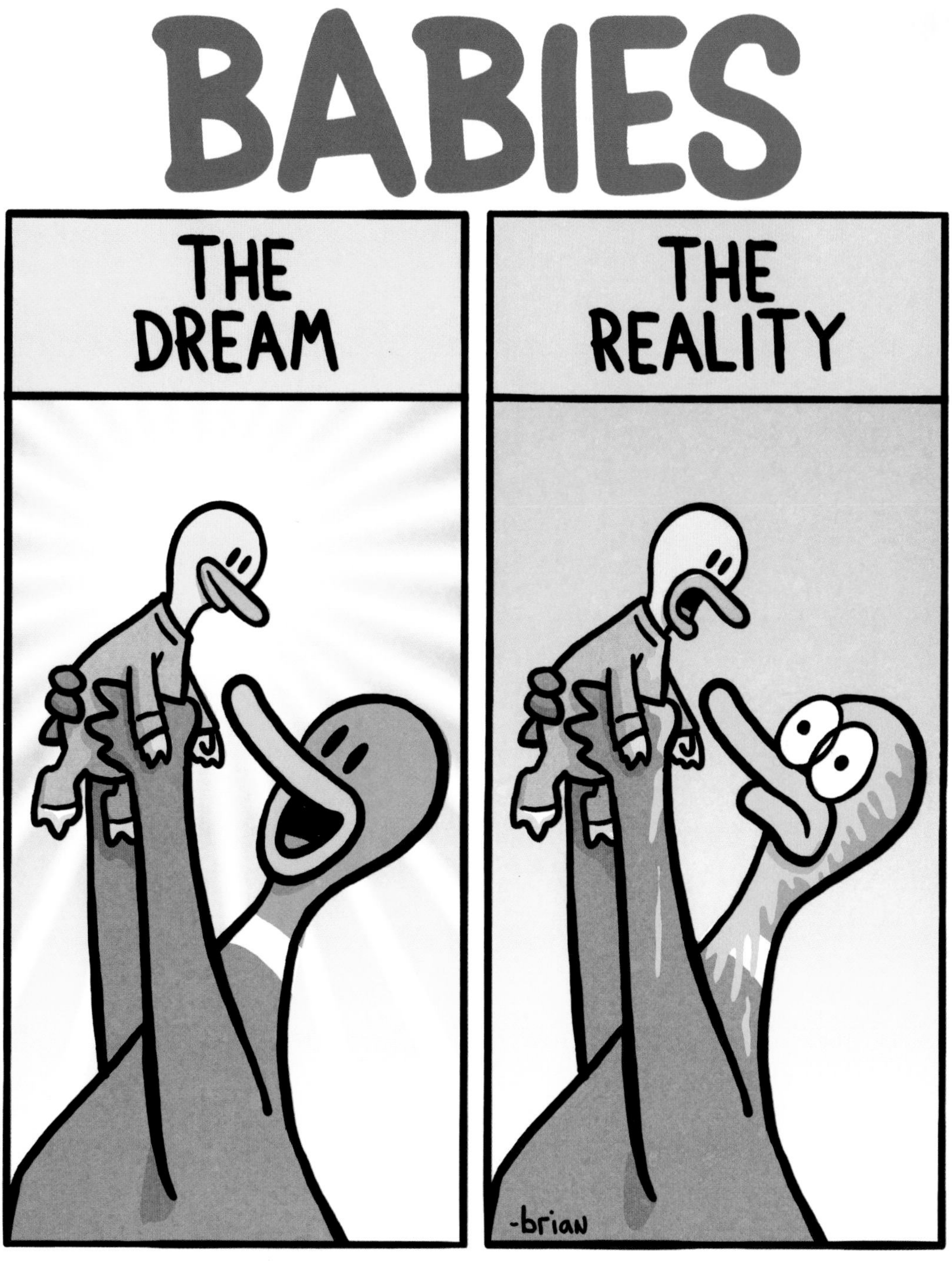
THE DREAM
THE REALITY
-brian

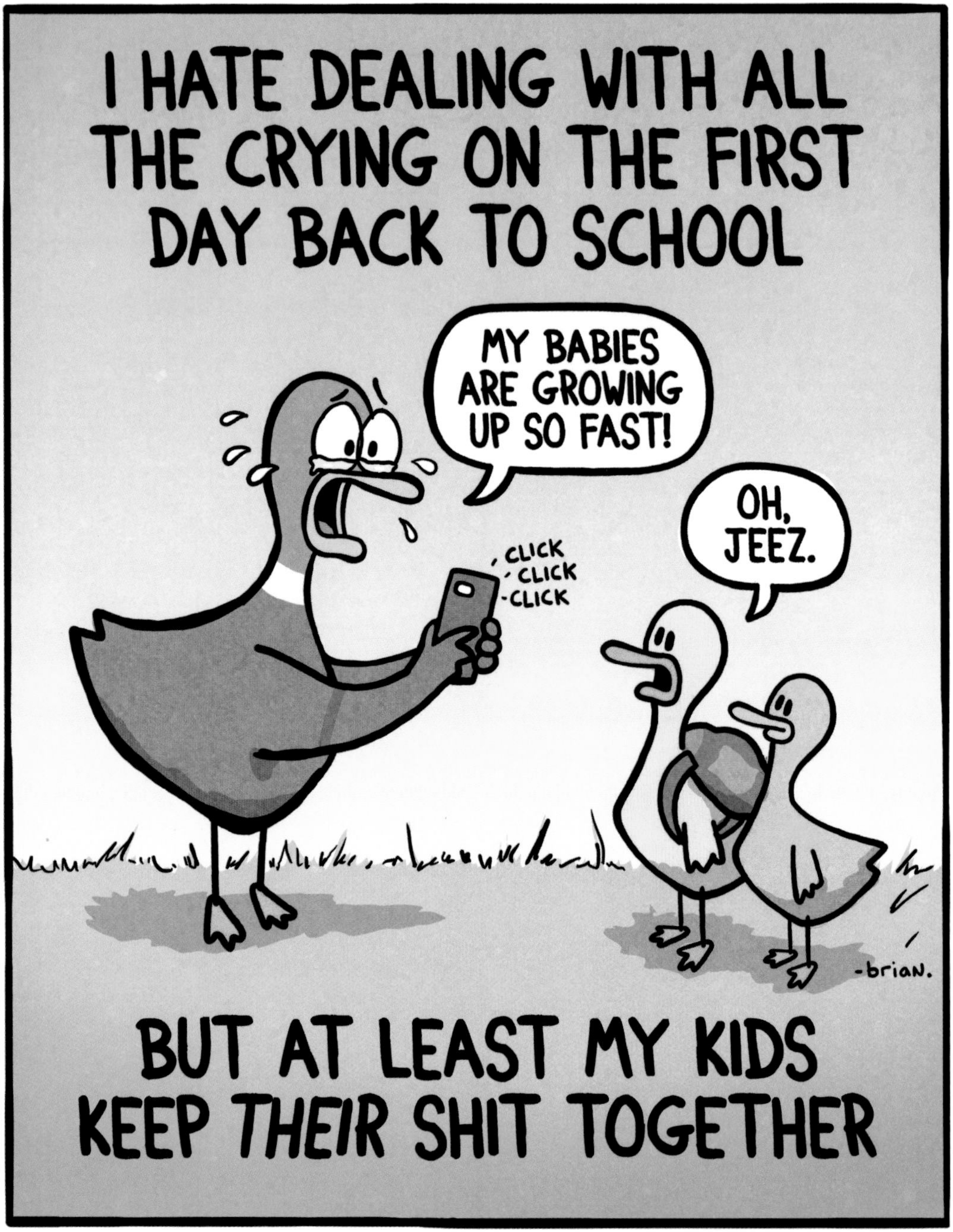
I HATE DEALING WITH ALL THE CRYING ON THE FIRST DAY BACK TO SCHOOL
MY BABIES ARE GROWING UP SO FAST!
CLICK CLICK CLICK
OH, JEEZ.
-brian.
BUT AT LEAST MY KIDS KEEP *THEIR* SHIT TOGETHER

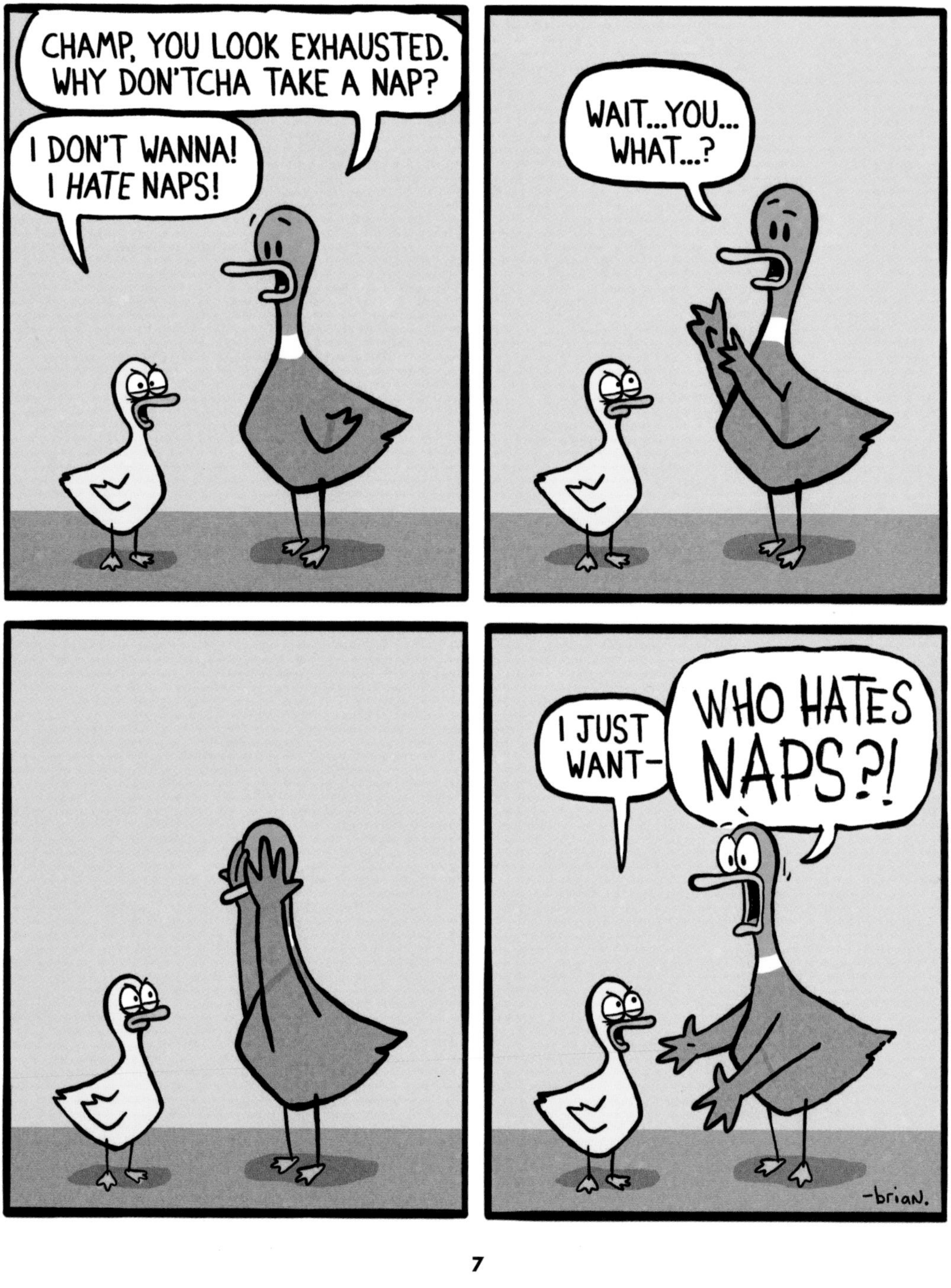
CHAMP, YOU LOOK EXHAUSTED. WHY DON'TCHA TAKE A NAP?
I DON'T WANNA! I *HATE* NAPS!
WAIT...YOU... WHAT...?
I JUST WANT-
WHO HATES NAPS?!
-brian.

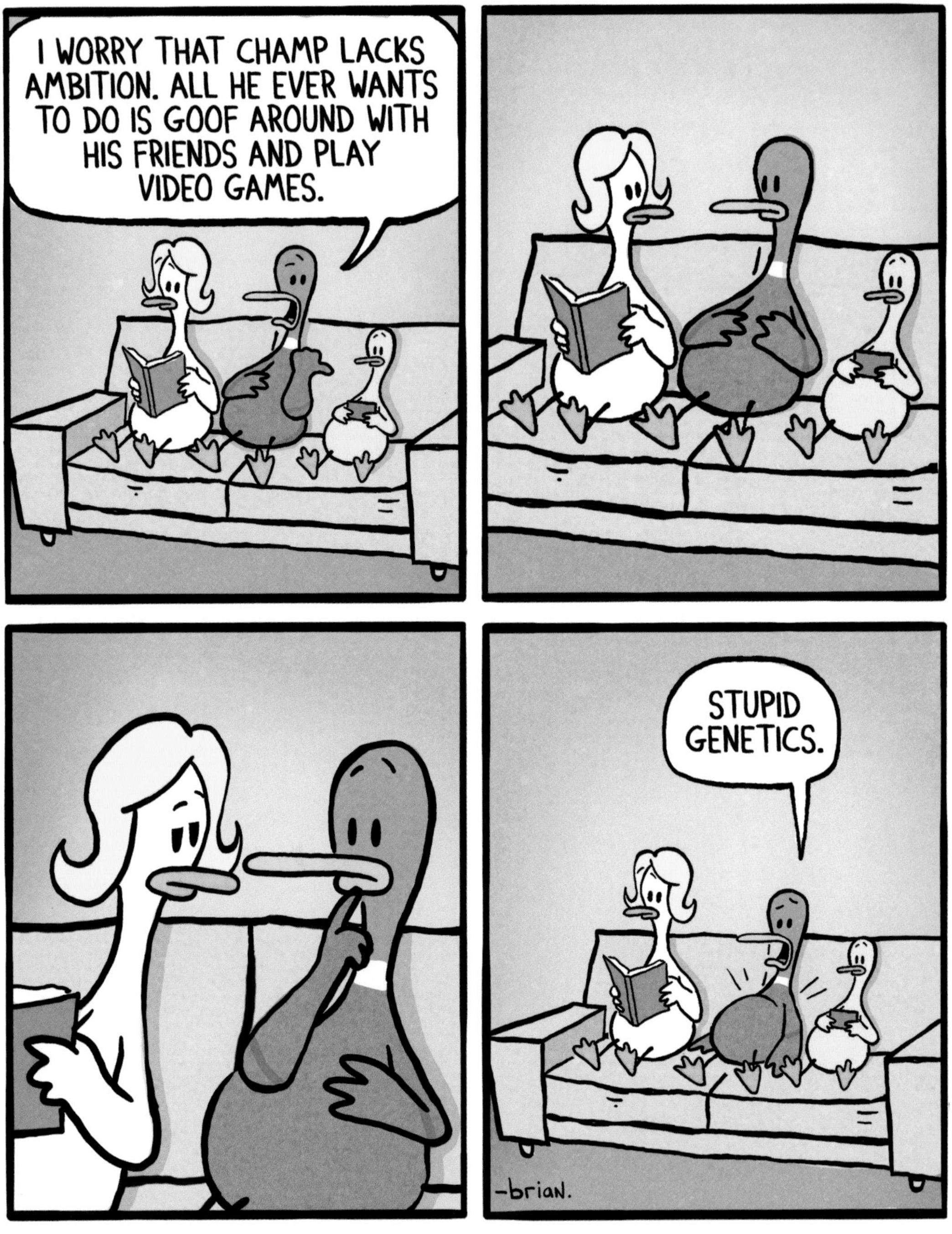
I WORRY THAT CHAMP LACKS AMBITION. ALL HE EVER WANTS TO DO IS GOOF AROUND WITH HIS FRIENDS AND PLAY VIDEO GAMES.
STUPID GENETICS.
-brian.

ANSWERING QUESTIONS FROM MY KID

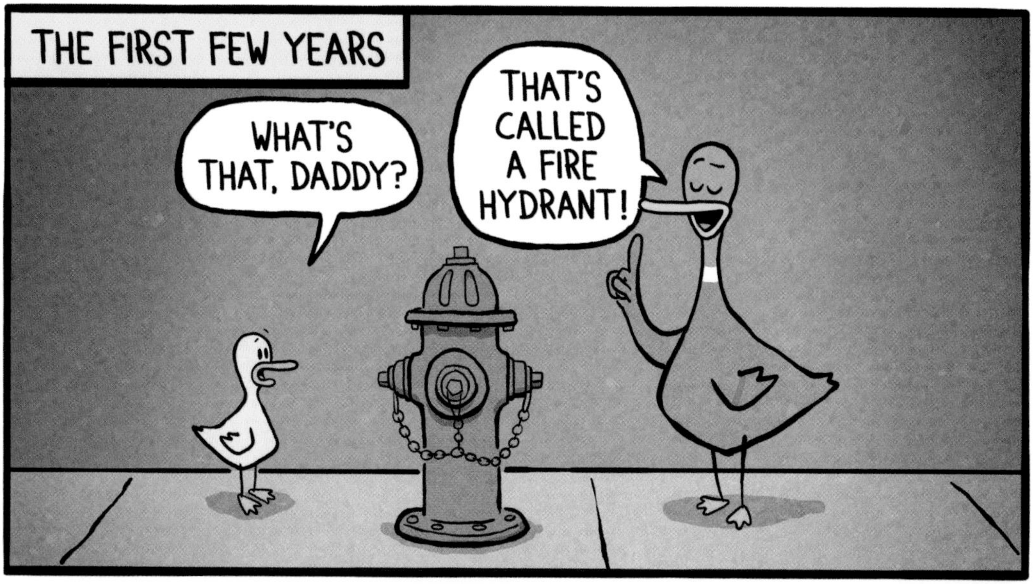
THE FIRST FEW YEARS
WHAT'S THAT, DADDY?
THAT'S CALLED A FIRE HYDRANT!

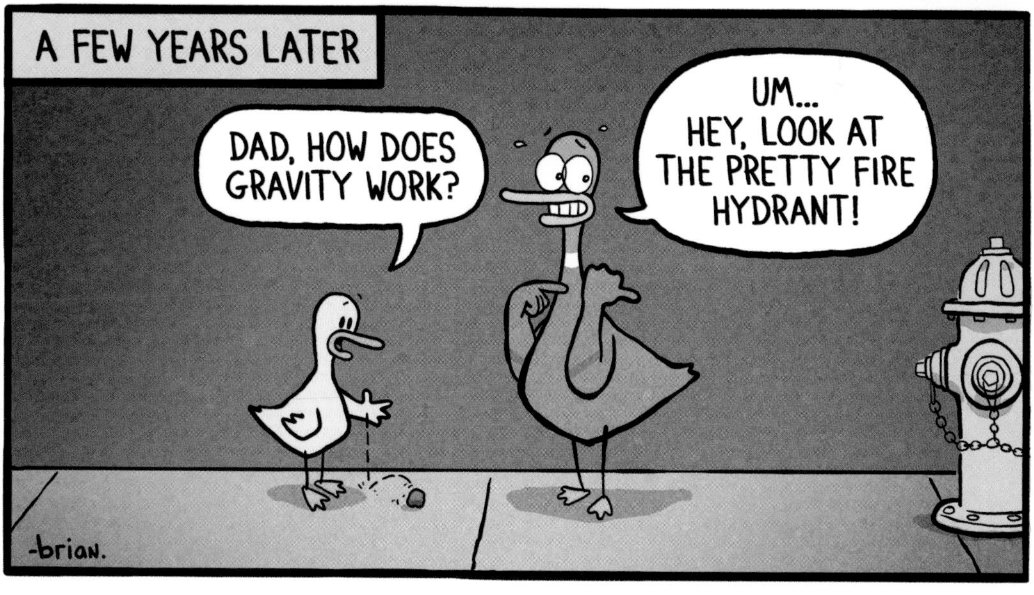
A FEW YEARS LATER
DAD, HOW DOES GRAVITY WORK?
UM... HEY, LOOK AT THE PRETTY FIRE HYDRANT!
-brian.

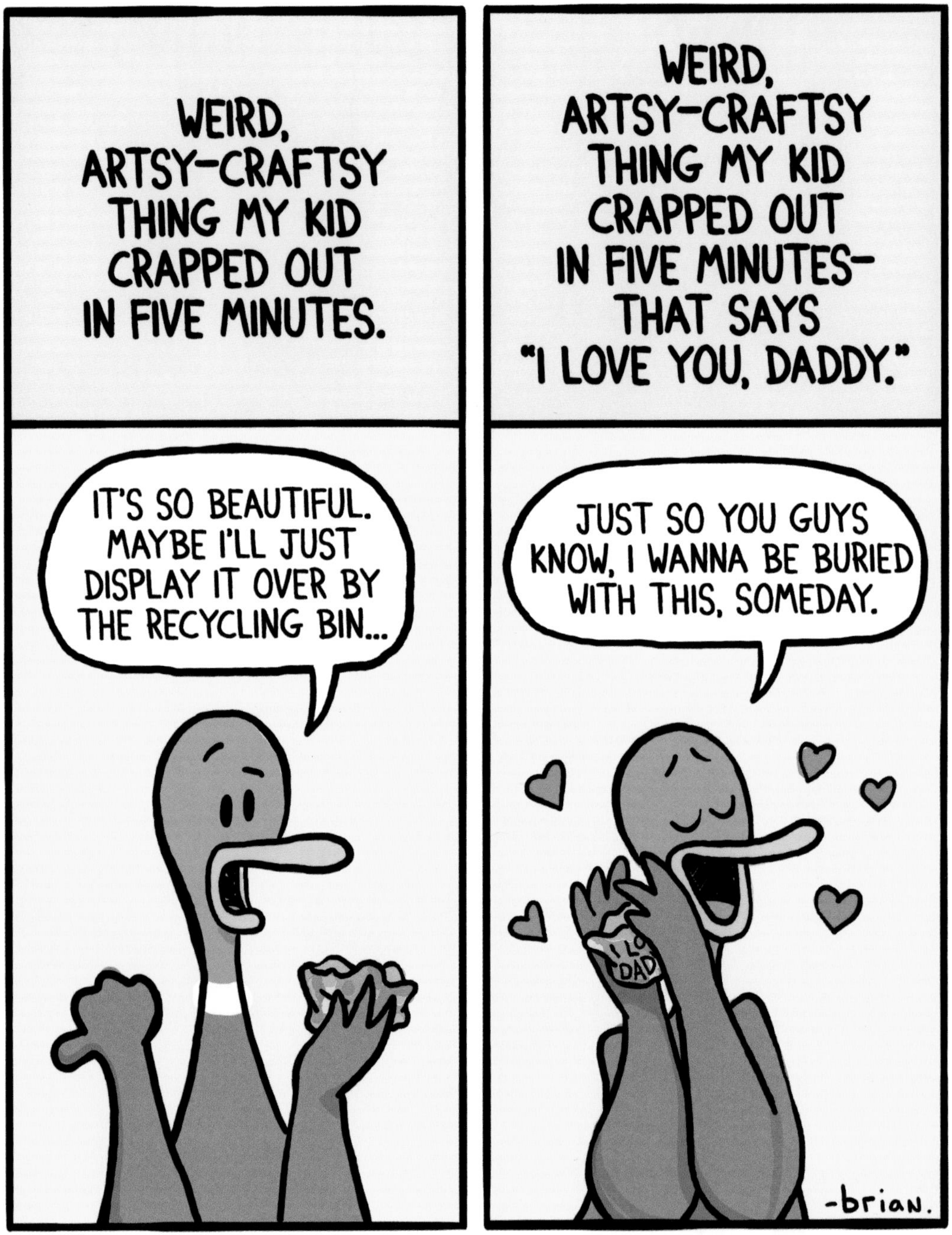
WEIRD, ARTSY-CRAFTSY THING MY KID CRAPPED OUT IN FIVE MINUTES.
IT'S SO BEAUTIFUL. MAYBE I'LL JUST DISPLAY IT OVER BY THE RECYCLING BIN...
WEIRD, ARTSY-CRAFTSY THING MY KID CRAPPED OUT IN FIVE MINUTES- THAT SAYS "I LOVE YOU, DADDY."
JUST SO YOU GUYS KNOW, I WANNA BE BURIED WITH THIS, SOMEDAY.
-brian.

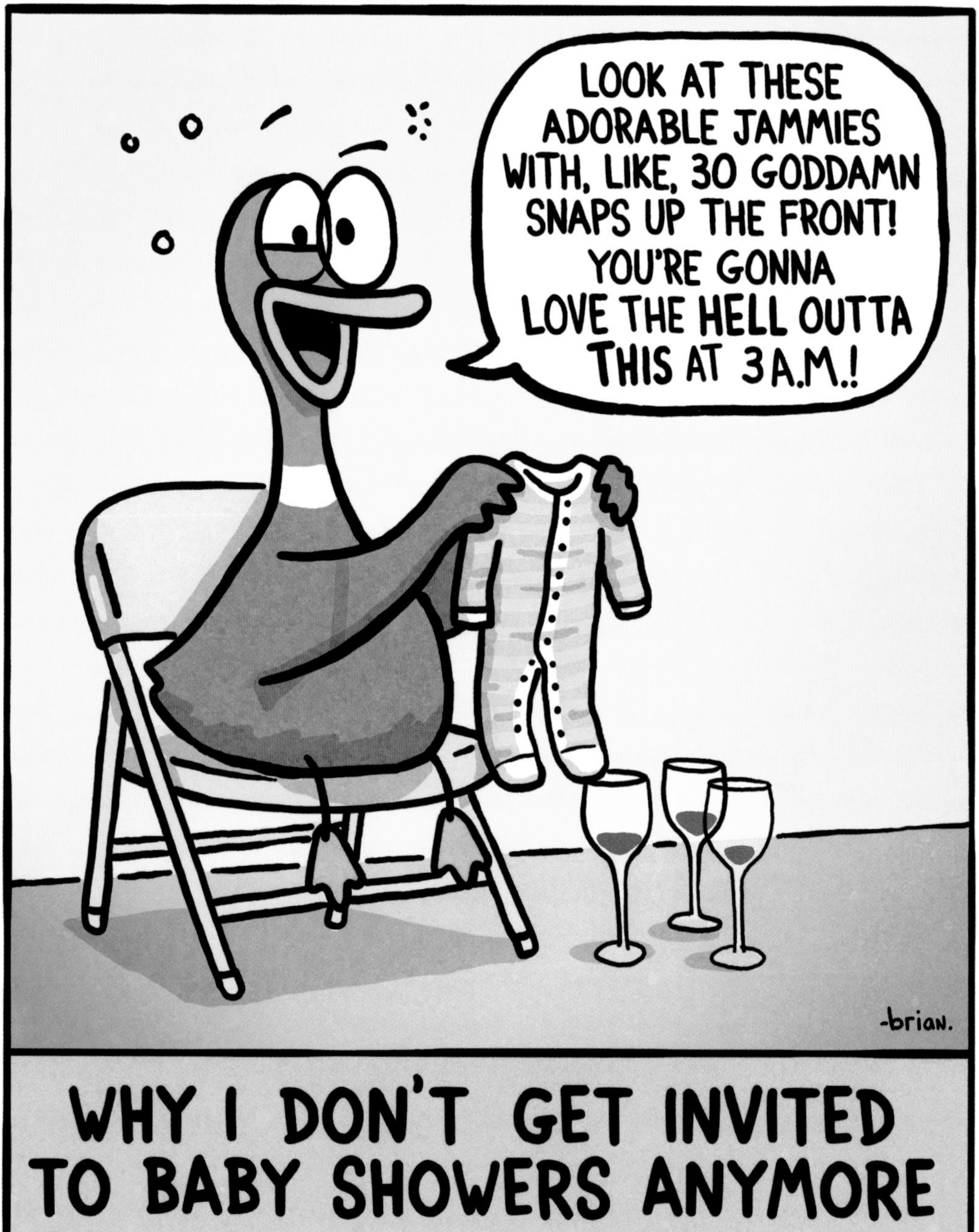
LOOK AT THESE ADORABLE JAMMIES WITH, LIKE, 30 GODDAMN SNAPS UP THE FRONT! YOU'RE GONNA LOVE THE HELL OUTTA THIS AT 3 A.M.!
-brian.

WHY I DON'T GET INVITED TO BABY SHOWERS ANYMORE

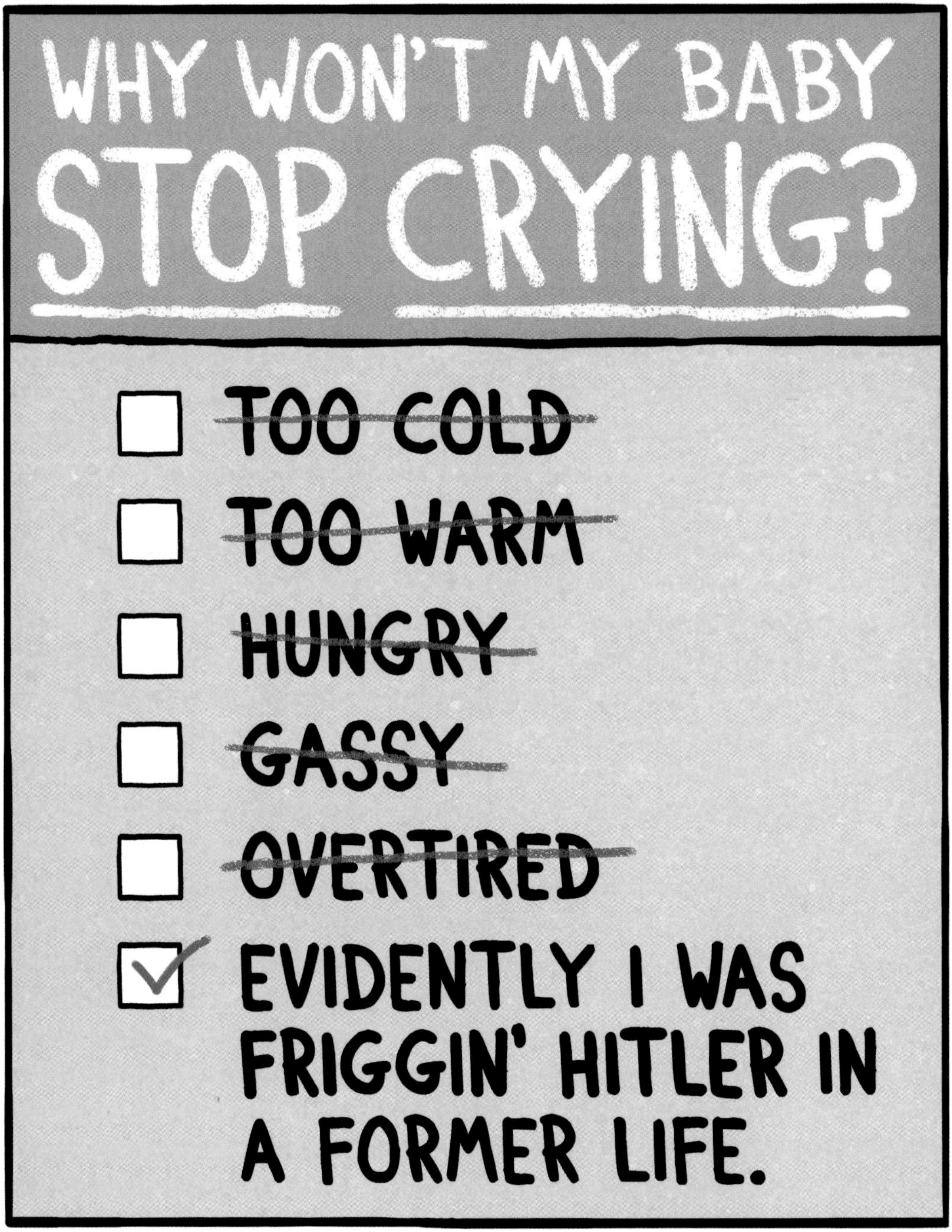
WHY WON'T MY BABY STOP CRYING?
~~TOO COLD~~
~~TOO WARM~~
~~HUNGRY~~
~~GASSY~~
~~OVERTIRED~~
EVIDENTLY I WAS FRIGGIN' HITLER IN A FORMER LIFE.

HOW I USED TO TALK TO MY KIDS
(BEFORE I LOST MY GODDAMN MIND)

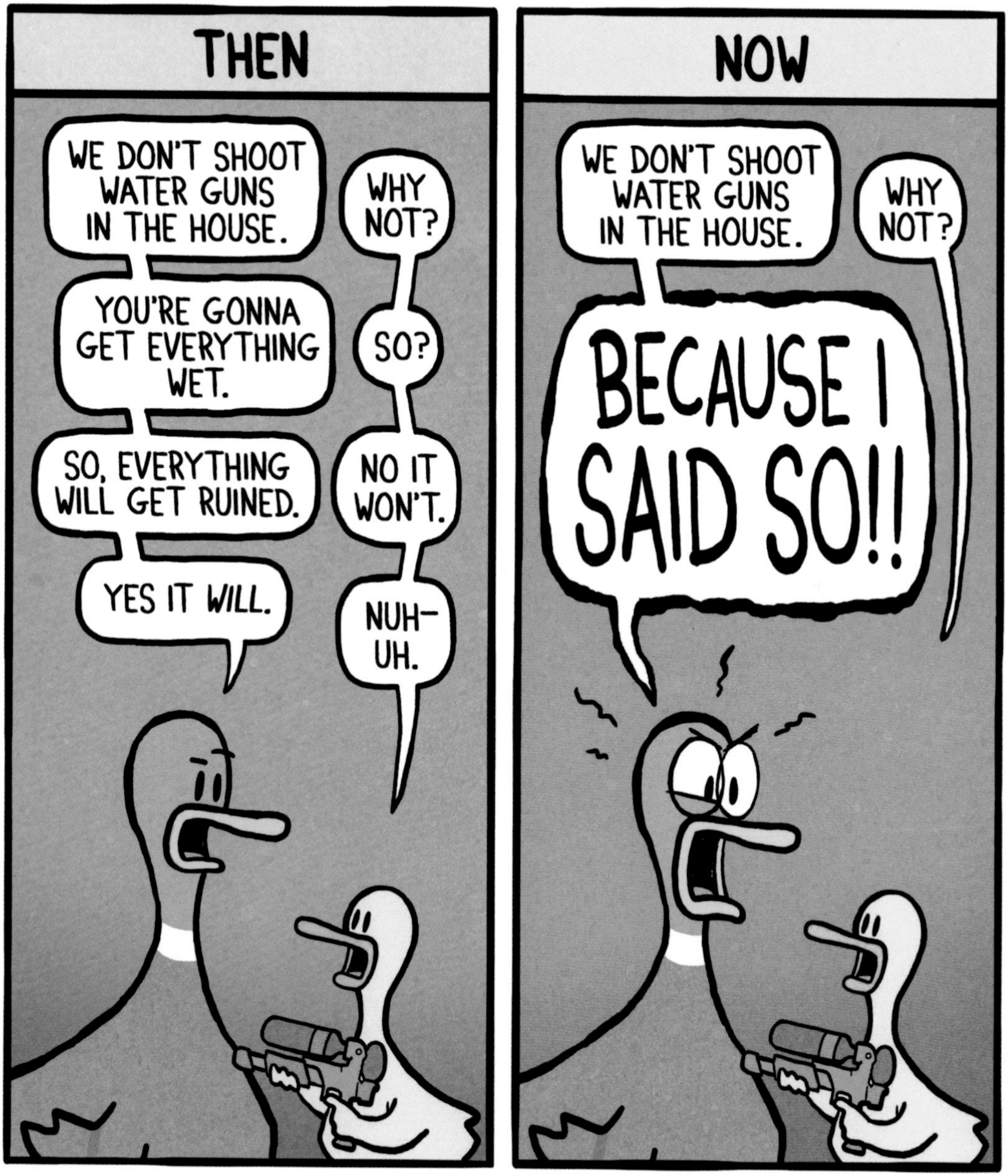
THEN
WE DON'T SHOOT WATER GUNS IN THE HOUSE.
WHY NOT?
YOU'RE GONNA GET EVERYTHING WET.
SO?
SO, EVERYTHING WILL GET RUINED.
NO IT WON'T.
YES IT WILL.
NUH-UH.
NOW
WE DON'T SHOOT WATER GUNS IN THE HOUSE.
WHY NOT?
BECAUSE I SAID SO!!

BEING SILLY WITH LITTLE KIDS

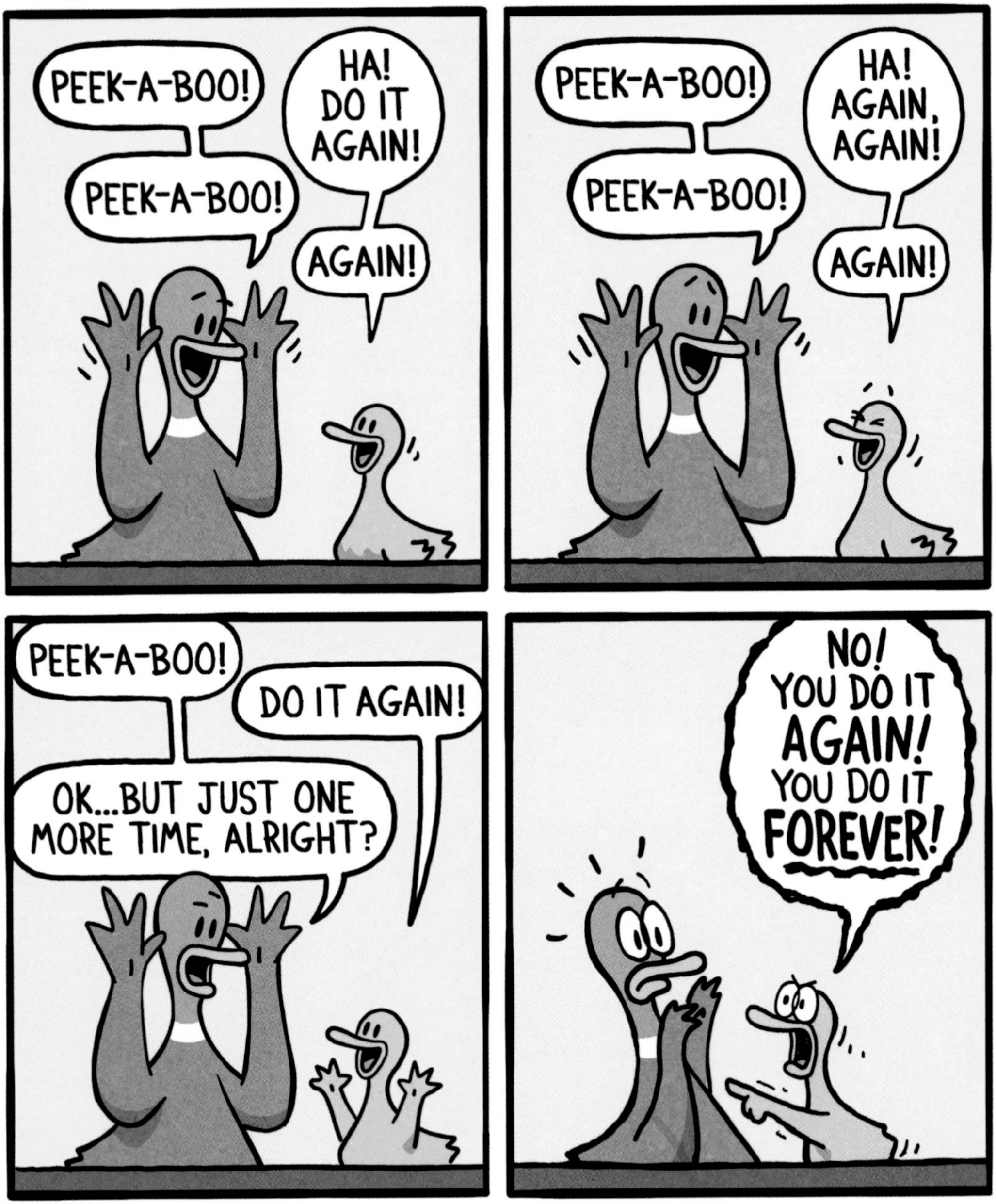
PEEK-A-BOO!
PEEK-A-BOO!
HA! DO IT AGAIN!
AGAIN!
PEEK-A-BOO!
PEEK-A-BOO!
HA! AGAIN, AGAIN!
AGAIN!
PEEK-A-BOO!
DO IT AGAIN!
OK...BUT JUST ONE MORE TIME, ALRIGHT?
NO! YOU DO IT AGAIN! YOU DO IT FOREVER!

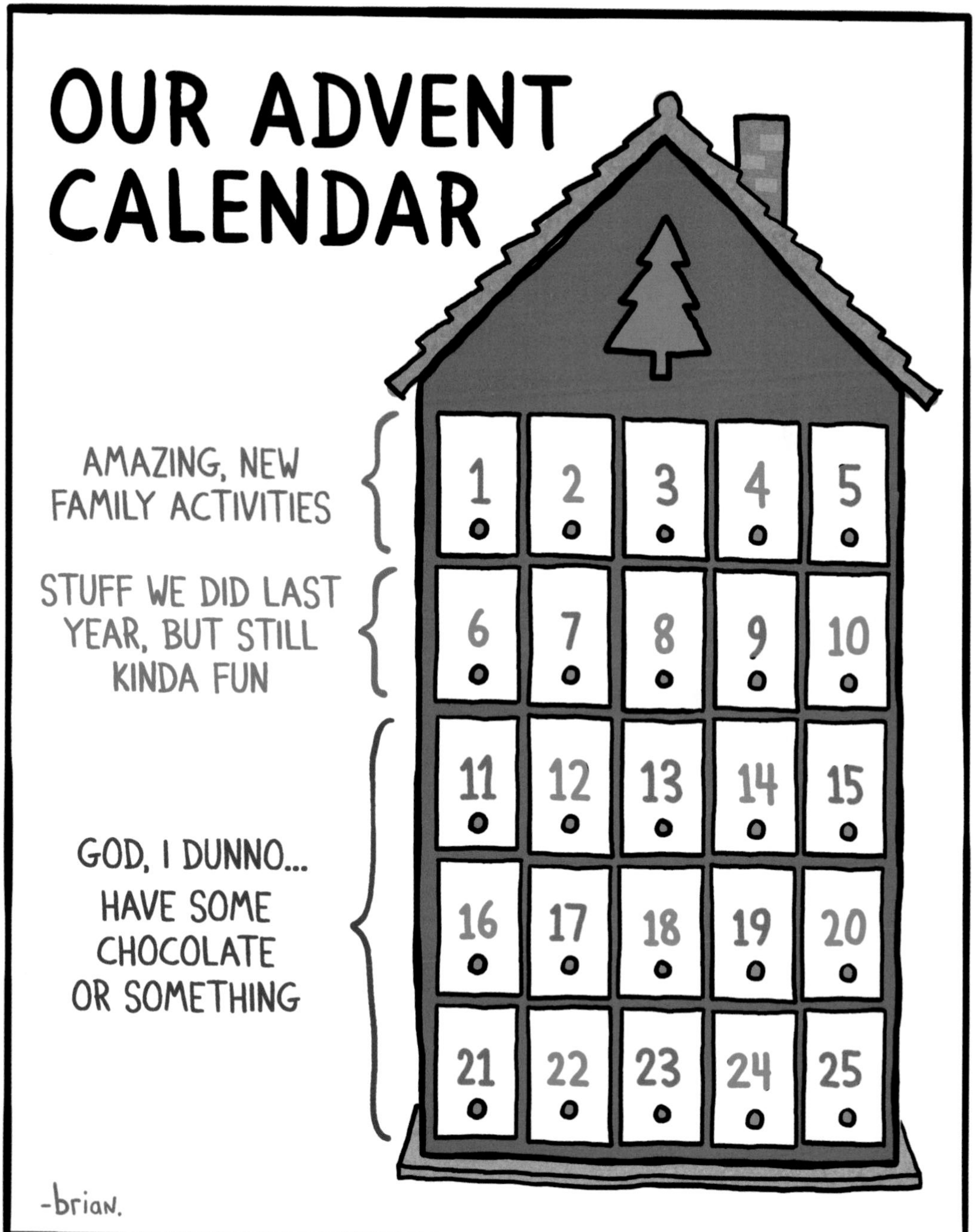
OUR ADVENT CALENDAR
AMAZING, NEW FAMILY ACTIVITIES
STUFF WE DID LAST YEAR, BUT STILL KINDA FUN
GOD, I DUNNO... HAVE SOME CHOCOLATE OR SOMETHING
1 2 3 4 5
6 7 8 9 10
11 12 13 14 15
16 17 18 19 20
21 22 23 24 25
-brian.

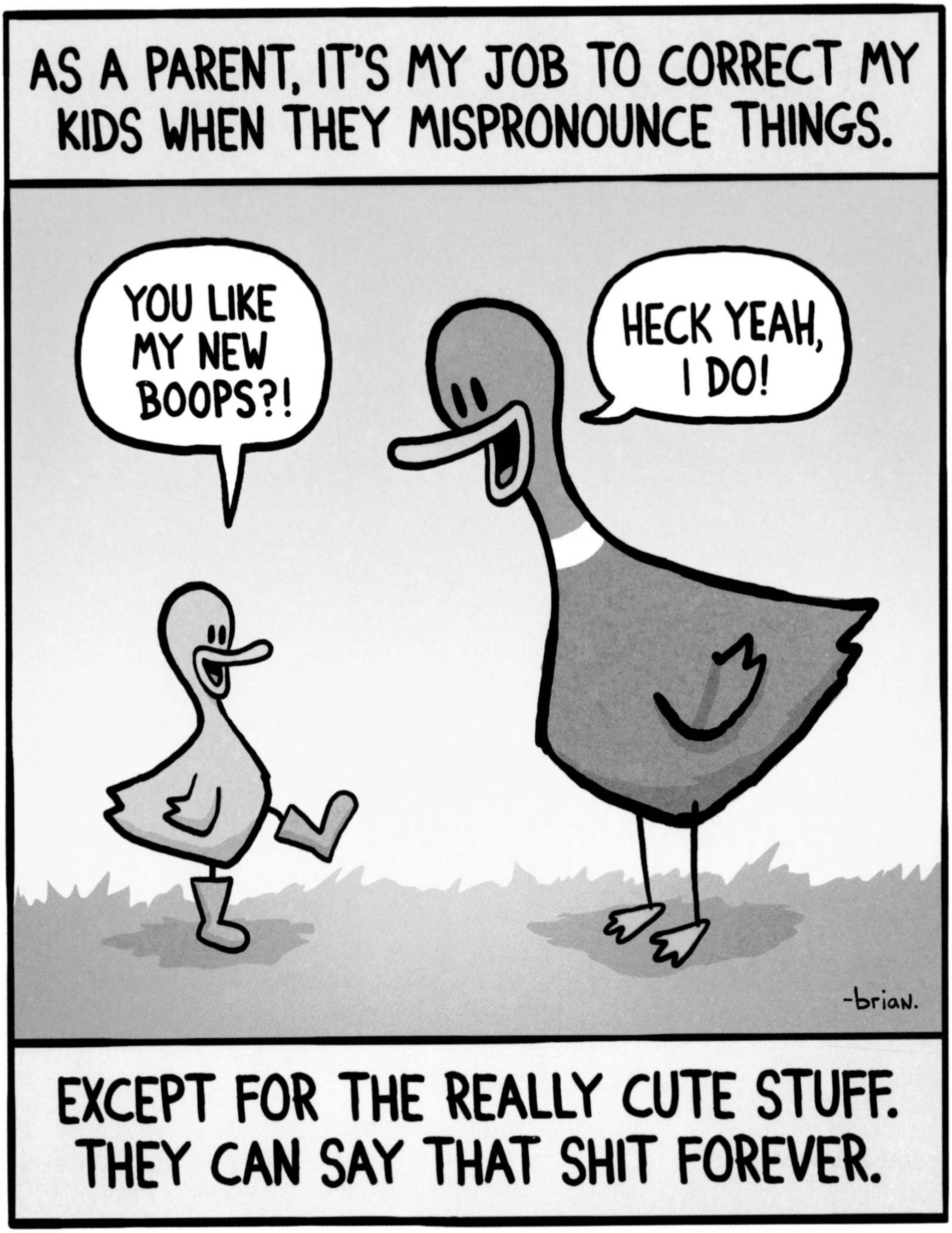
AS A PARENT, IT'S MY JOB TO CORRECT MY KIDS WHEN THEY MISPRONOUNCE THINGS.
YOU LIKE MY NEW BOOPS?!
HECK YEAH, I DO!
-brian.
EXCEPT FOR THE REALLY CUTE STUFF. THEY CAN SAY THAT SHIT FOREVER.

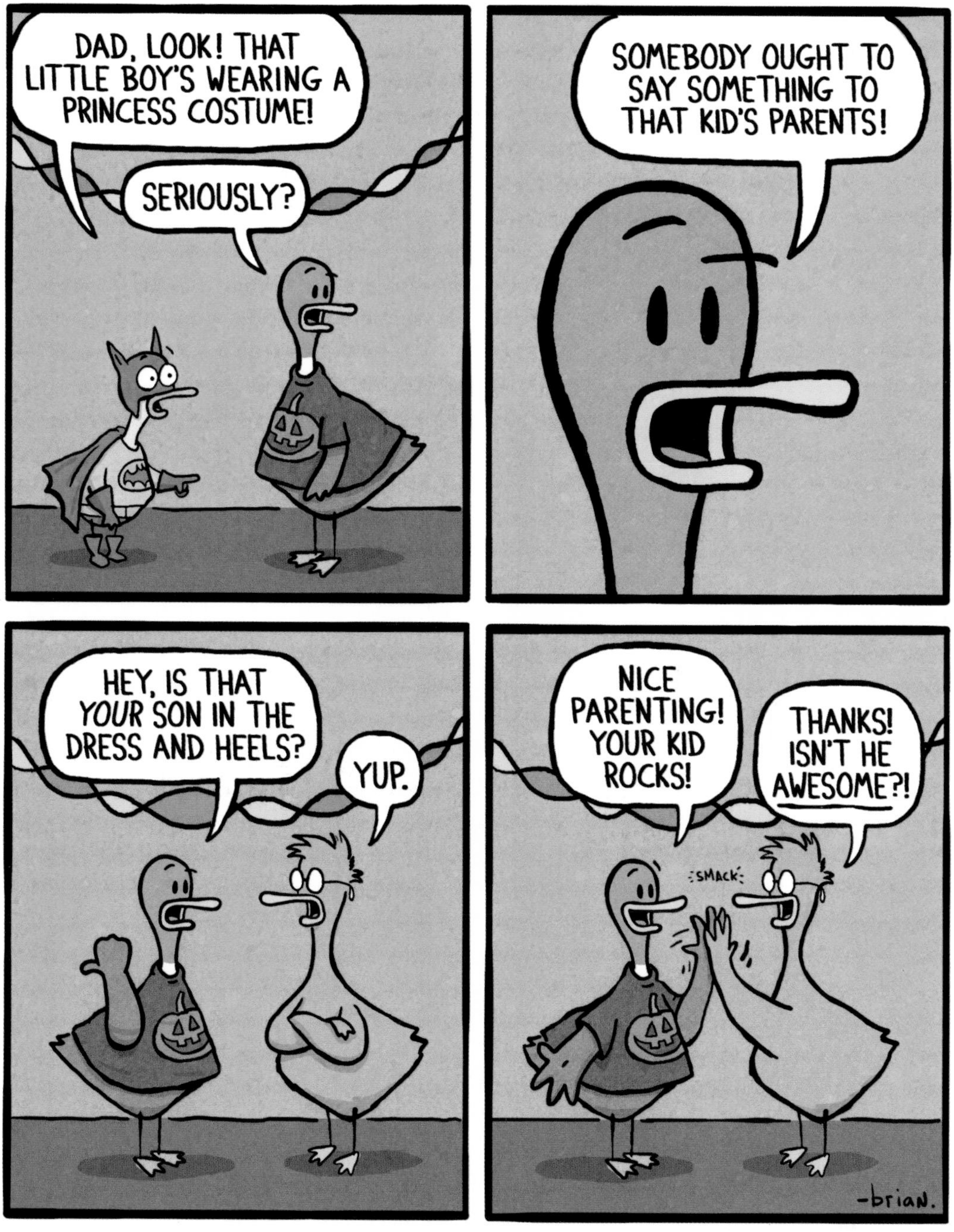
DAD, LOOK! THAT LITTLE BOY'S WEARING A PRINCESS COSTUME!
SERIOUSLY?
SOMEBODY OUGHT TO SAY SOMETHING TO THAT KID'S PARENTS!
HEY, IS THAT *YOUR* SON IN THE DRESS AND HEELS?
YUP.
NICE PARENTING! YOUR KID ROCKS!
THANKS! ISN'T HE AWESOME?!
SMACK
-brian.

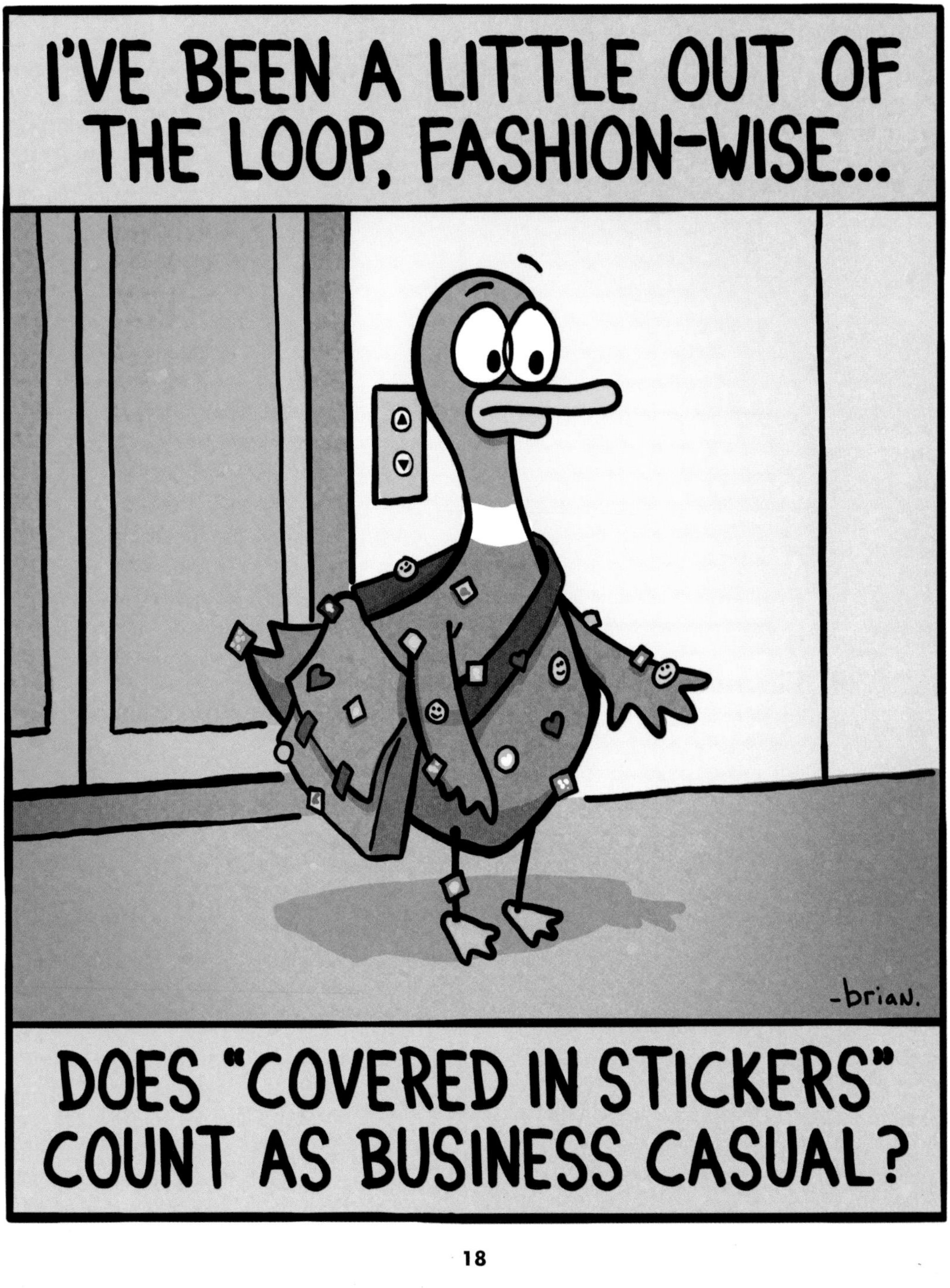
I'VE BEEN A LITTLE OUT OF THE LOOP, FASHION-WISE...
-brian.
DOES "COVERED IN STICKERS" COUNT AS BUSINESS CASUAL?

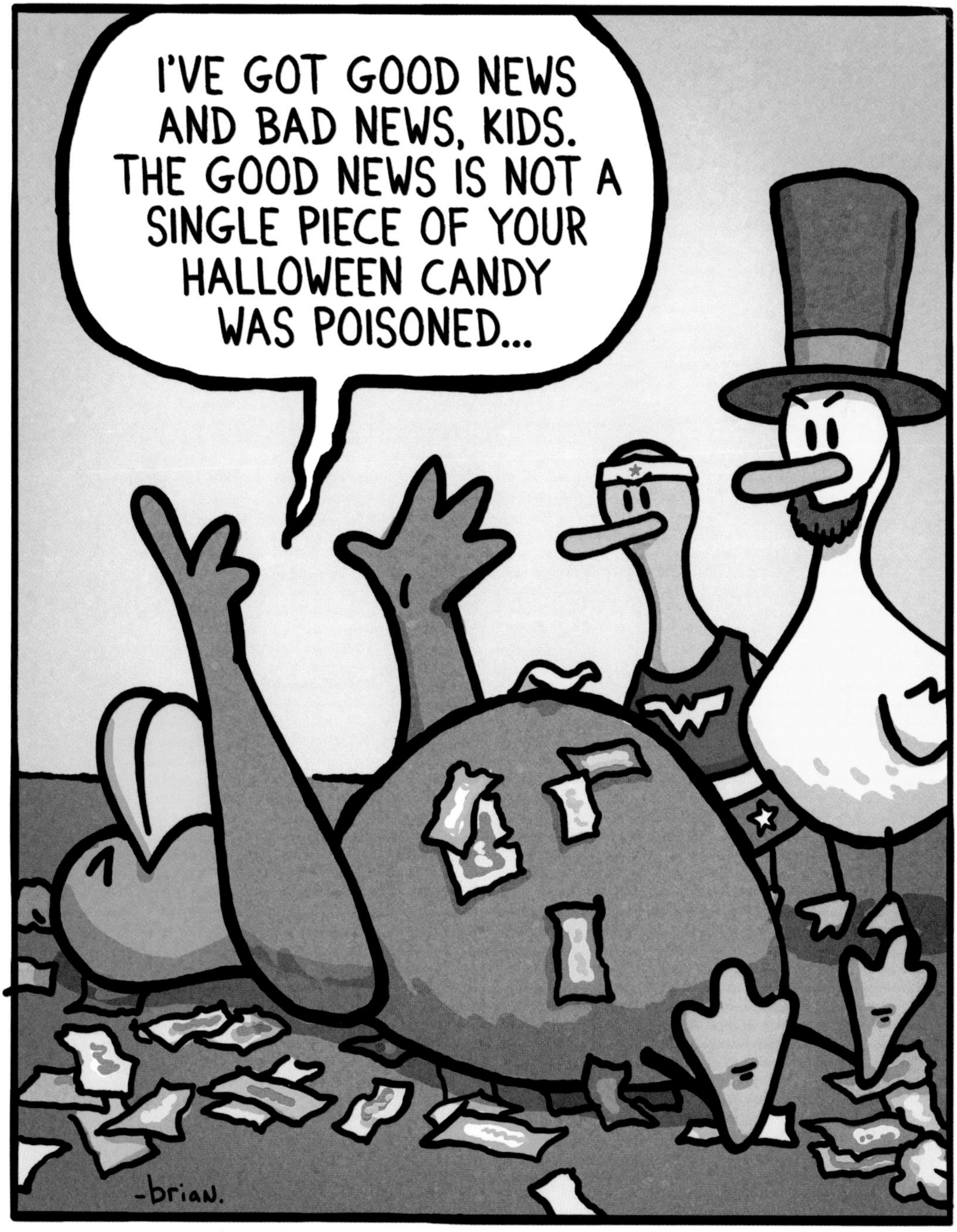
I'VE GOT GOOD NEWS AND BAD NEWS, KIDS. THE GOOD NEWS IS NOT A SINGLE PIECE OF YOUR HALLOWEEN CANDY WAS POISONED...
-brian.

CAR SAFETY FOR CHILDREN

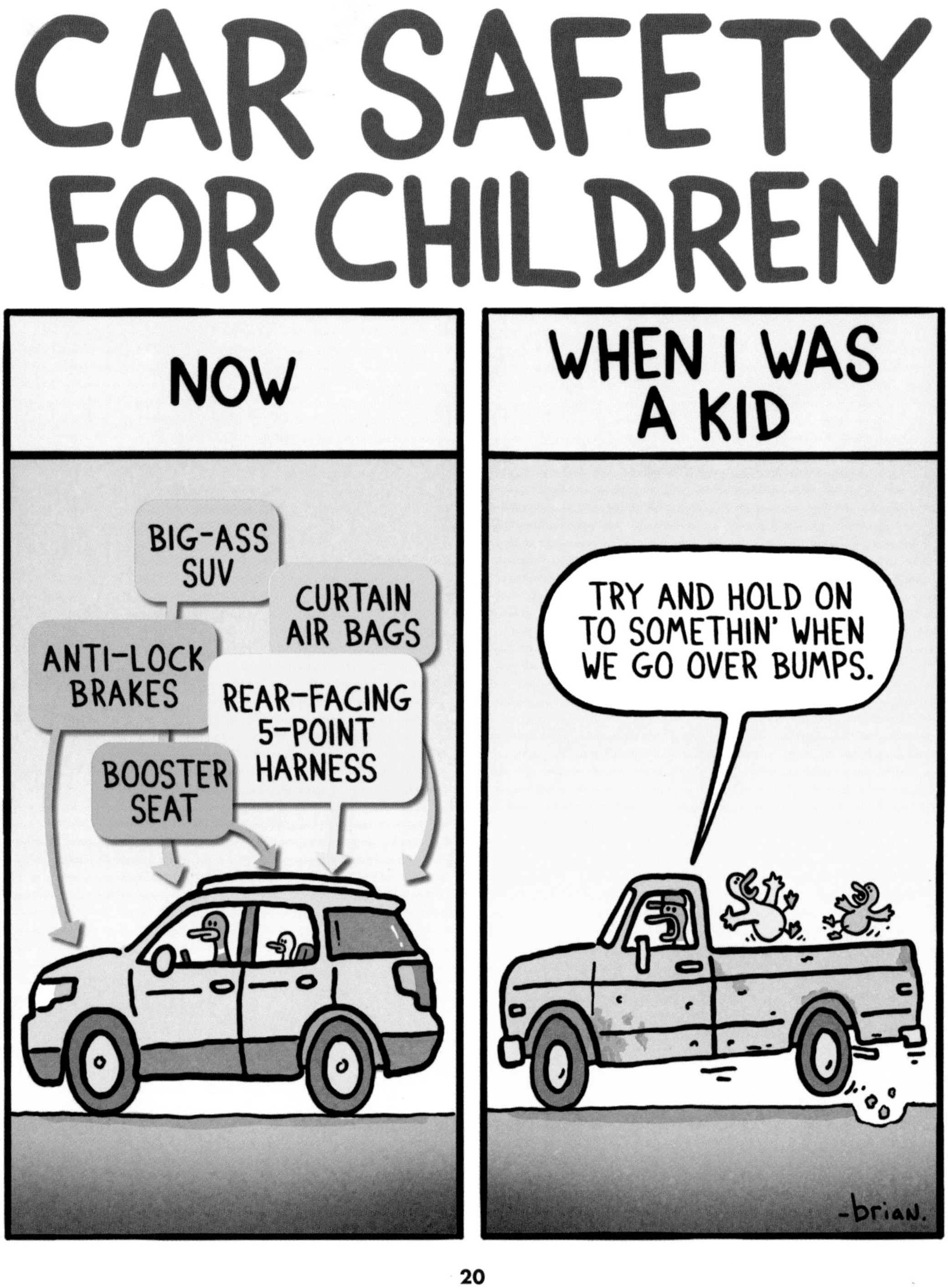
NOW
BIG-ASS SUV
CURTAIN AIR BAGS
ANTI-LOCK BRAKES
REAR-FACING 5-POINT HARNESS
BOOSTER SEAT
WHEN I WAS A KID
TRY AND HOLD ON TO SOMETHIN' WHEN WE GO OVER BUMPS.
-brian.

THE POST-CHRISTMAS CLEANUP

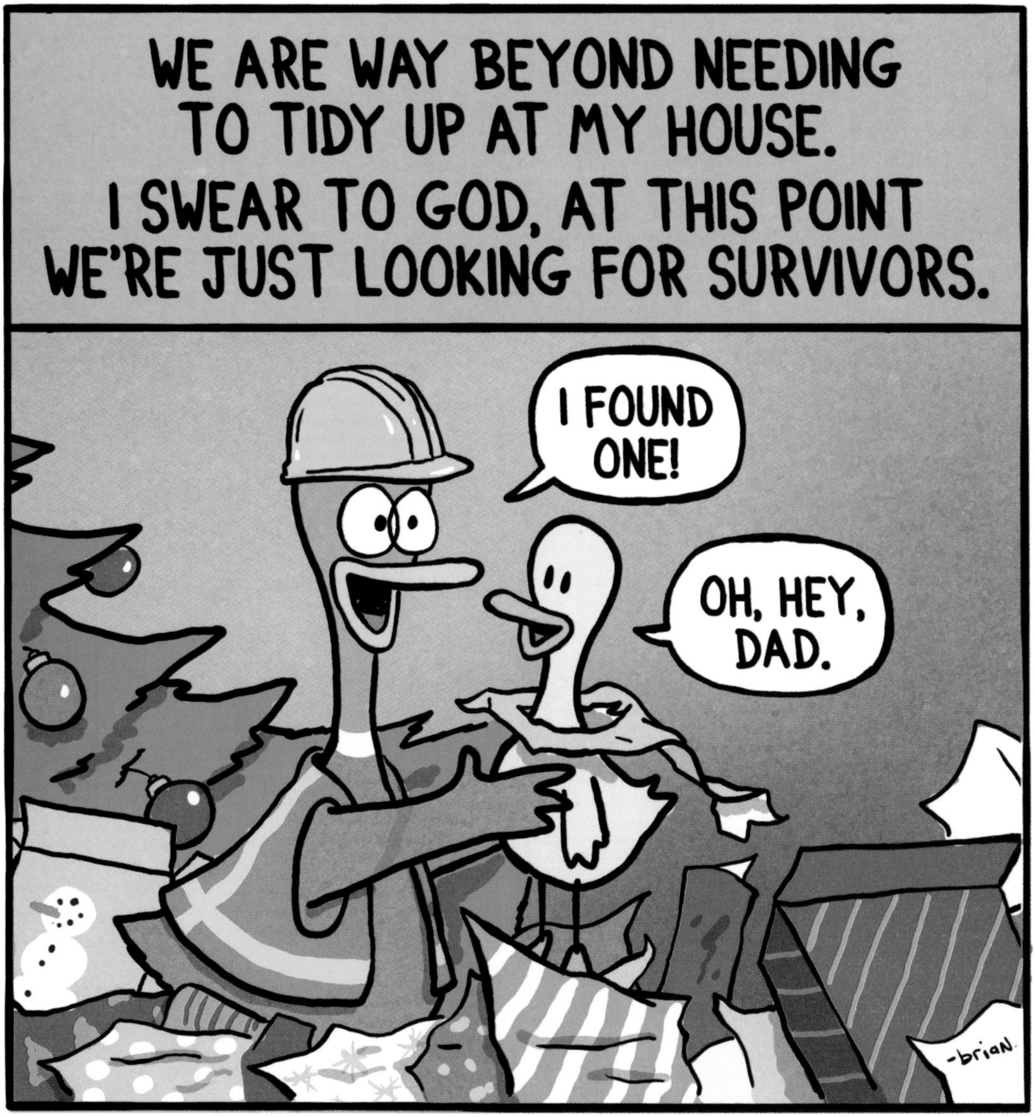
WE ARE WAY BEYOND NEEDING TO TIDY UP AT MY HOUSE.
I SWEAR TO GOD, AT THIS POINT WE'RE JUST LOOKING FOR SURVIVORS.
I FOUND ONE!
OH, HEY, DAD.
-brian.

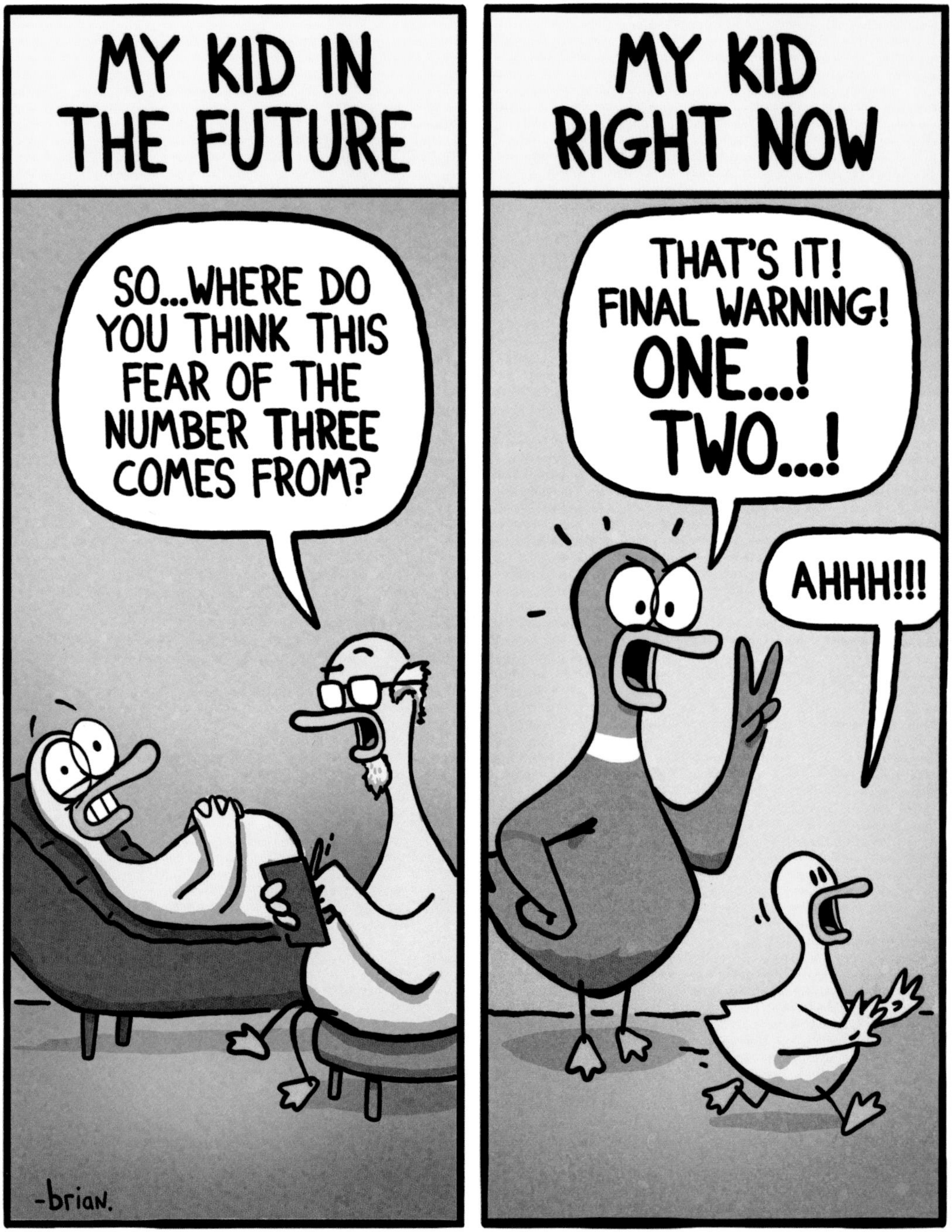
MY KID IN THE FUTURE
SO...WHERE DO YOU THINK THIS FEAR OF THE NUMBER THREE COMES FROM?
-brian.
MY KID RIGHT NOW
THAT'S IT! FINAL WARNING! ONE...! TWO...!
AHHH!!!

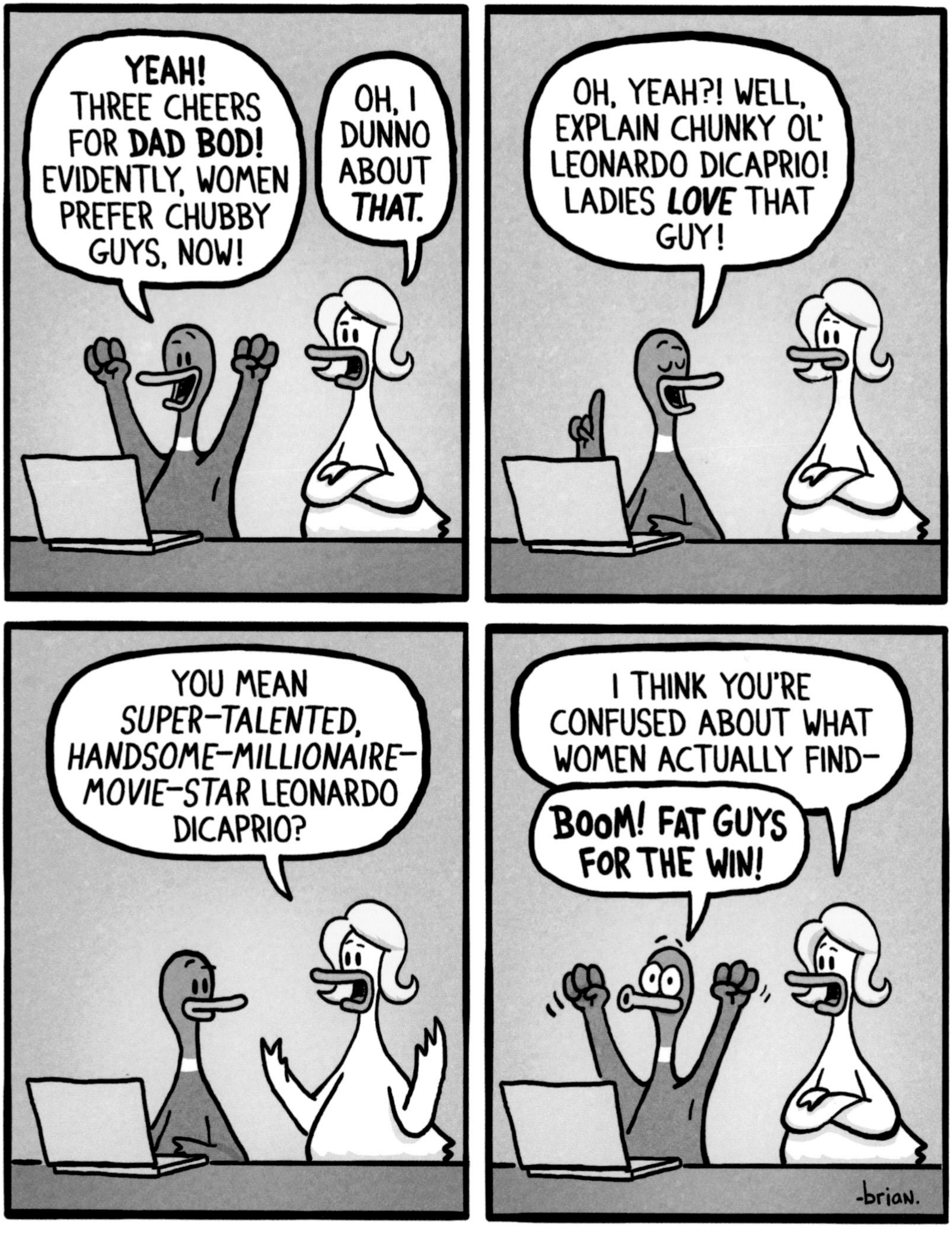
YEAH! THREE CHEERS FOR DAD BOD! EVIDENTLY, WOMEN PREFER CHUBBY GUYS, NOW!
OH, I DUNNO ABOUT THAT.
OH, YEAH?! WELL, EXPLAIN CHUNKY OL' LEONARDO DICAPRIO! LADIES LOVE THAT GUY!
YOU MEAN SUPER-TALENTED, HANDSOME-MILLIONAIRE-MOVIE-STAR LEONARDO DICAPRIO?
I THINK YOU'RE CONFUSED ABOUT WHAT WOMEN ACTUALLY FIND-
BOOM! FAT GUYS FOR THE WIN!
-brian.

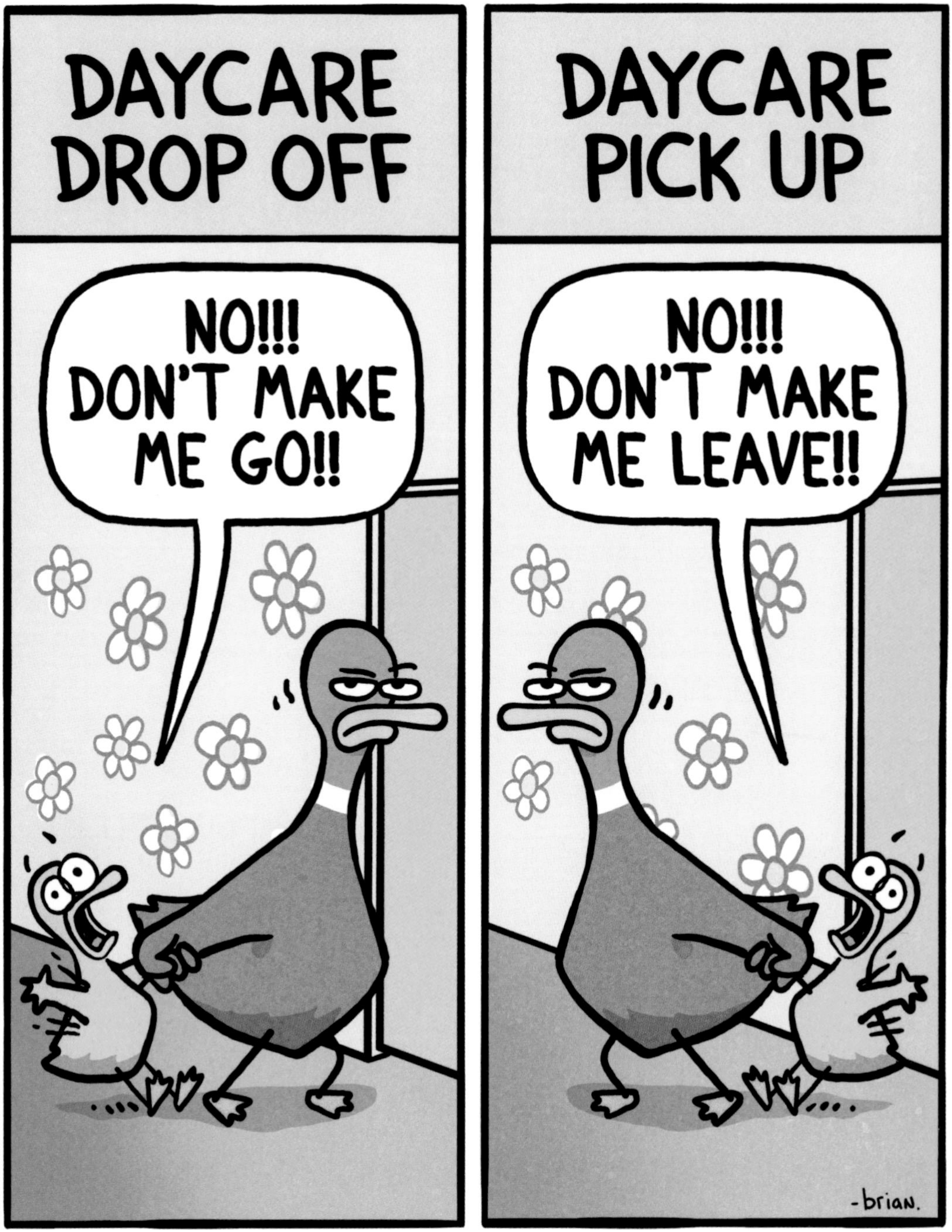
DAYCARE DROP OFF
NO!!! DON'T MAKE ME GO!!
DAYCARE PICK UP
NO!!! DON'T MAKE ME LEAVE!!
-brian.

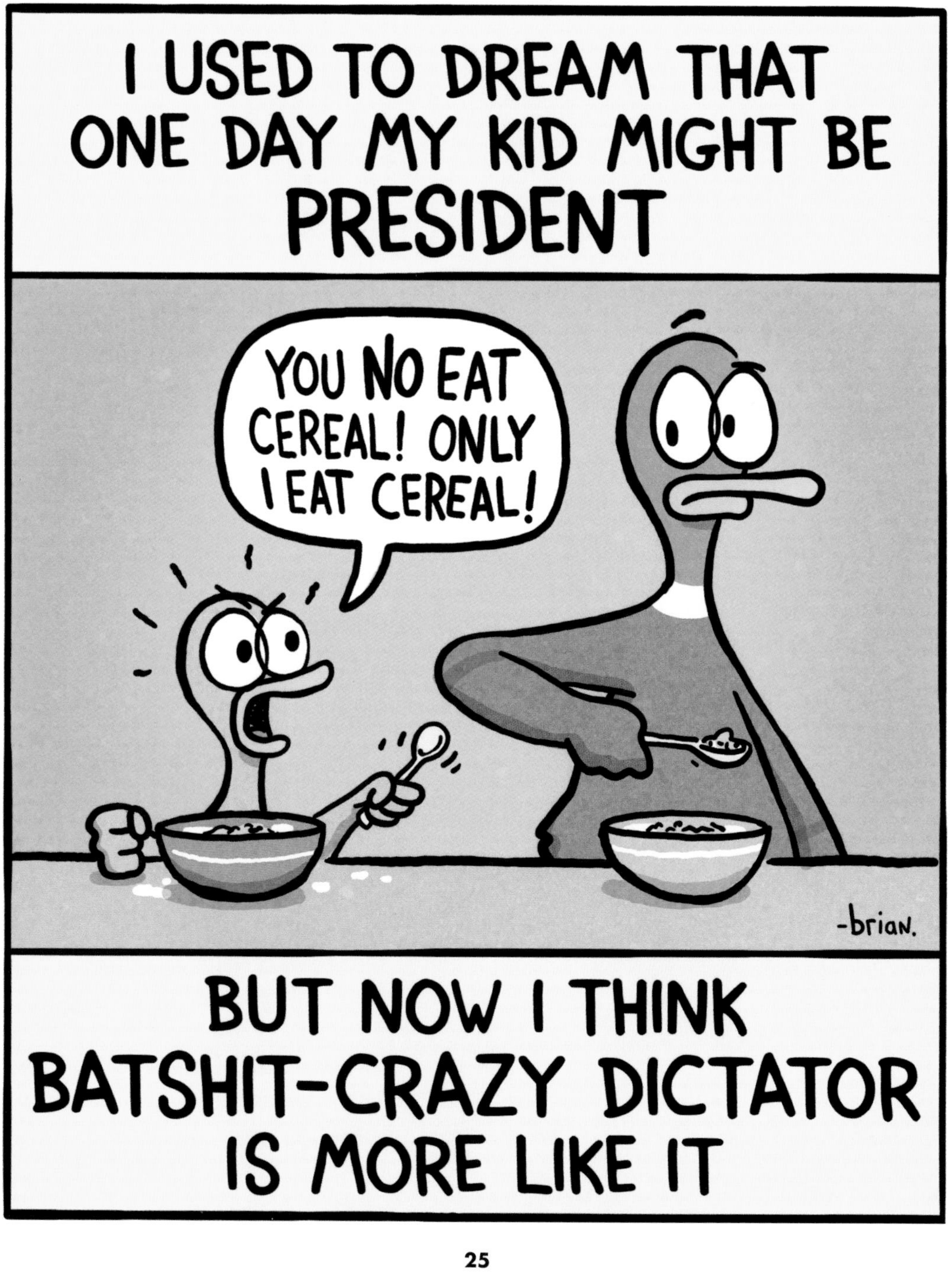
I USED TO DREAM THAT ONE DAY MY KID MIGHT BE PRESIDENT
YOU NO EAT CEREAL! ONLY I EAT CEREAL!
-brian.
BUT NOW I THINK BATSHIT-CRAZY DICTATOR IS MORE LIKE IT

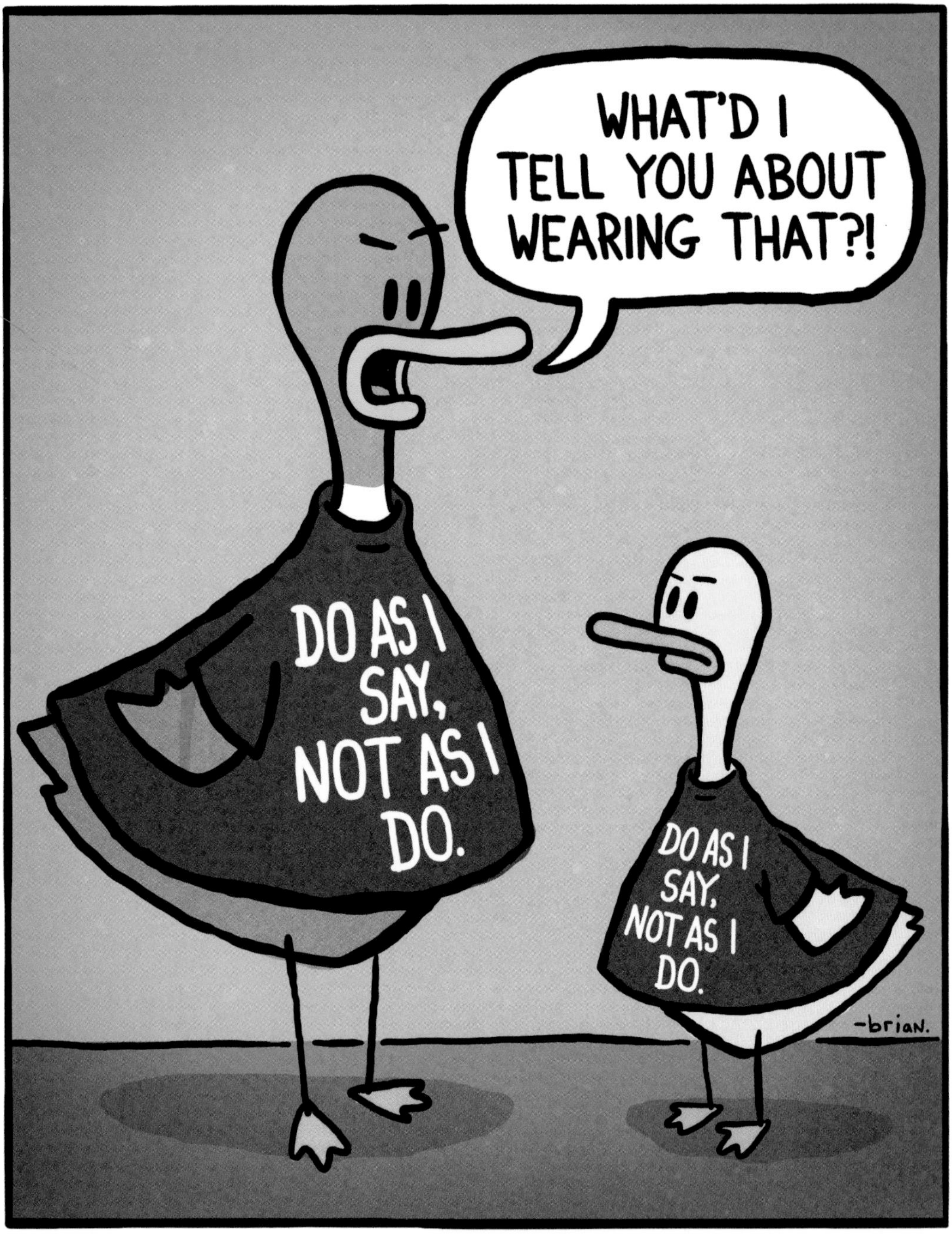
WHAT'D I TELL YOU ABOUT WEARING THAT?!
DO AS I SAY, NOT AS I DO.
DO AS I SAY, NOT AS I DO.
-brian.

KIDS DRINKING WATER

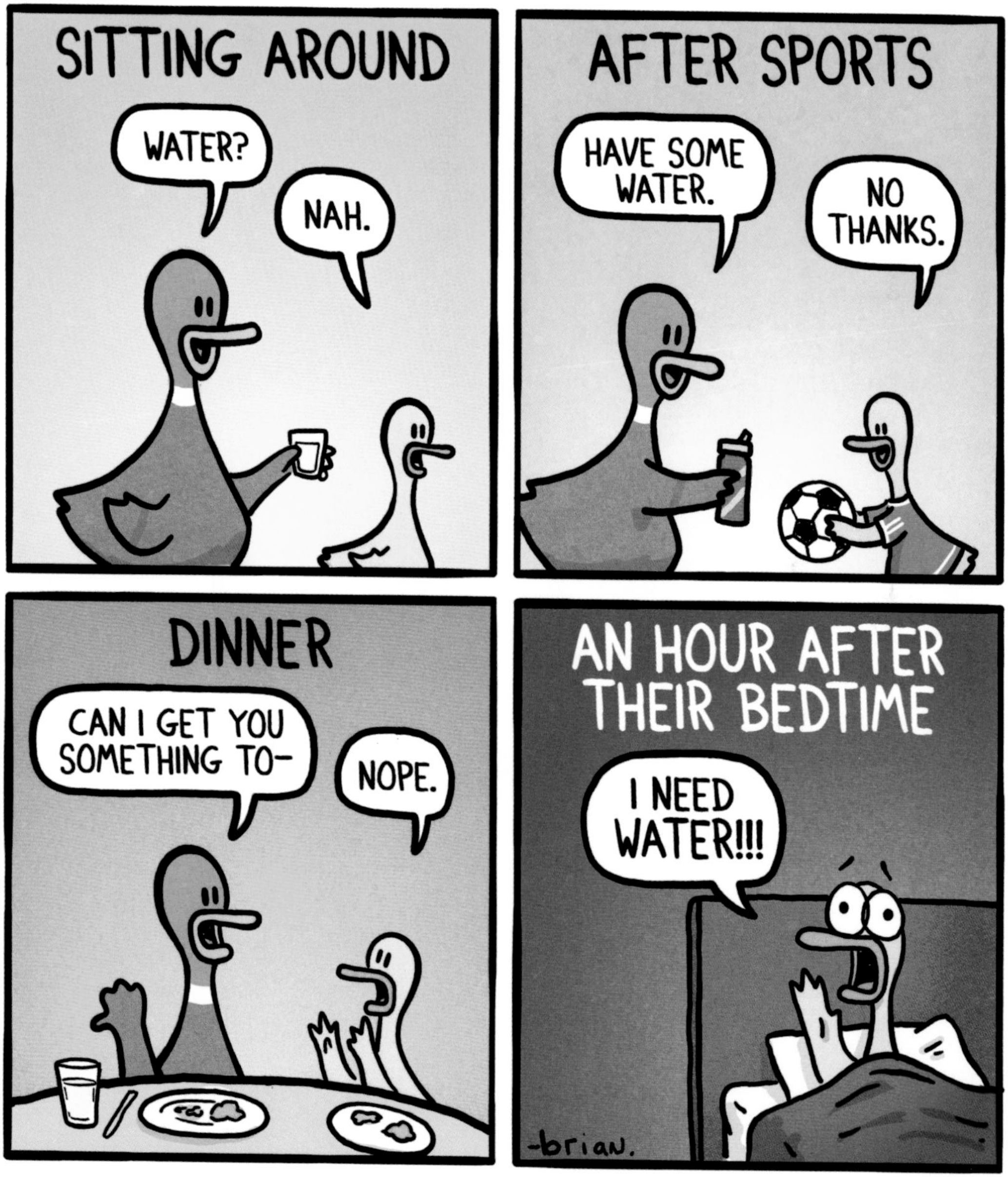
SITTING AROUND
WATER?
NAH.
AFTER SPORTS
HAVE SOME WATER.
NO THANKS.
DINNER
CAN I GET YOU SOMETHING TO–
NOPE.
AN HOUR AFTER THEIR BEDTIME
I NEED WATER!!!
-brian.

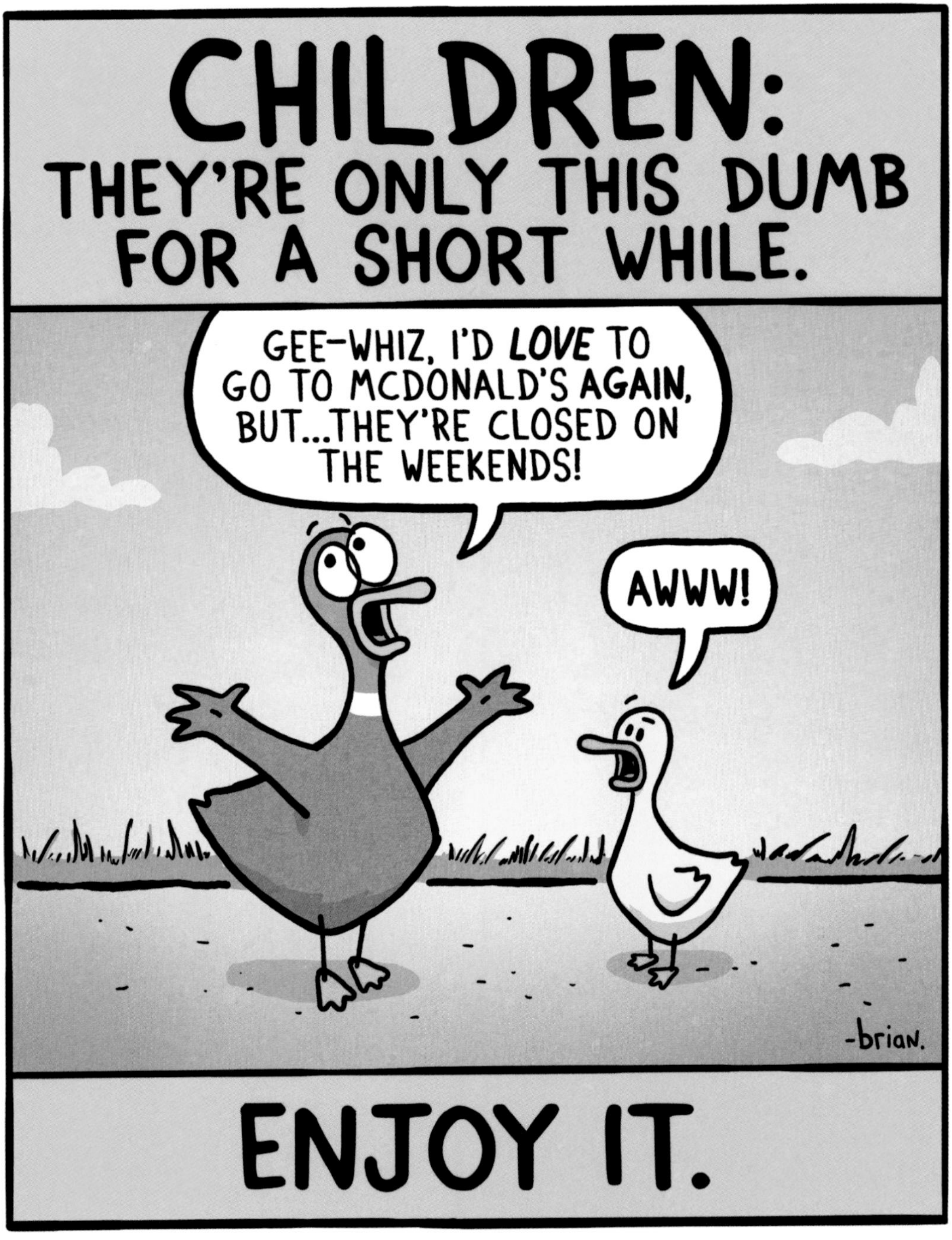
CHILDREN:
THEY'RE ONLY THIS DUMB FOR A SHORT WHILE.
GEE-WHIZ, I'D LOVE TO GO TO MCDONALD'S AGAIN, BUT...THEY'RE CLOSED ON THE WEEKENDS!
AWWW!
-brian.
ENJOY IT.

ELF ON THE SHELF

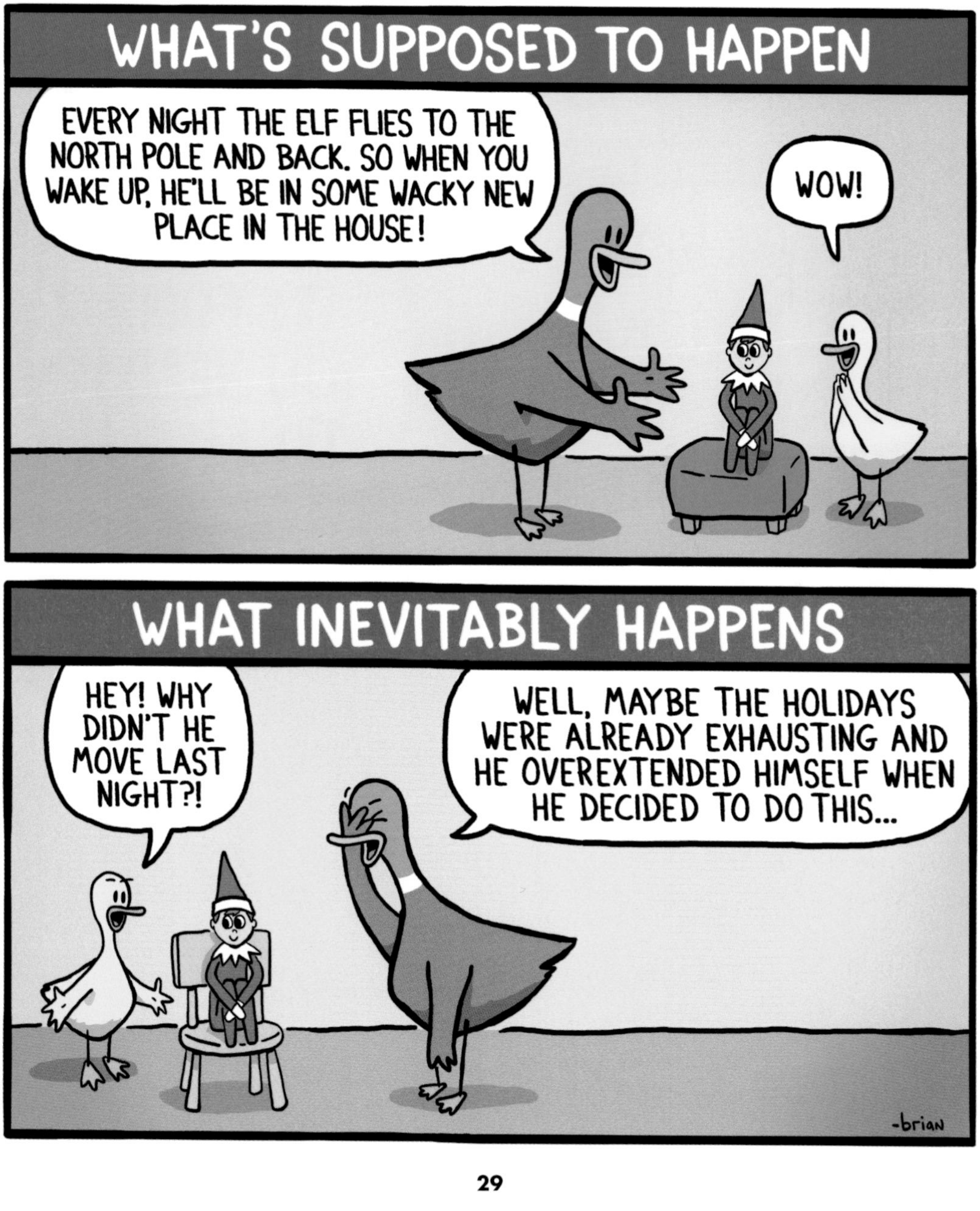
WHAT'S SUPPOSED TO HAPPEN
EVERY NIGHT THE ELF FLIES TO THE NORTH POLE AND BACK. SO WHEN YOU WAKE UP, HE'LL BE IN SOME WACKY NEW PLACE IN THE HOUSE!
WOW!
WHAT INEVITABLY HAPPENS
HEY! WHY DIDN'T HE MOVE LAST NIGHT?!
WELL, MAYBE THE HOLIDAYS WERE ALREADY EXHAUSTING AND HE OVEREXTENDED HIMSELF WHEN HE DECIDED TO DO THIS...
-brian

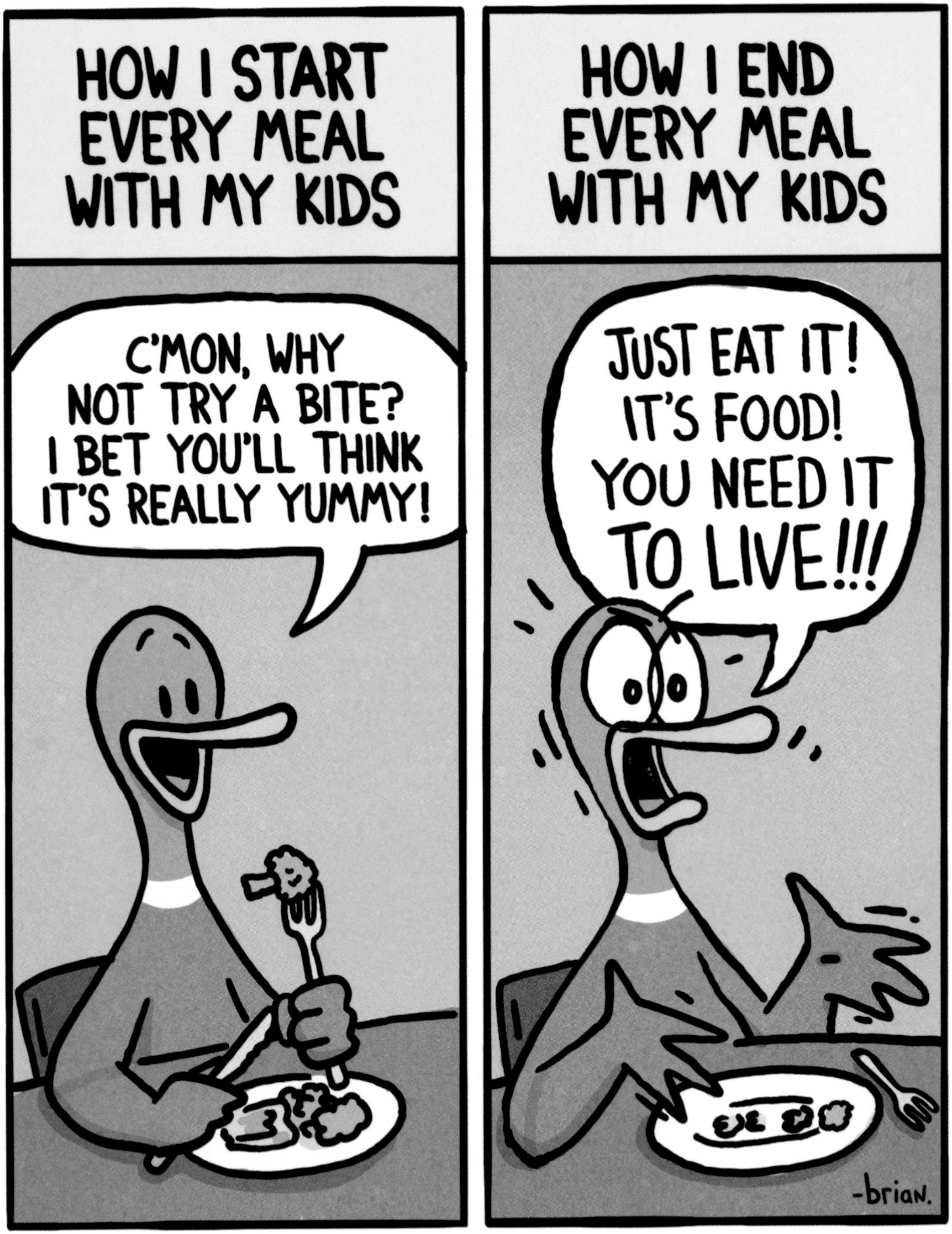
HOW I START EVERY MEAL WITH MY KIDS
C'MON, WHY NOT TRY A BITE? I BET YOU'LL THINK IT'S REALLY YUMMY!
HOW I END EVERY MEAL WITH MY KIDS
JUST EAT IT! IT'S FOOD! YOU NEED IT TO LIVE!!!
-brian.

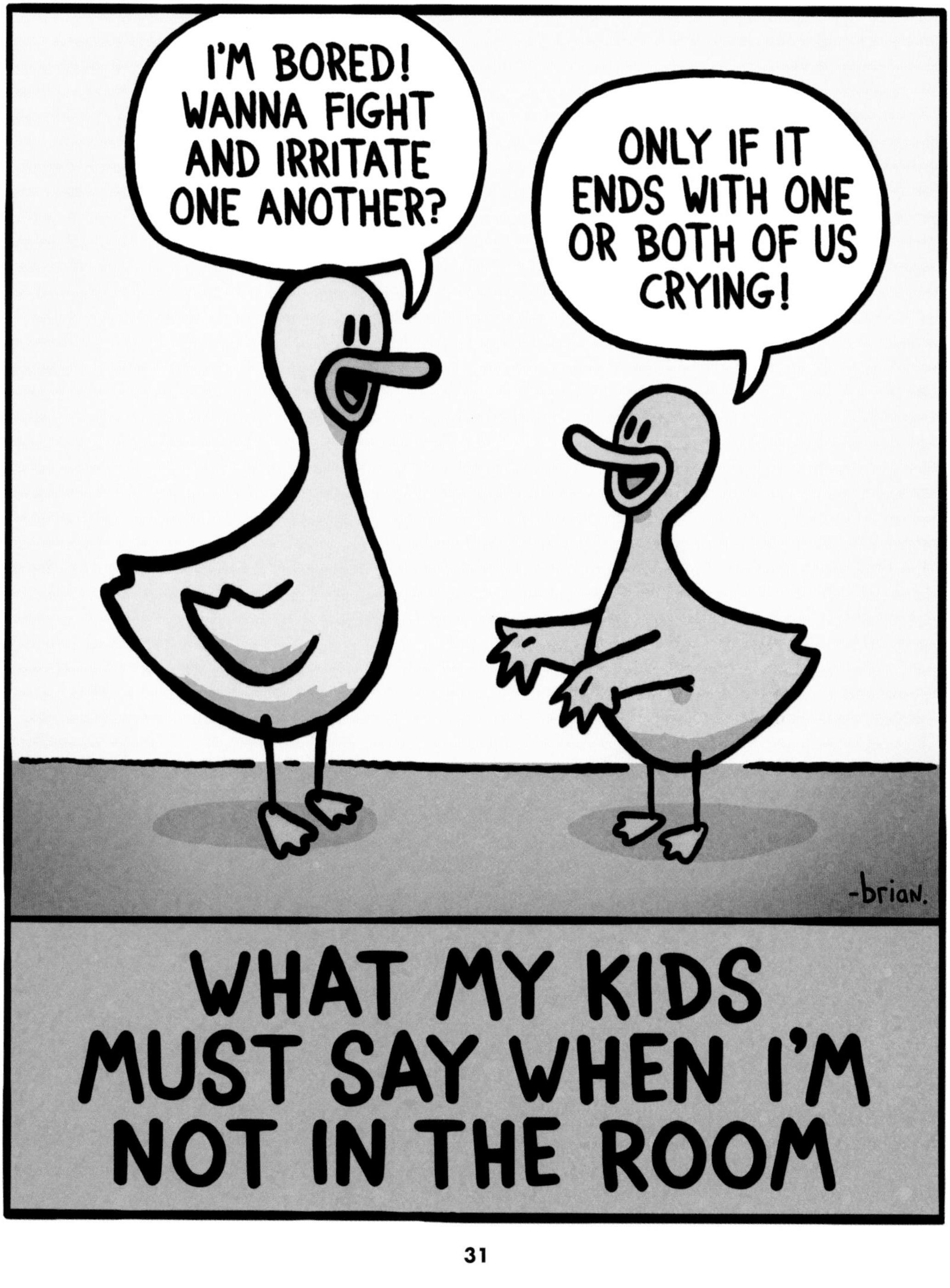
I'M BORED! WANNA FIGHT AND IRRITATE ONE ANOTHER?
ONLY IF IT ENDS WITH ONE OR BOTH OF US CRYING!
-brian.
WHAT MY KIDS MUST SAY WHEN I'M NOT IN THE ROOM

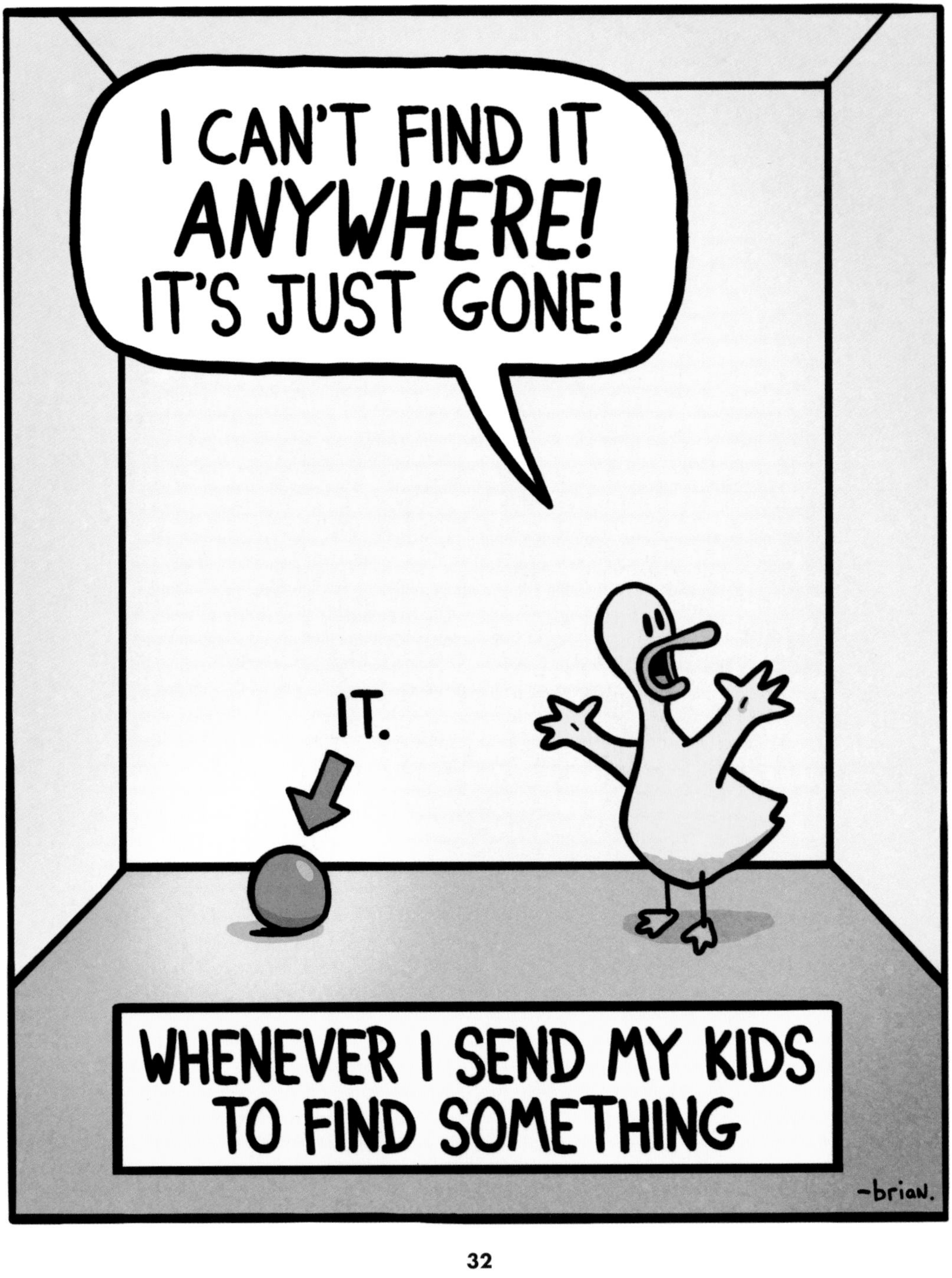
I CAN'T FIND IT ANYWHERE! IT'S JUST GONE!
IT.
WHENEVER I SEND MY KIDS TO FIND SOMETHING
-brian.

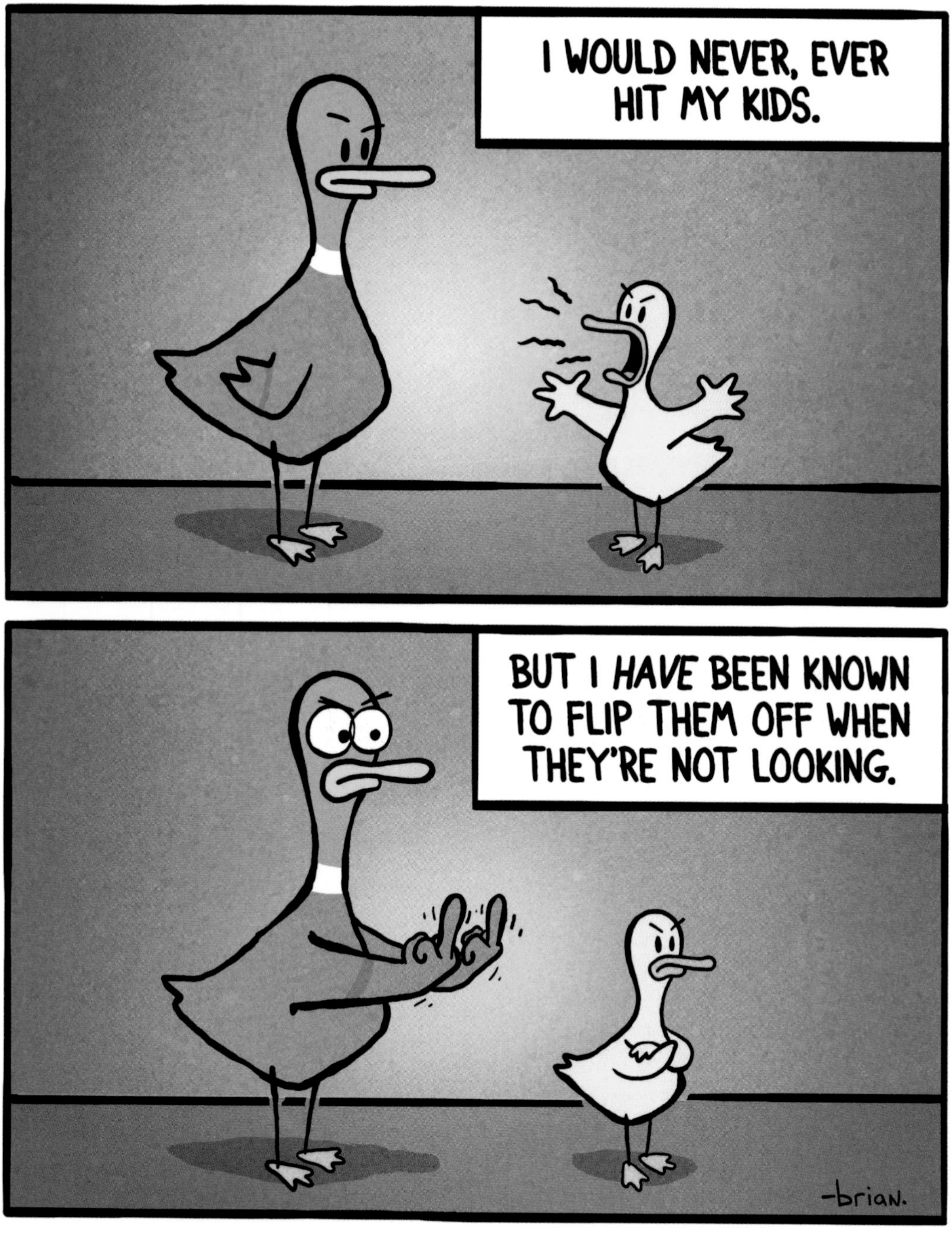
I WOULD NEVER, EVER HIT MY KIDS.
BUT I *HAVE* BEEN KNOWN TO FLIP THEM OFF WHEN THEY'RE NOT LOOKING.
-brian.

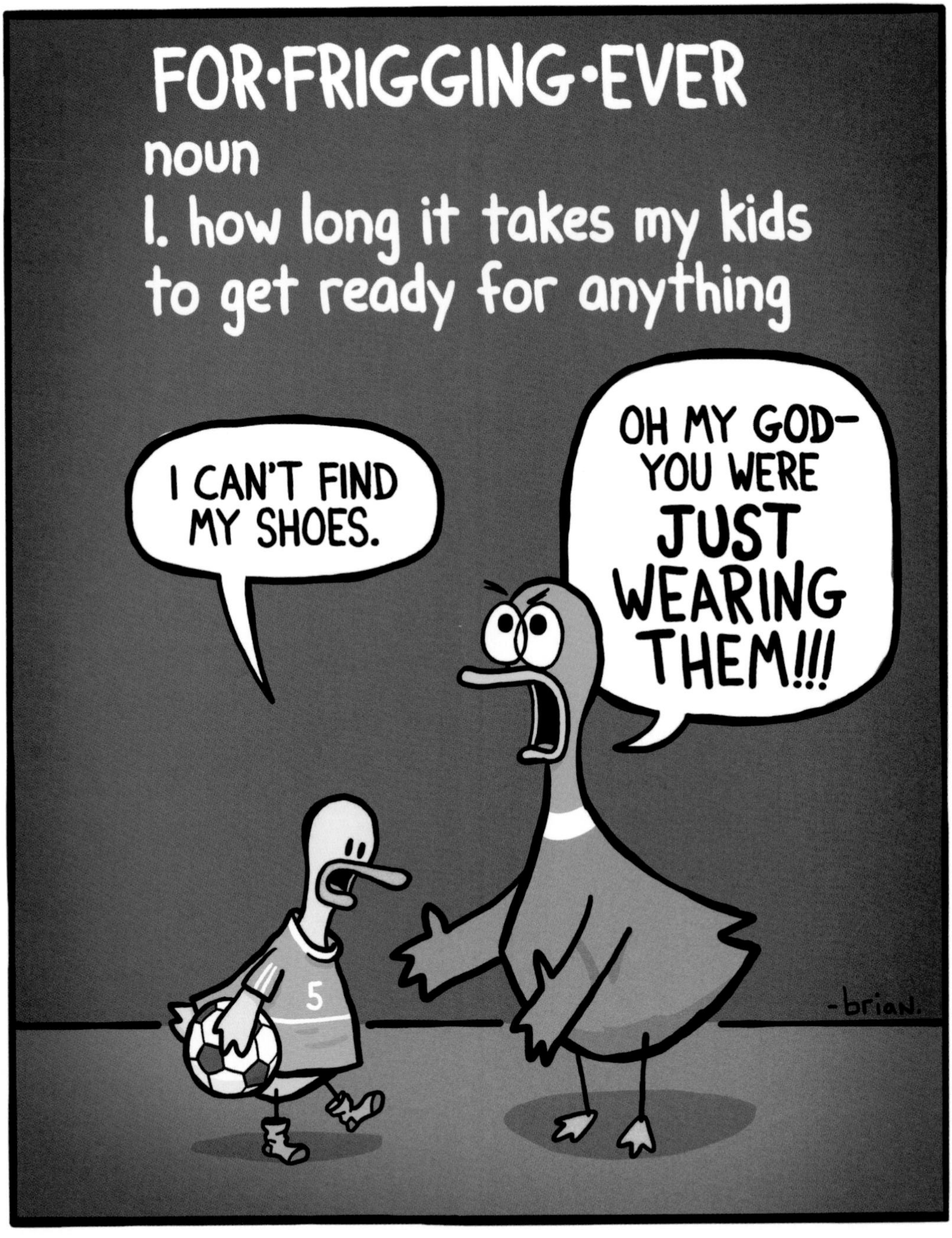
FOR·FRIGGING·EVER
noun
1. how long it takes my kids to get ready for anything
I CAN'T FIND MY SHOES.
OH MY GOD- YOU WERE JUST WEARING THEM!!!
5
-brian.

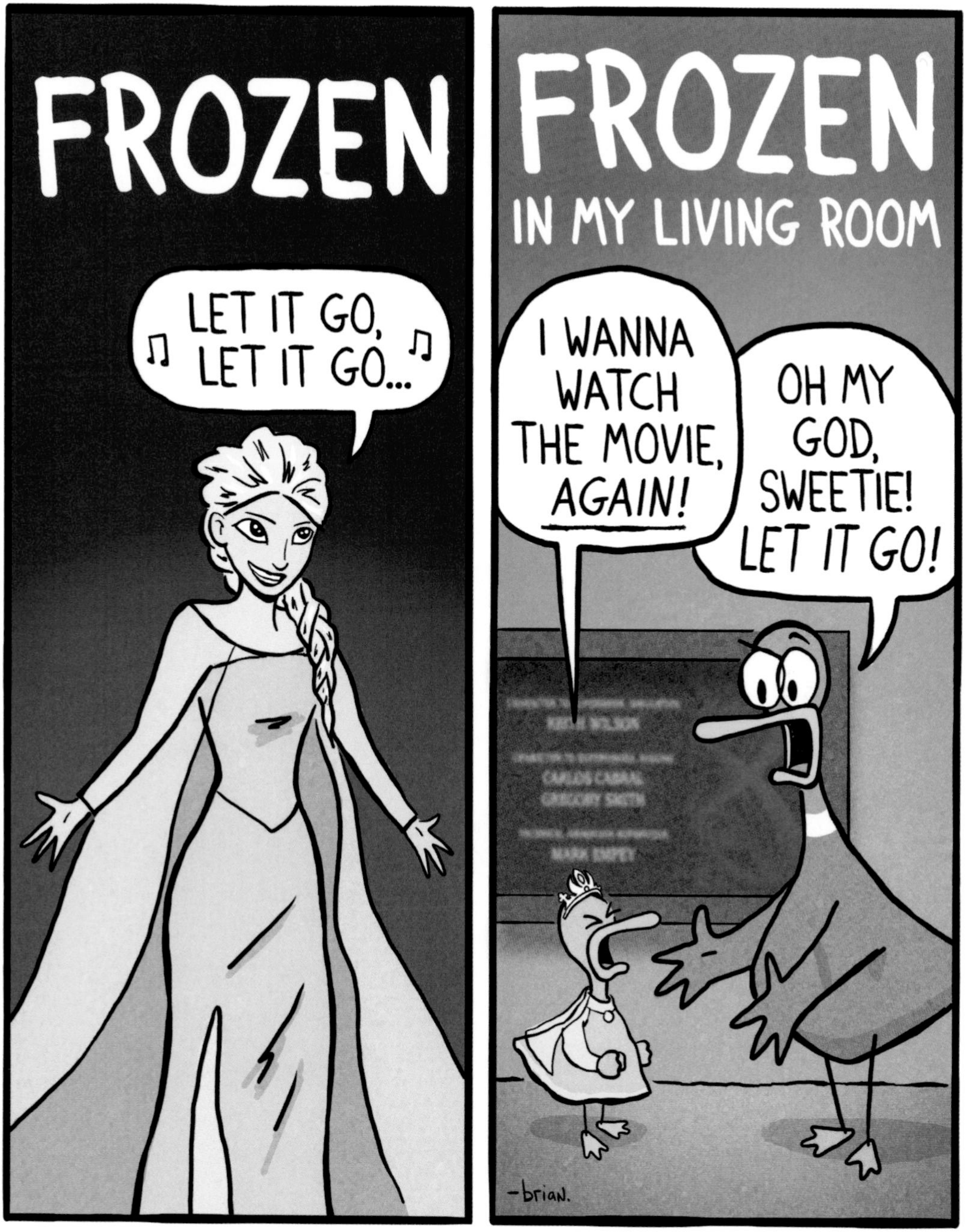
FROZEN
♫ LET IT GO, LET IT GO... ♫
FROZEN
IN MY LIVING ROOM
I WANNA WATCH THE MOVIE, AGAIN!
OH MY GOD, SWEETIE! LET IT GO!
-brian.

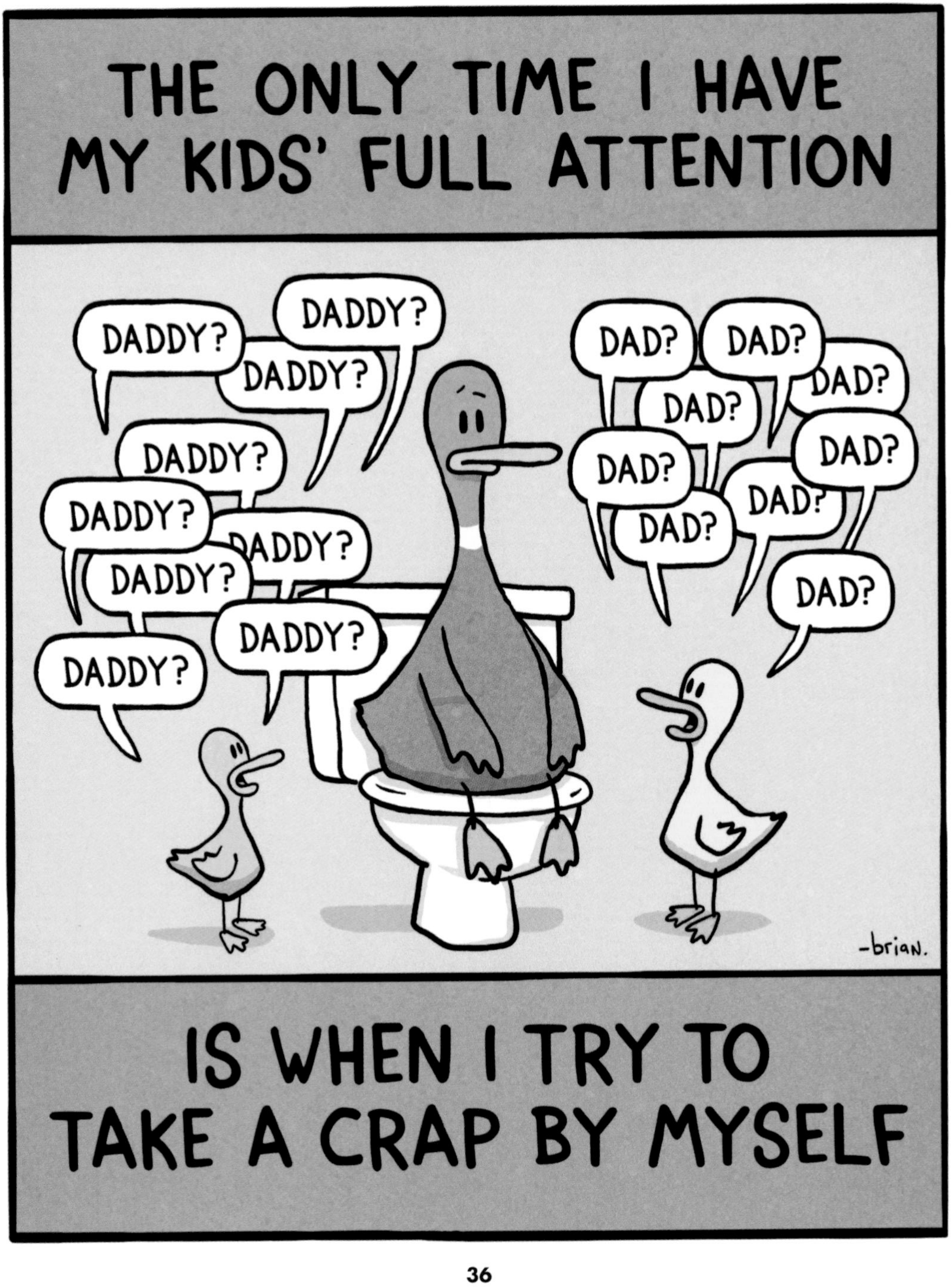
THE ONLY TIME I HAVE MY KIDS' FULL ATTENTION
DADDY?
DADDY?
DADDY?
DADDY?
DADDY?
DADDY?
DADDY?
DADDY?
DADDY?
DAD?
DAD?
DAD?
DAD?
DAD?
DAD?
DAD?
DAD?
DAD?
-brian.
IS WHEN I TRY TO TAKE A CRAP BY MYSELF

A STEP-BY-STEP GUIDE TO EXPLAINING GAY MARRIAGE TO CHILDREN

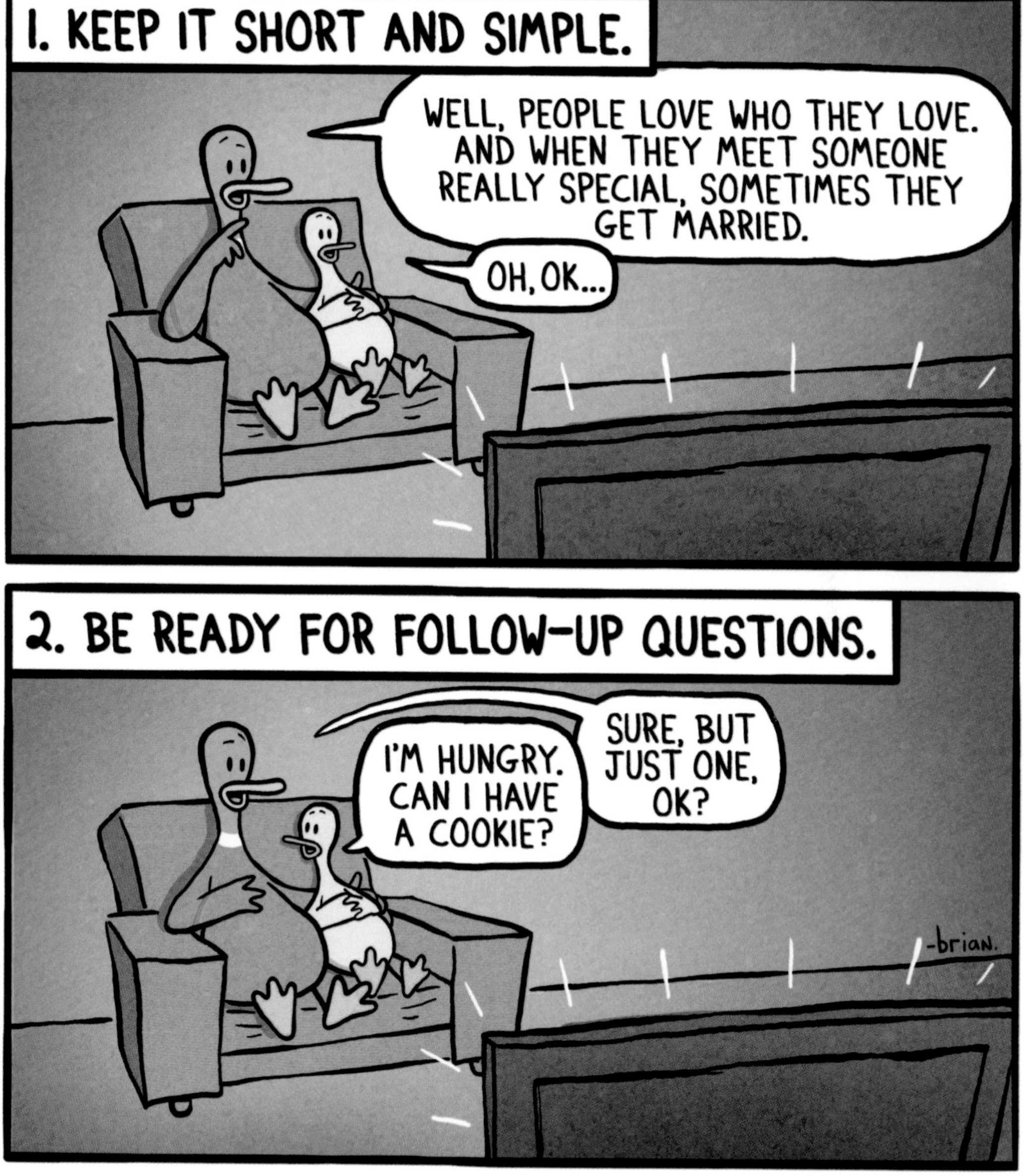
1. KEEP IT SHORT AND SIMPLE.
WELL, PEOPLE LOVE WHO THEY LOVE. AND WHEN THEY MEET SOMEONE REALLY SPECIAL, SOMETIMES THEY GET MARRIED.
OH, OK...
2. BE READY FOR FOLLOW-UP QUESTIONS.
I'M HUNGRY. CAN I HAVE A COOKIE?
SURE, BUT JUST ONE, OK?
-brian.

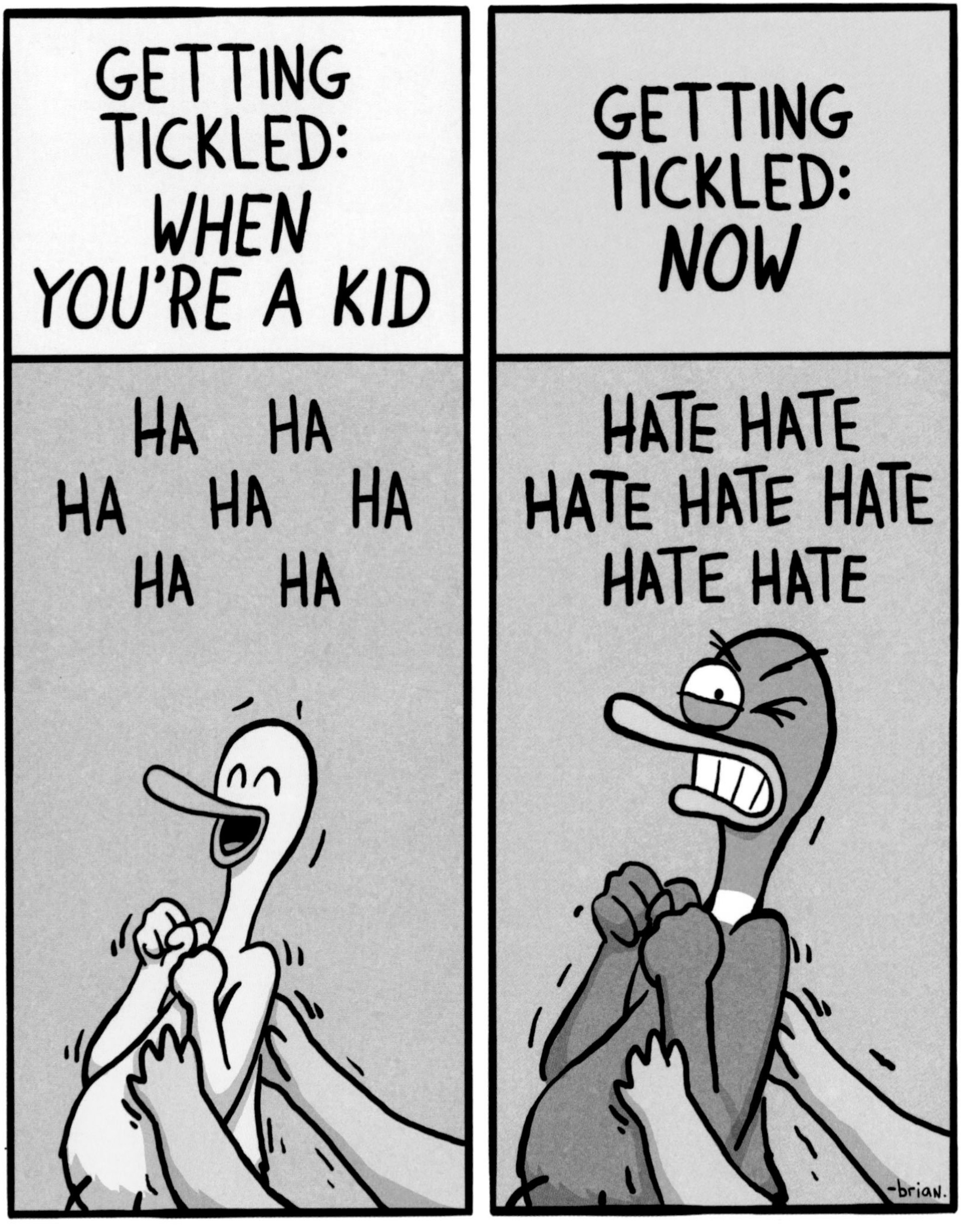
GETTING TICKLED: WHEN YOU'RE A KID
HA HA HA HA HA HA HA
GETTING TICKLED: NOW
HATE HATE HATE HATE HATE HATE HATE
-brian.

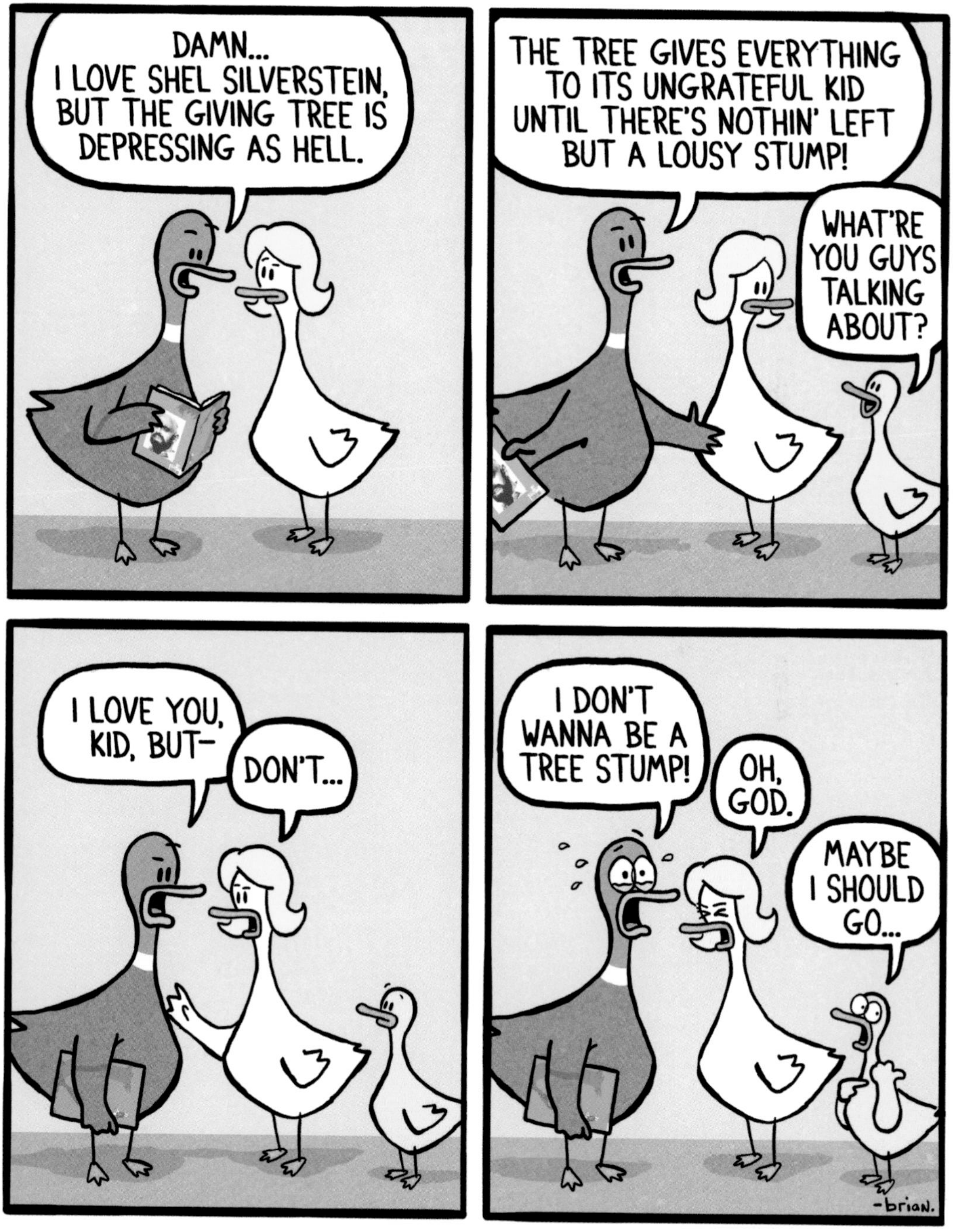
DAMN... I LOVE SHEL SILVERSTEIN, BUT THE GIVING TREE IS DEPRESSING AS HELL.
THE TREE GIVES EVERYTHING TO ITS UNGRATEFUL KID UNTIL THERE'S NOTHIN' LEFT BUT A LOUSY STUMP!
WHAT'RE YOU GUYS TALKING ABOUT?
I LOVE YOU, KID, BUT–
DON'T...
I DON'T WANNA BE A TREE STUMP!
OH, GOD.
MAYBE I SHOULD GO...
-brian.

A HOW-TO GUIDE FOR A HALLOWEEN CANDY WIN

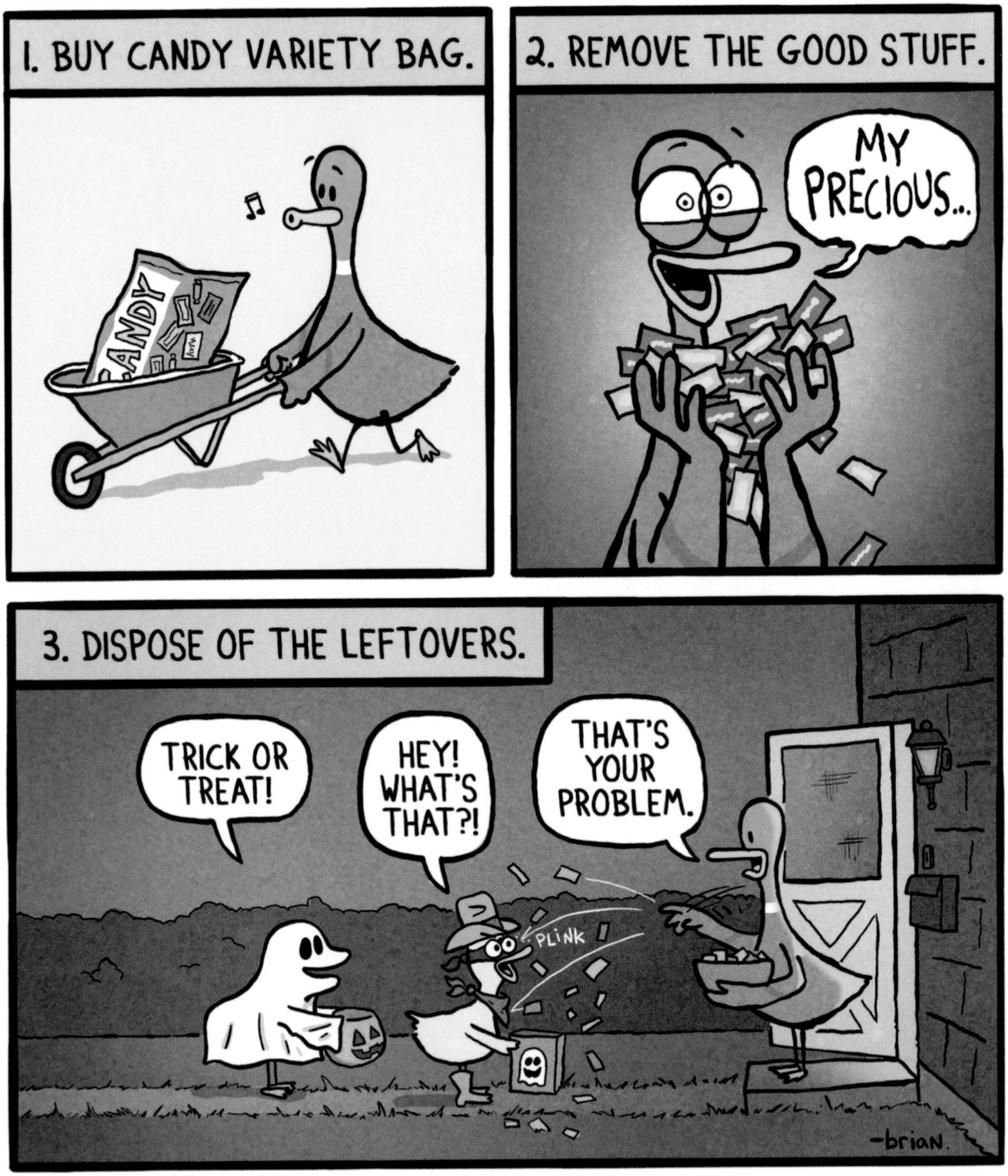
1. BUY CANDY VARIETY BAG.
CANDY
2. REMOVE THE GOOD STUFF.
MY PRECIOUS...
3. DISPOSE OF THE LEFTOVERS.
TRICK OR TREAT!
HEY! WHAT'S THAT?!
THAT'S YOUR PROBLEM.
PLINK
-brian.

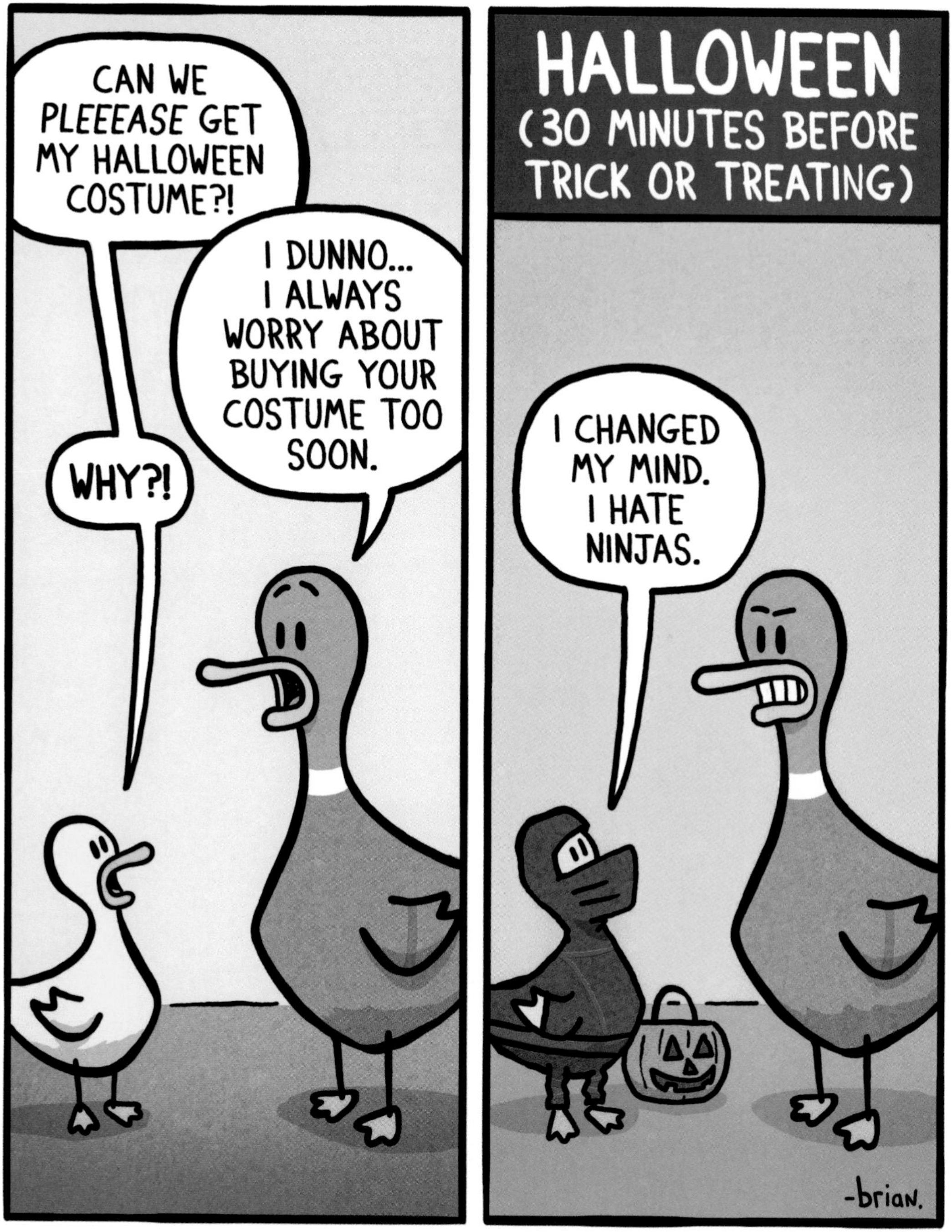
CAN WE PLEEEASE GET MY HALLOWEEN COSTUME?!
I DUNNO... I ALWAYS WORRY ABOUT BUYING YOUR COSTUME TOO SOON.
WHY?!
HALLOWEEN (30 MINUTES BEFORE TRICK OR TREATING)
I CHANGED MY MIND. I HATE NINJAS.
-brian.

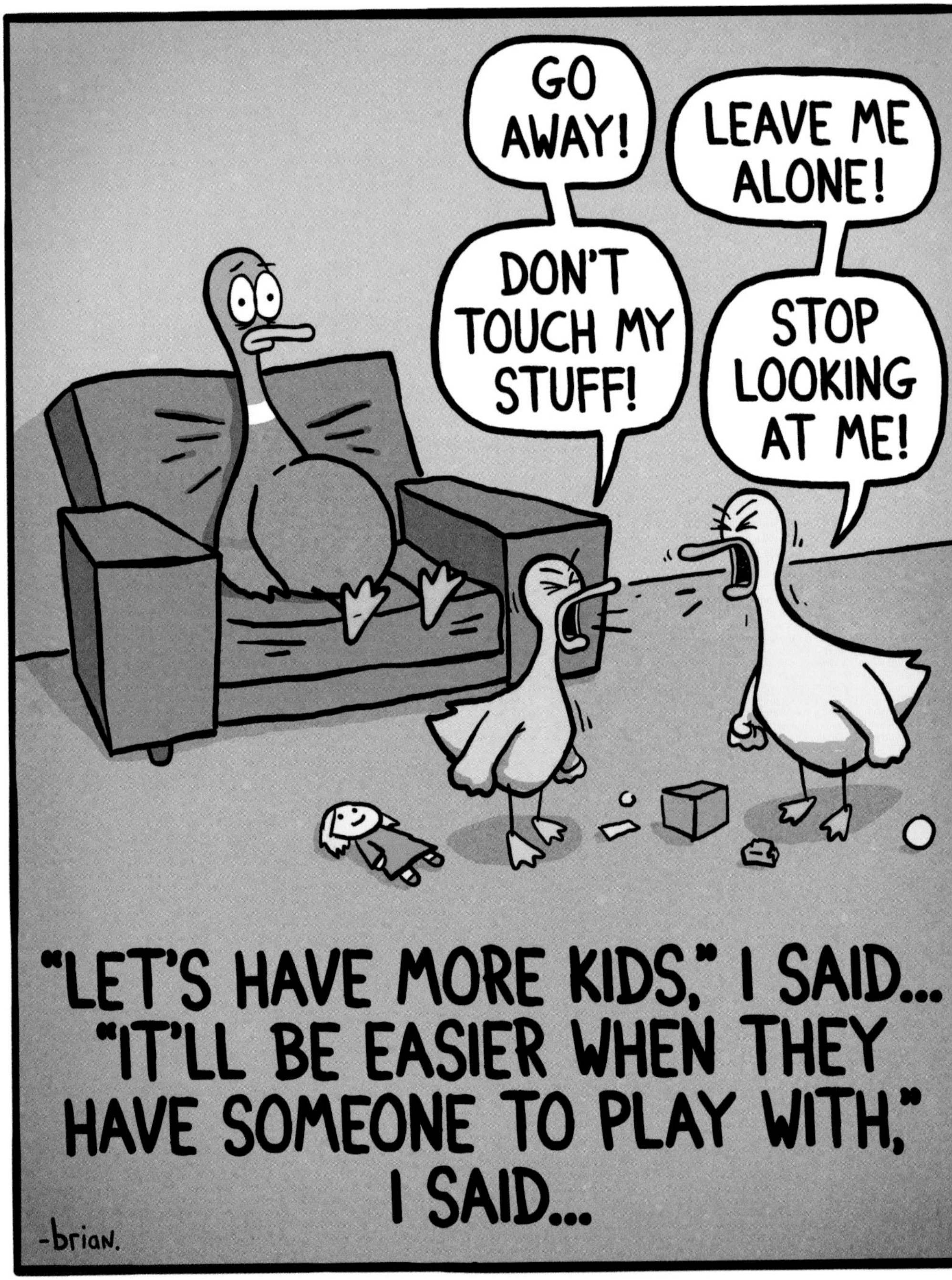
GO AWAY!
DON'T TOUCH MY STUFF!
LEAVE ME ALONE!
STOP LOOKING AT ME!
"LET'S HAVE MORE KIDS," I SAID... "IT'LL BE EASIER WHEN THEY HAVE SOMEONE TO PLAY WITH," I SAID...
-brian.

HOW TO RAISE HEALTHY KIDS

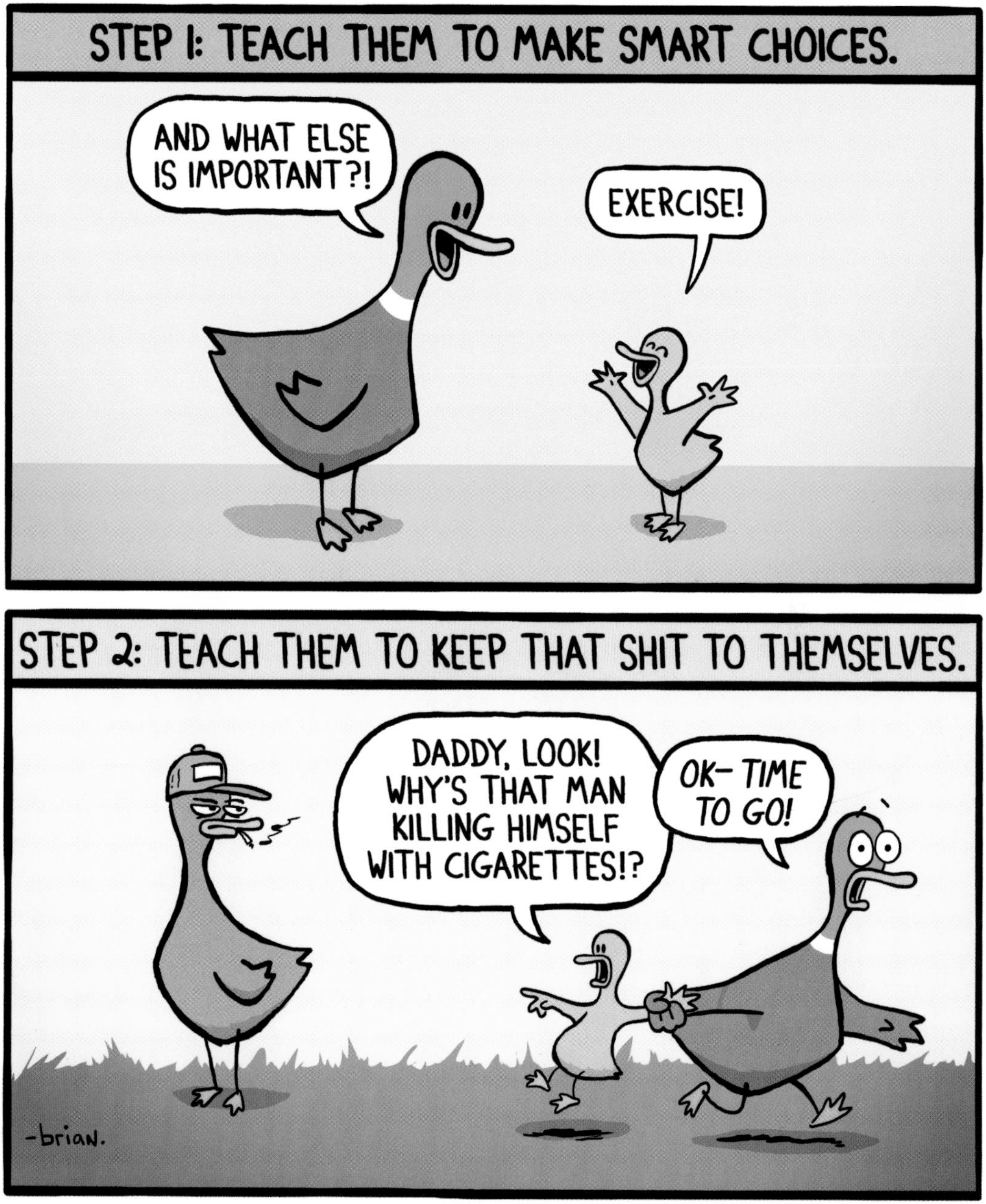
STEP 1: TEACH THEM TO MAKE SMART CHOICES.
AND WHAT ELSE IS IMPORTANT?!
EXERCISE!
STEP 2: TEACH THEM TO KEEP THAT SHIT TO THEMSELVES.
DADDY, LOOK! WHY'S THAT MAN KILLING HIMSELF WITH CIGARETTES!?
OK– TIME TO GO!
-brian.

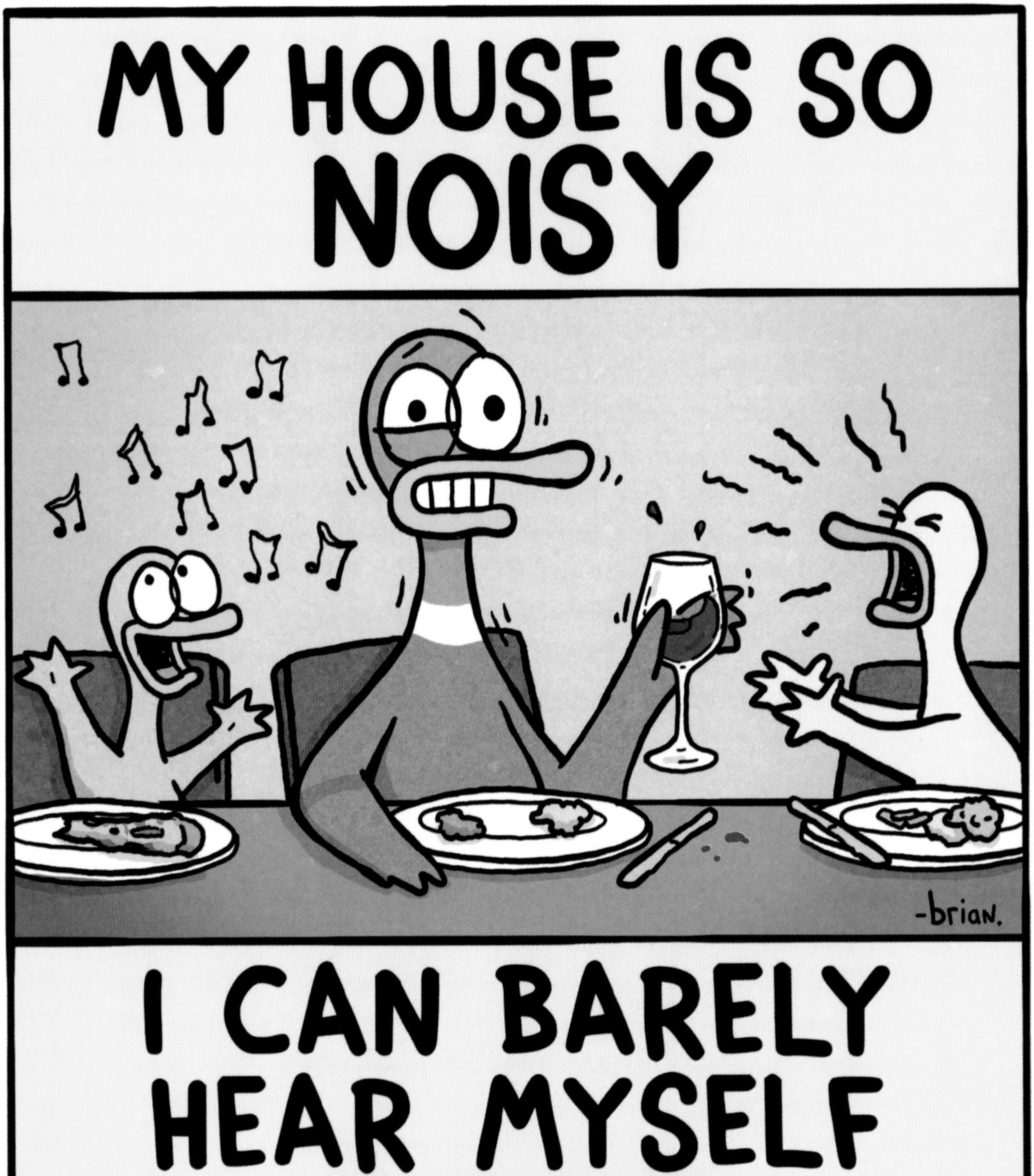
MY HOUSE IS SO
NOISY
-brian.
I CAN BARELY
HEAR MYSELF
DRINK

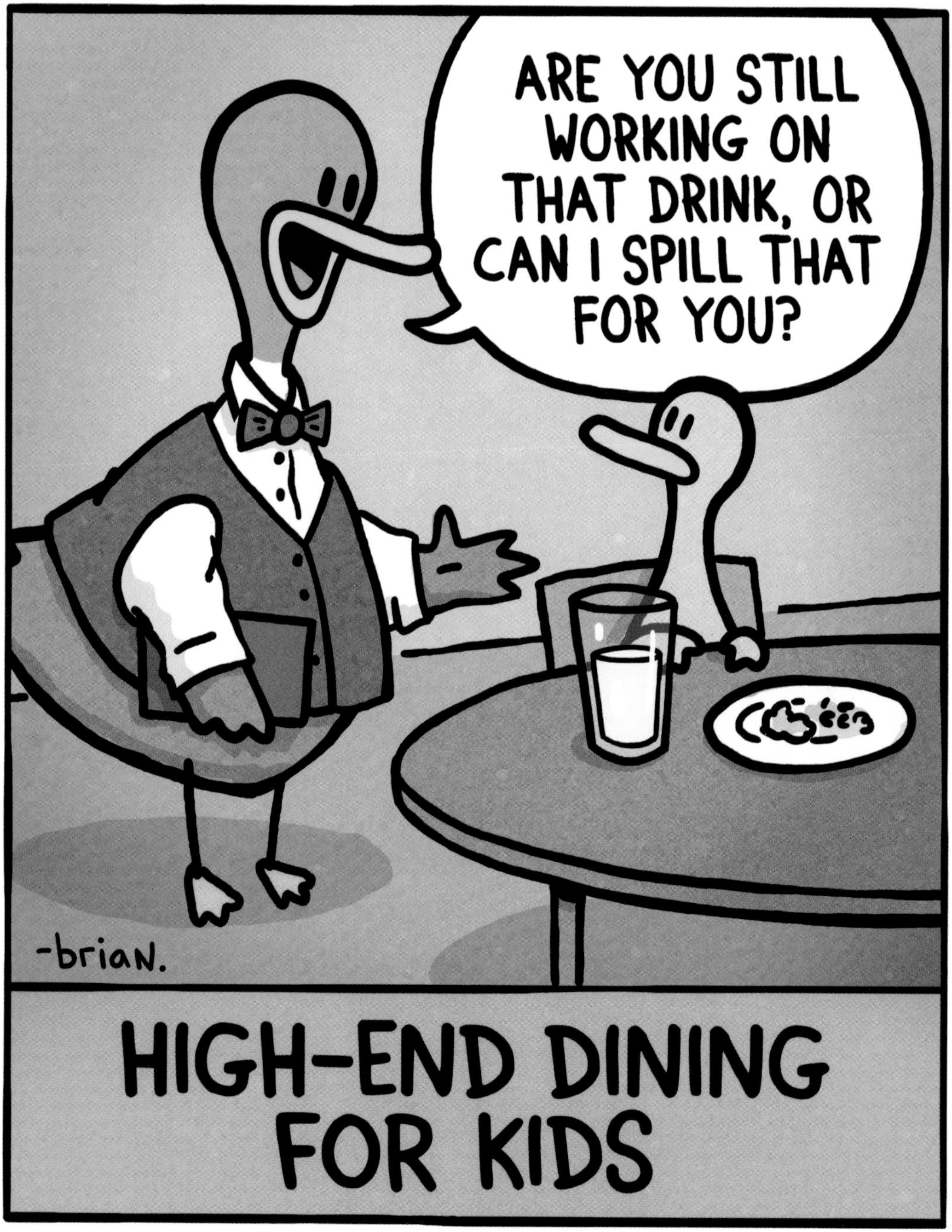
ARE YOU STILL WORKING ON THAT DRINK, OR CAN I SPILL THAT FOR YOU?
-brian.
HIGH-END DINING FOR KIDS

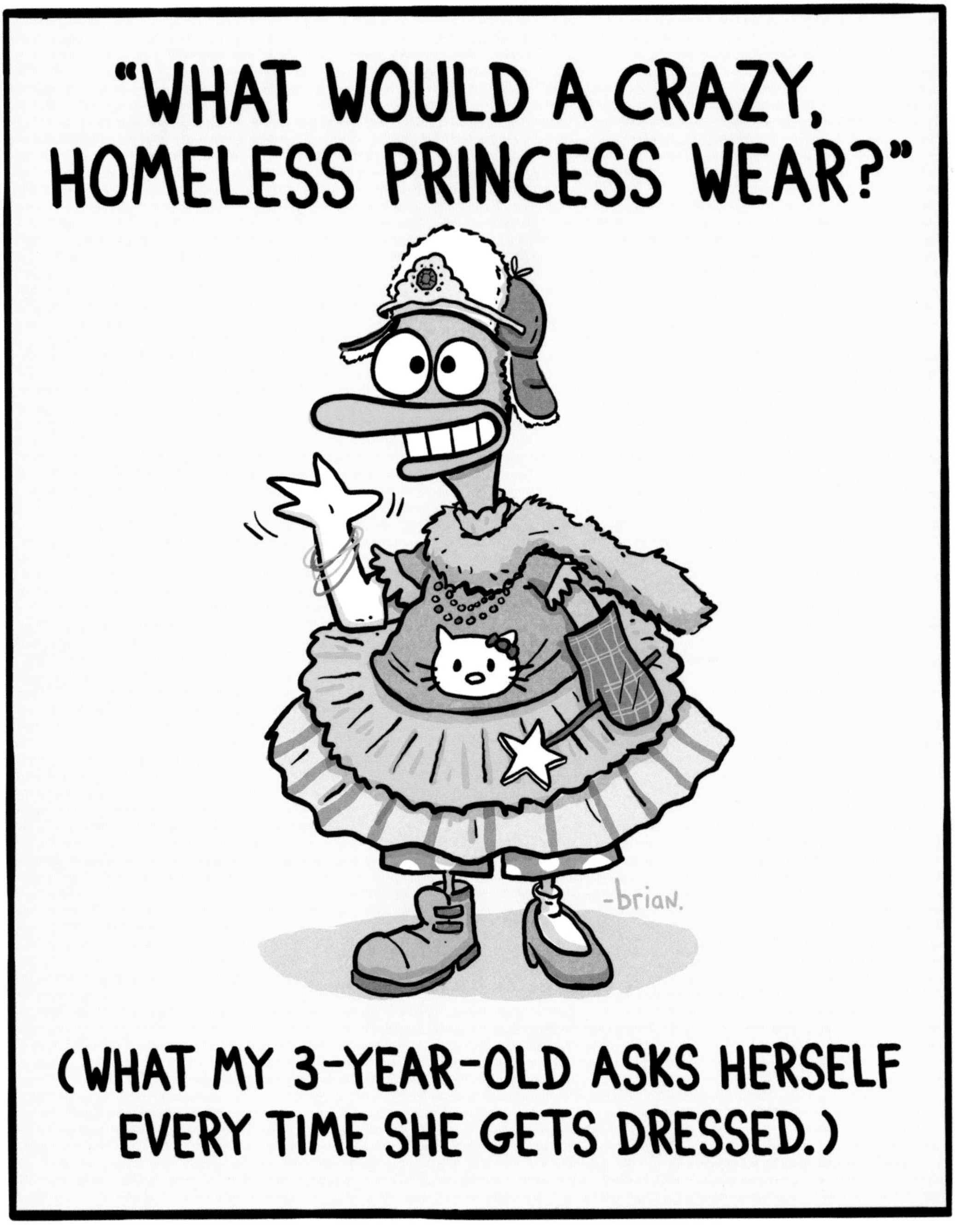
"WHAT WOULD A CRAZY, HOMELESS PRINCESS WEAR?"
-brian.
(WHAT MY 3-YEAR-OLD ASKS HERSELF EVERY TIME SHE GETS DRESSED.)

HOW WELL I SLEEP

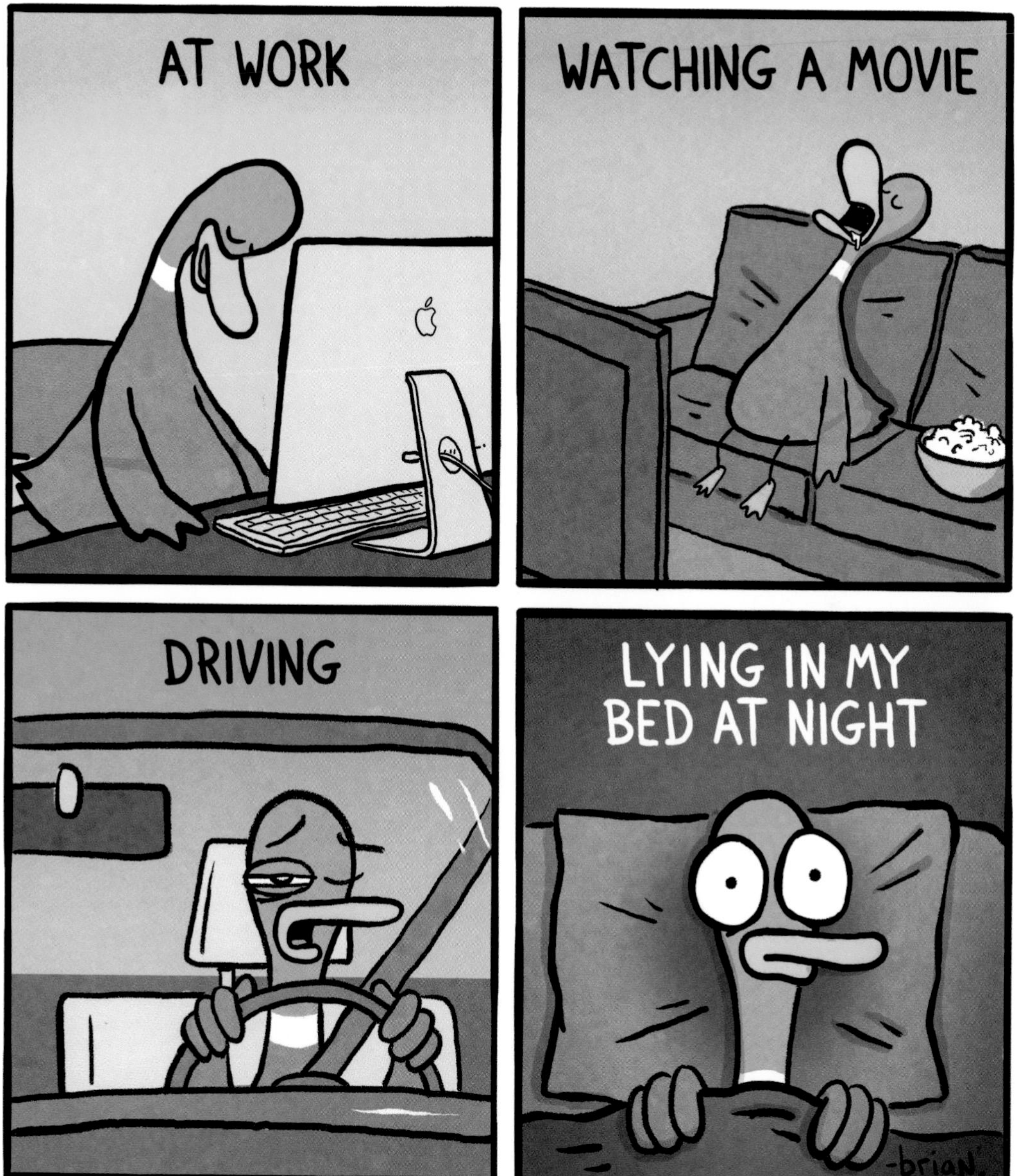
AT WORK
WATCHING A MOVIE
DRIVING
LYING IN MY BED AT NIGHT
-brian.

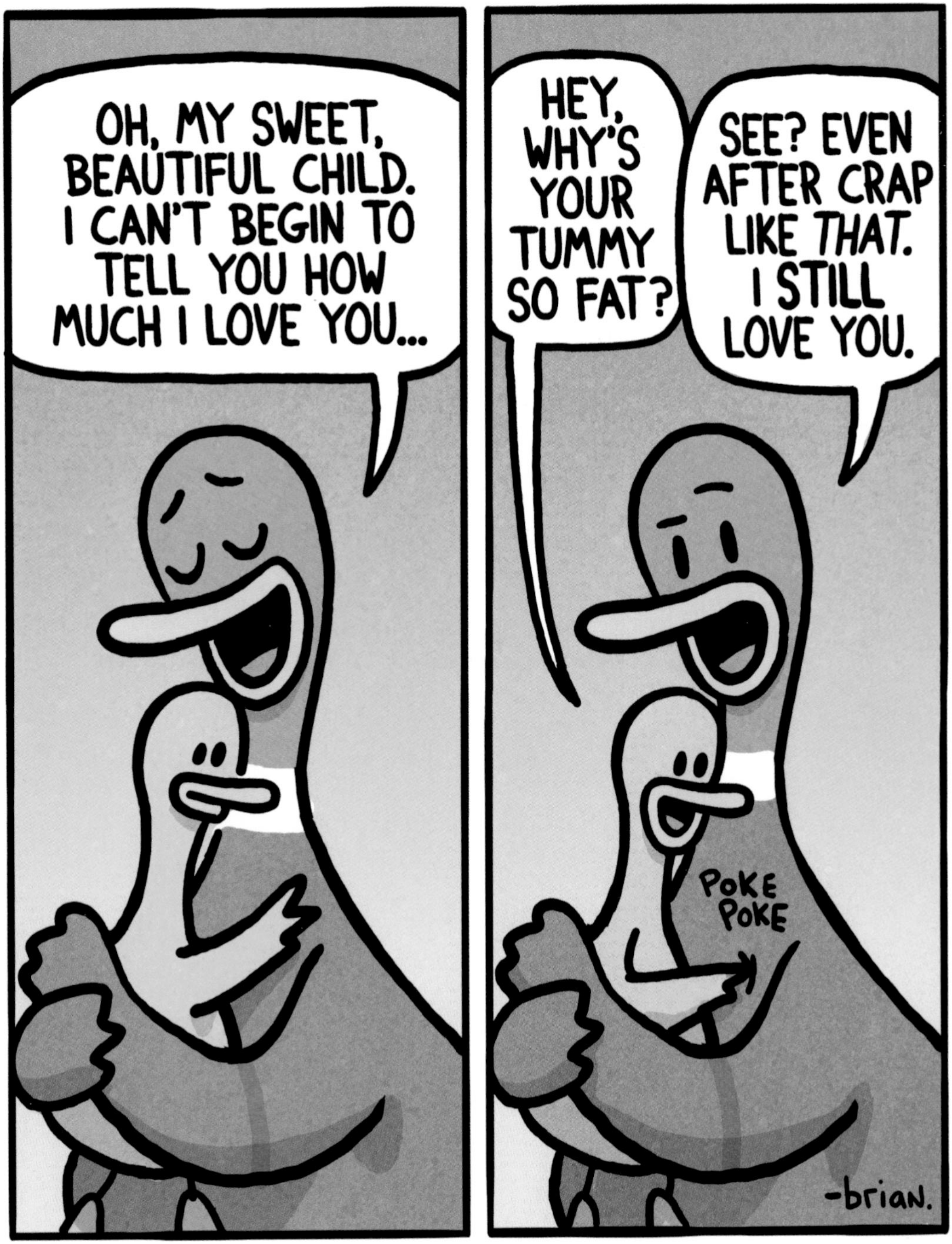
OH, MY SWEET, BEAUTIFUL CHILD. I CAN'T BEGIN TO TELL YOU HOW MUCH I LOVE YOU...
HEY, WHY'S YOUR TUMMY SO FAT?
SEE? EVEN AFTER CRAP LIKE *THAT*. I STILL LOVE YOU.
POKE POKE
-brian.

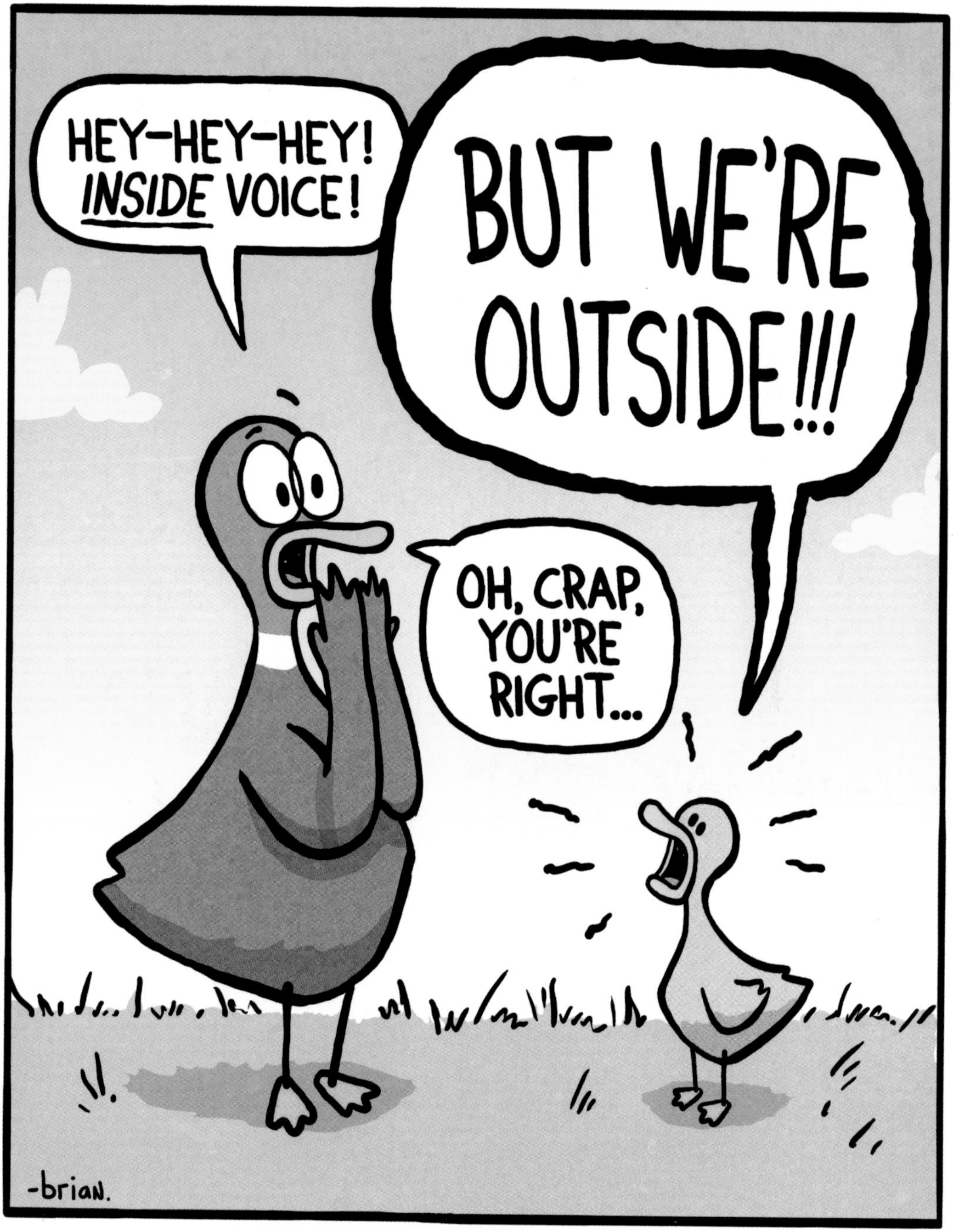
HEY—HEY—HEY! INSIDE VOICE!
BUT WE'RE OUTSIDE!!!
OH, CRAP, YOU'RE RIGHT...
-brian.

INTERROGATION

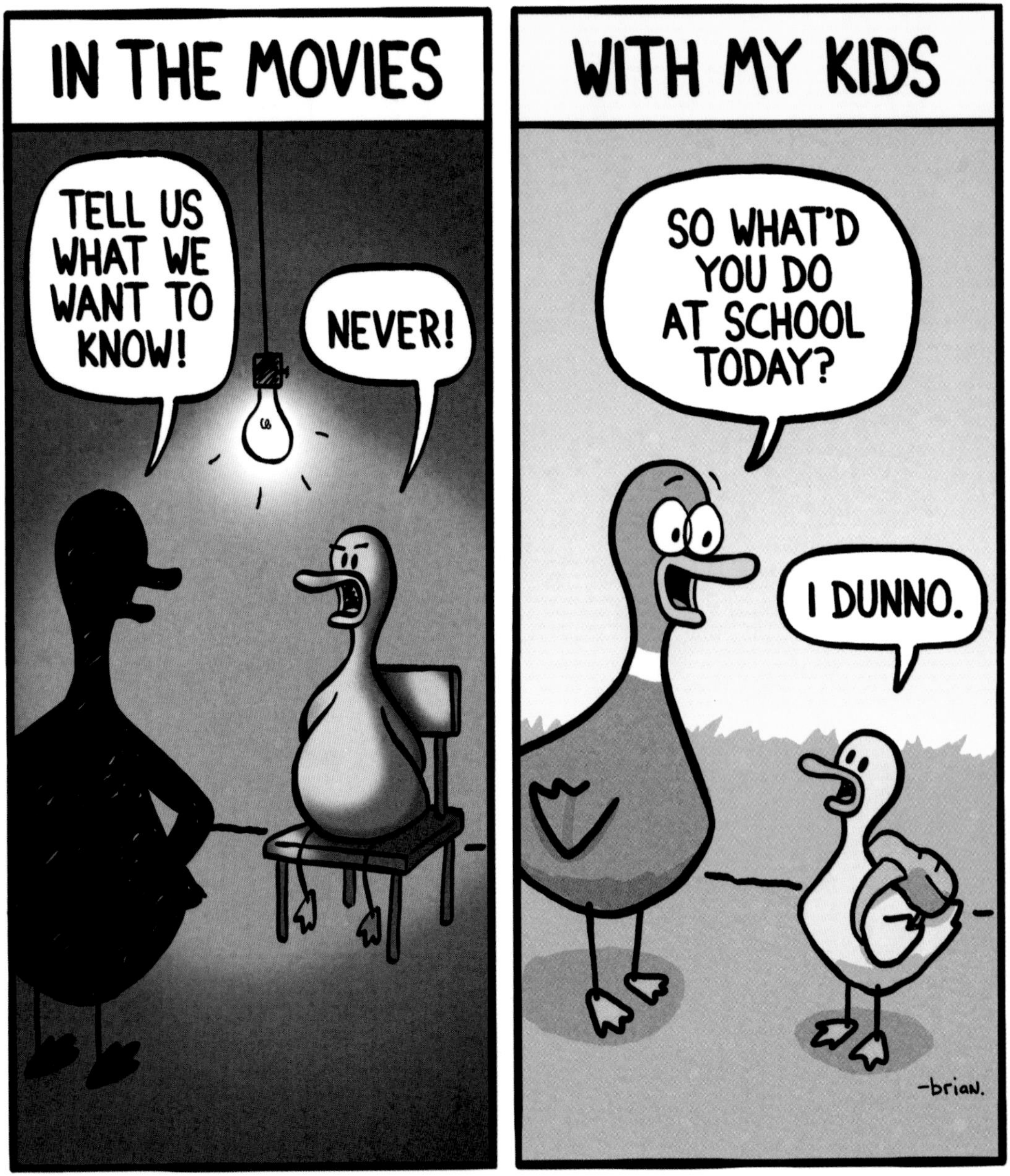
IN THE MOVIES
TELL US WHAT WE WANT TO KNOW!
NEVER!
WITH MY KIDS
SO WHAT'D YOU DO AT SCHOOL TODAY?
I DUNNO.
-brian.

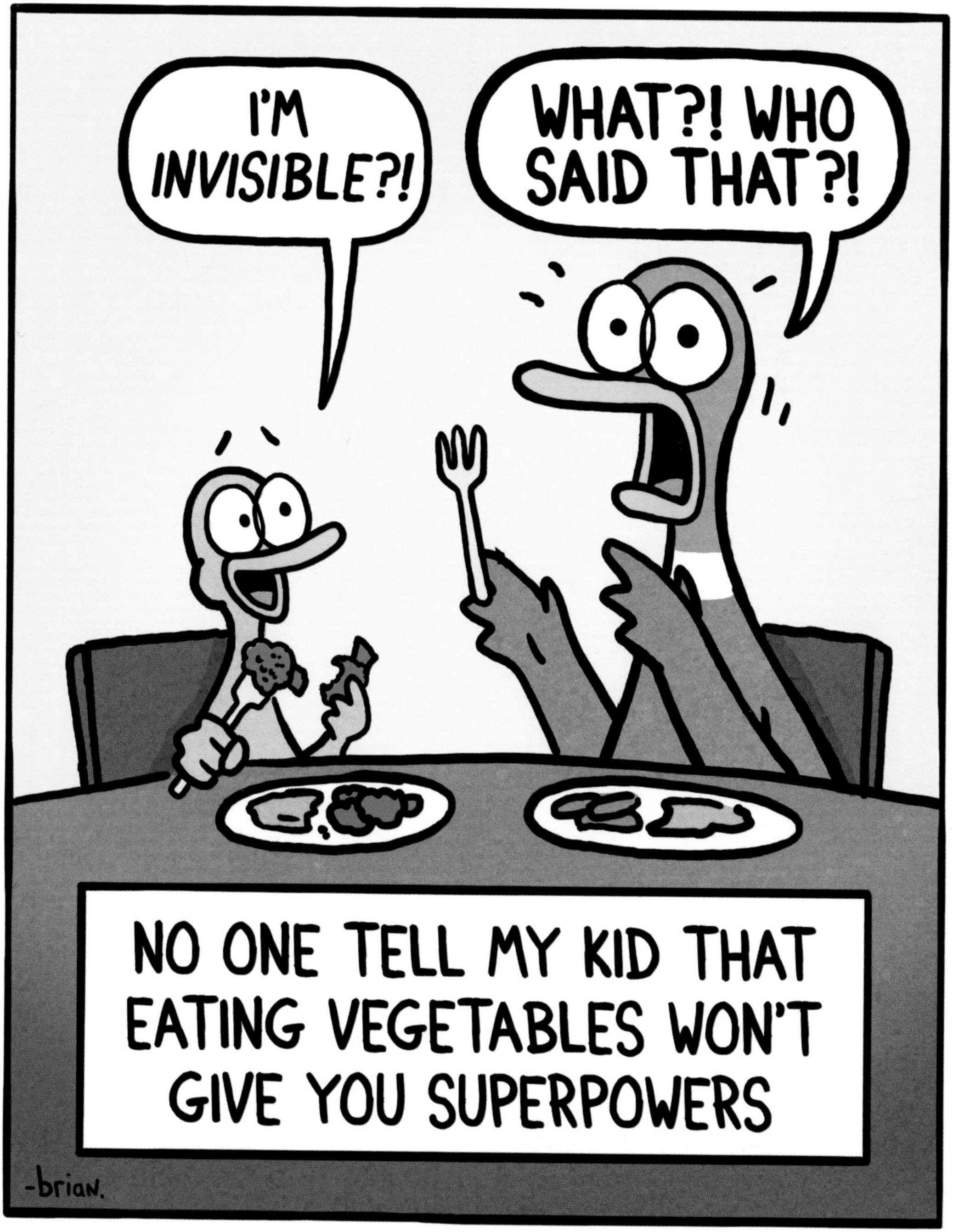
I'M INVISIBLE?!
WHAT?! WHO SAID THAT?!
NO ONE TELL MY KID THAT EATING VEGETABLES WON'T GIVE YOU SUPERPOWERS
-brian.

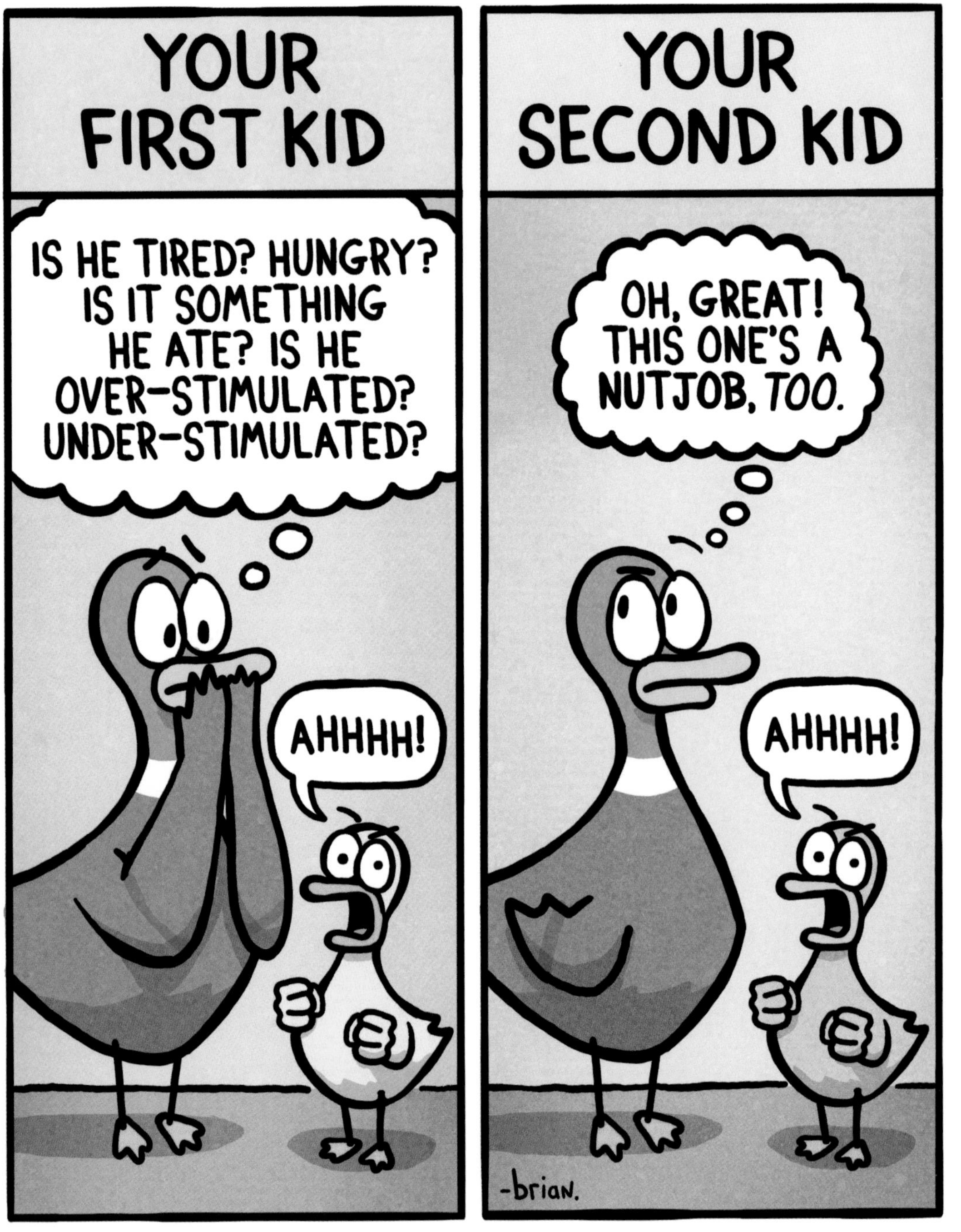
YOUR FIRST KID
IS HE TIRED? HUNGRY? IS IT SOMETHING HE ATE? IS HE OVER-STIMULATED? UNDER-STIMULATED?
AHHHH!
YOUR SECOND KID
OH, GREAT! THIS ONE'S A NUTJOB, *TOO.*
AHHHH!
-brian.

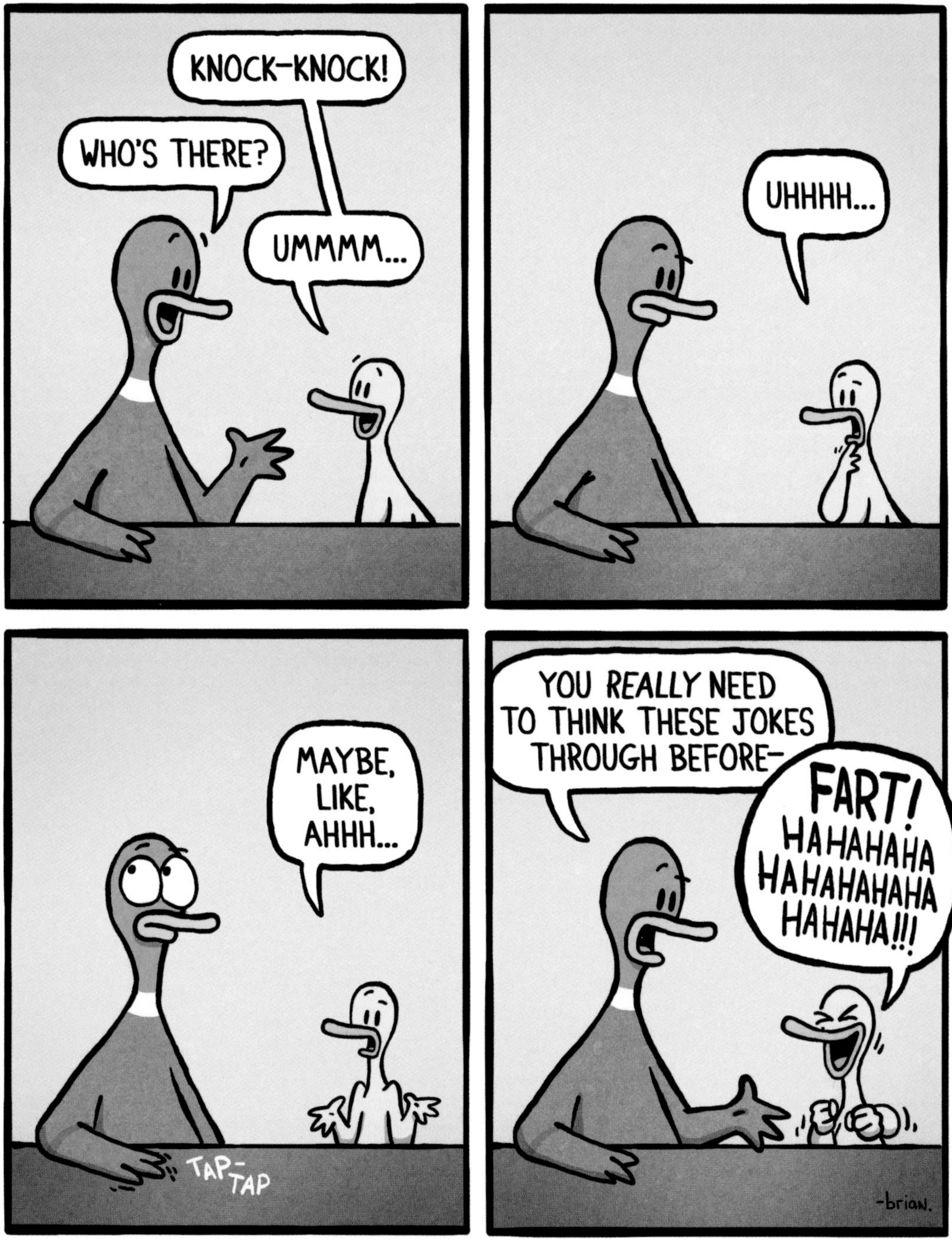
KNOCK–KNOCK!
WHO'S THERE?
UMMMM...
UHHHH...
MAYBE, LIKE, AHHH...
TAP-TAP
YOU REALLY NEED TO THINK THESE JOKES THROUGH BEFORE–
FART! HAHAHAHA HAHAHAHAHA HAHAHA!!!
-brian.

TAKING KIDS TO THE DOCTOR

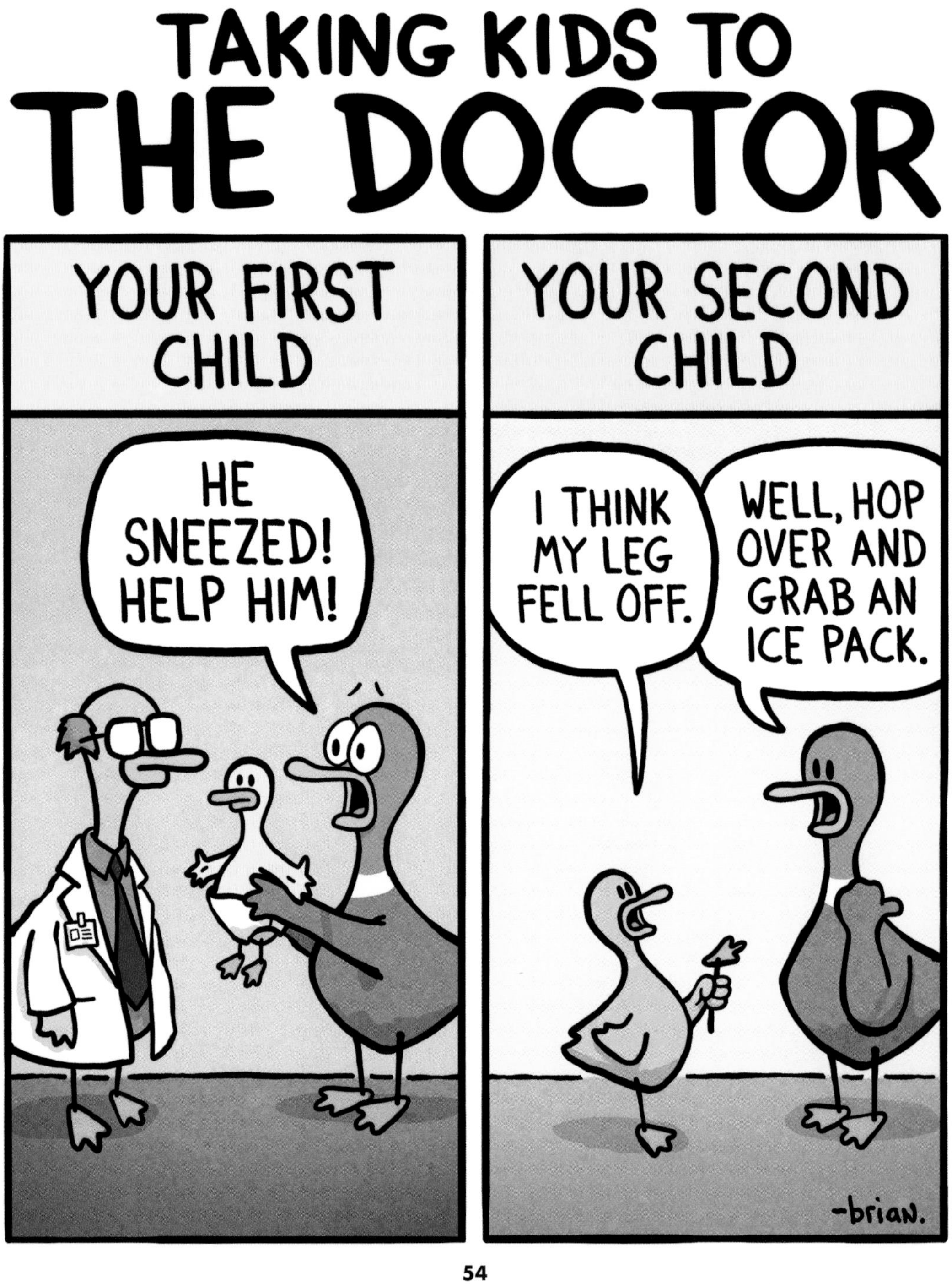

YOUR FIRST CHILD
HE SNEEZED! HELP HIM!
YOUR SECOND CHILD
I THINK MY LEG FELL OFF.
WELL, HOP OVER AND GRAB AN ICE PACK.
-brian.

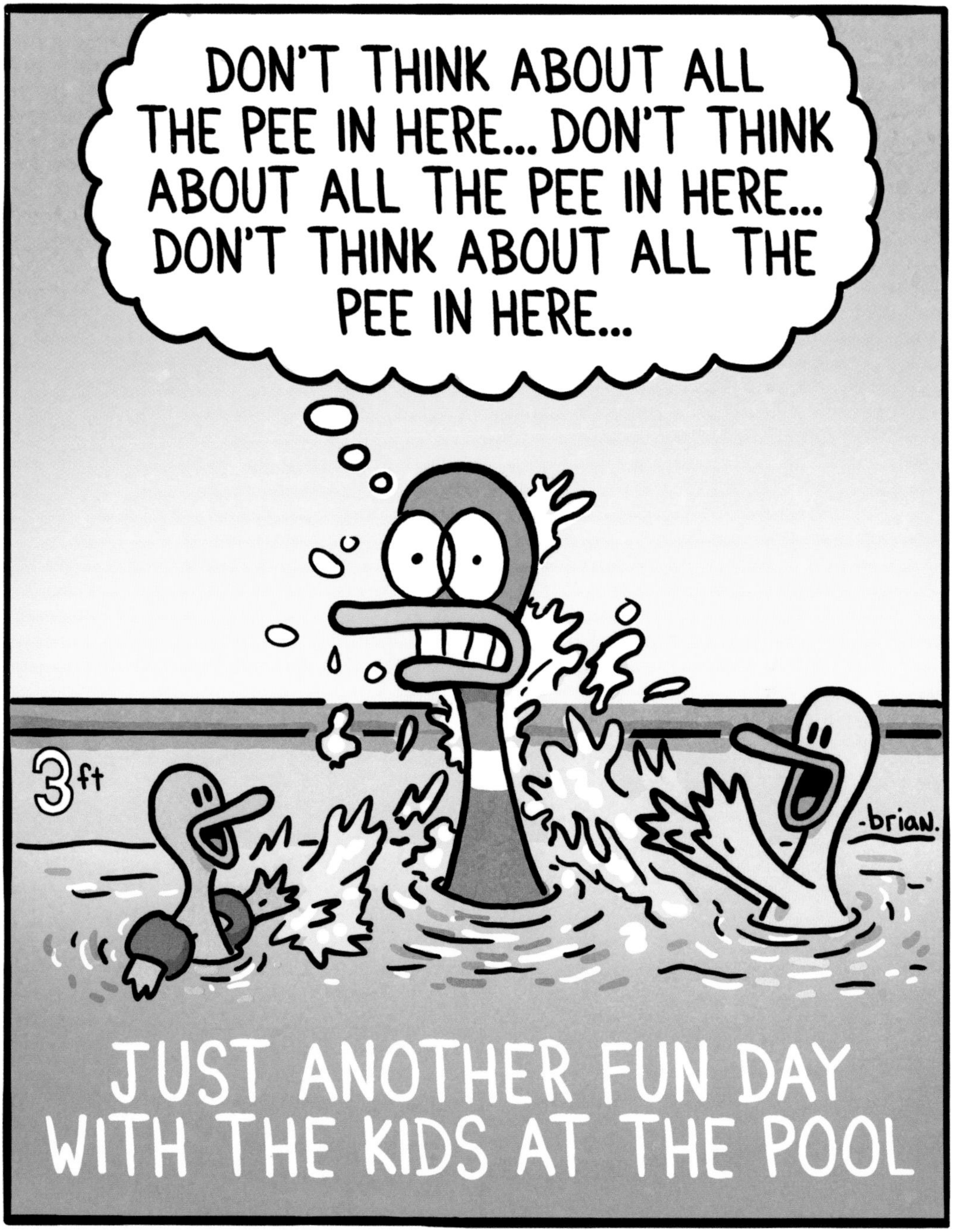
DON'T THINK ABOUT ALL THE PEE IN HERE... DON'T THINK ABOUT ALL THE PEE IN HERE... DON'T THINK ABOUT ALL THE PEE IN HERE...
3 ft
-brian.
JUST ANOTHER FUN DAY WITH THE KIDS AT THE POOL

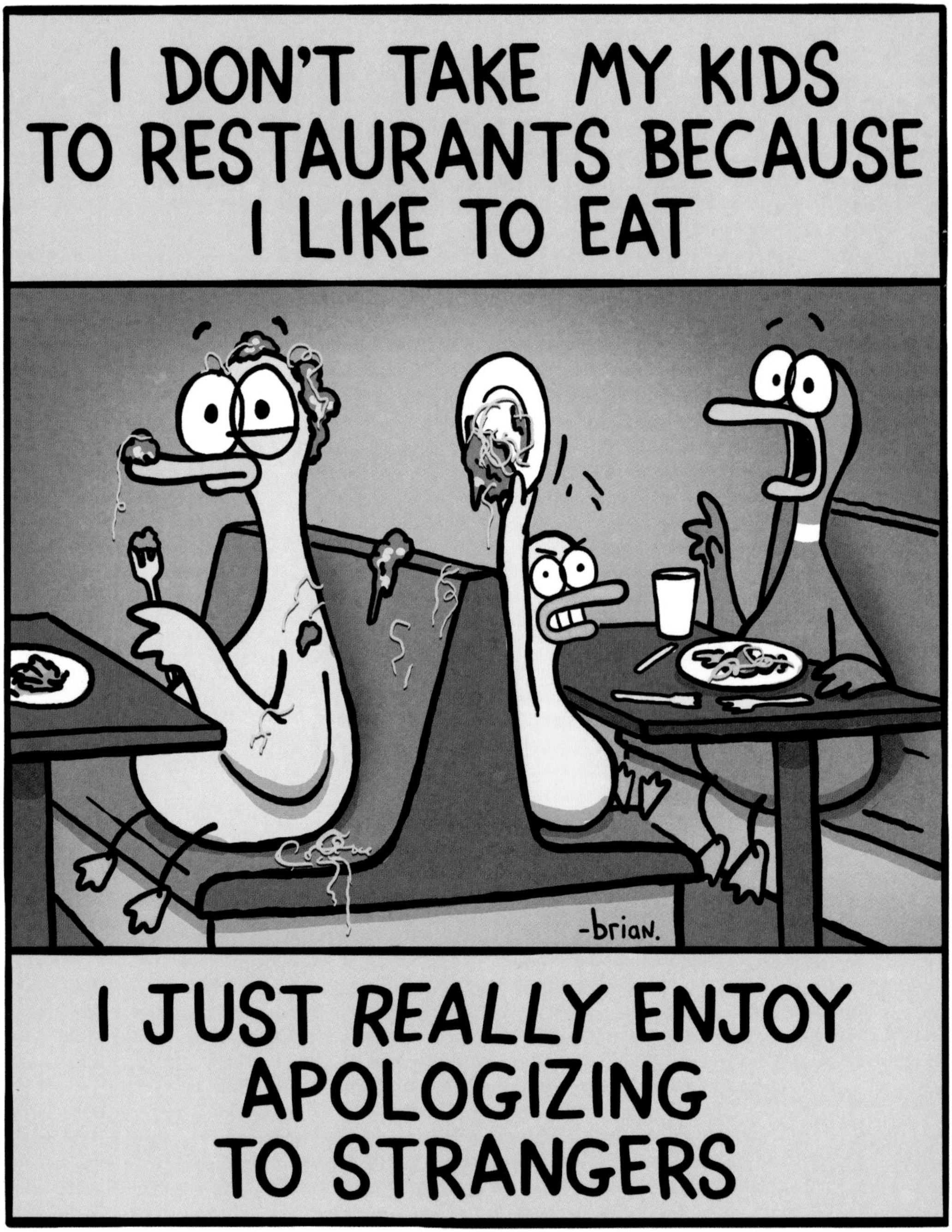
I DON'T TAKE MY KIDS TO RESTAURANTS BECAUSE I LIKE TO EAT
-brian.
I JUST *REALLY* ENJOY APOLOGIZING TO STRANGERS

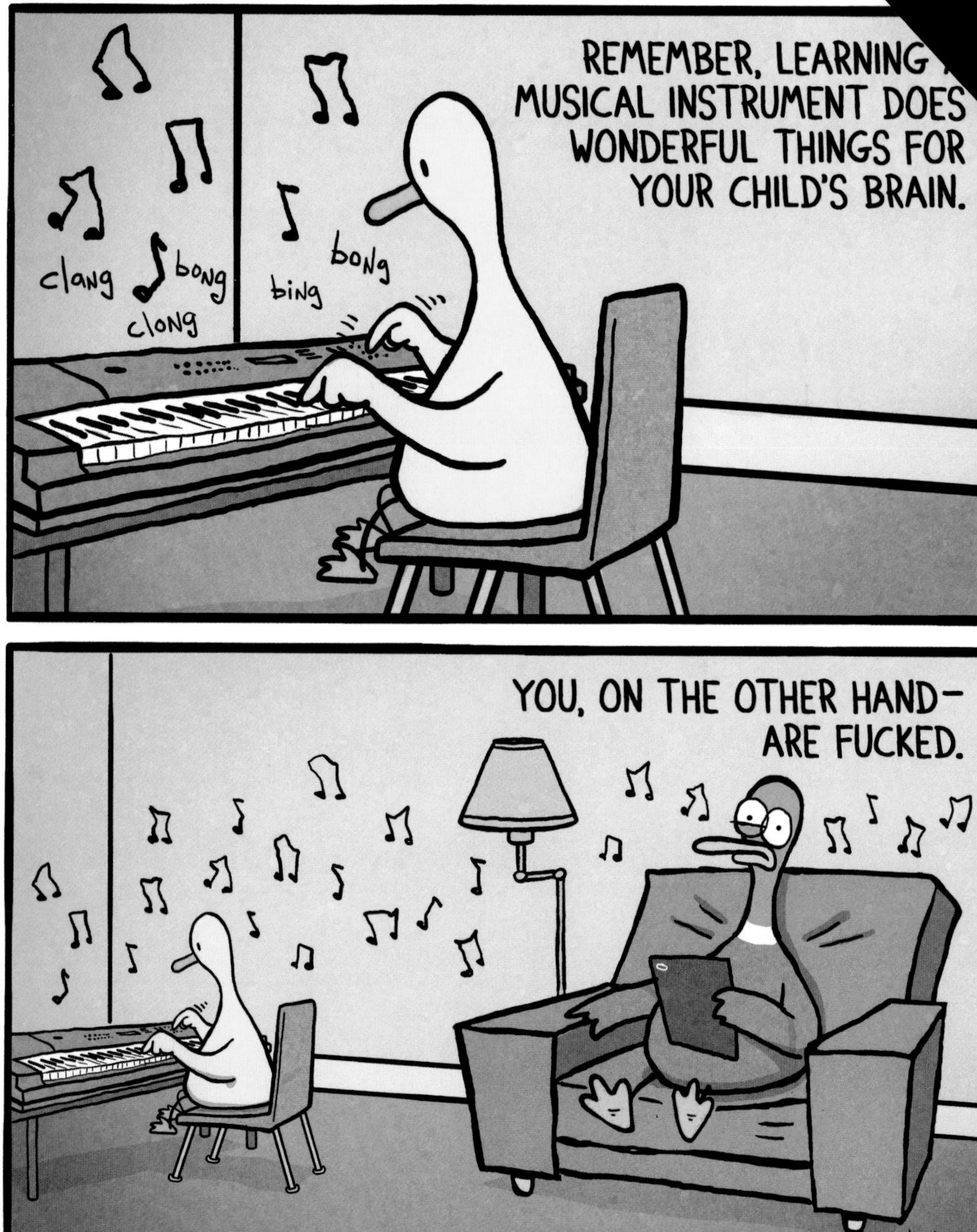
REMEMBER, LEARNING
MUSICAL INSTRUMENT DOES
WONDERFUL THINGS FOR
YOUR CHILD'S BRAIN.
clang
bong
clong
bing
bong
YOU, ON THE OTHER HAND-
ARE FUCKED.
-brian.

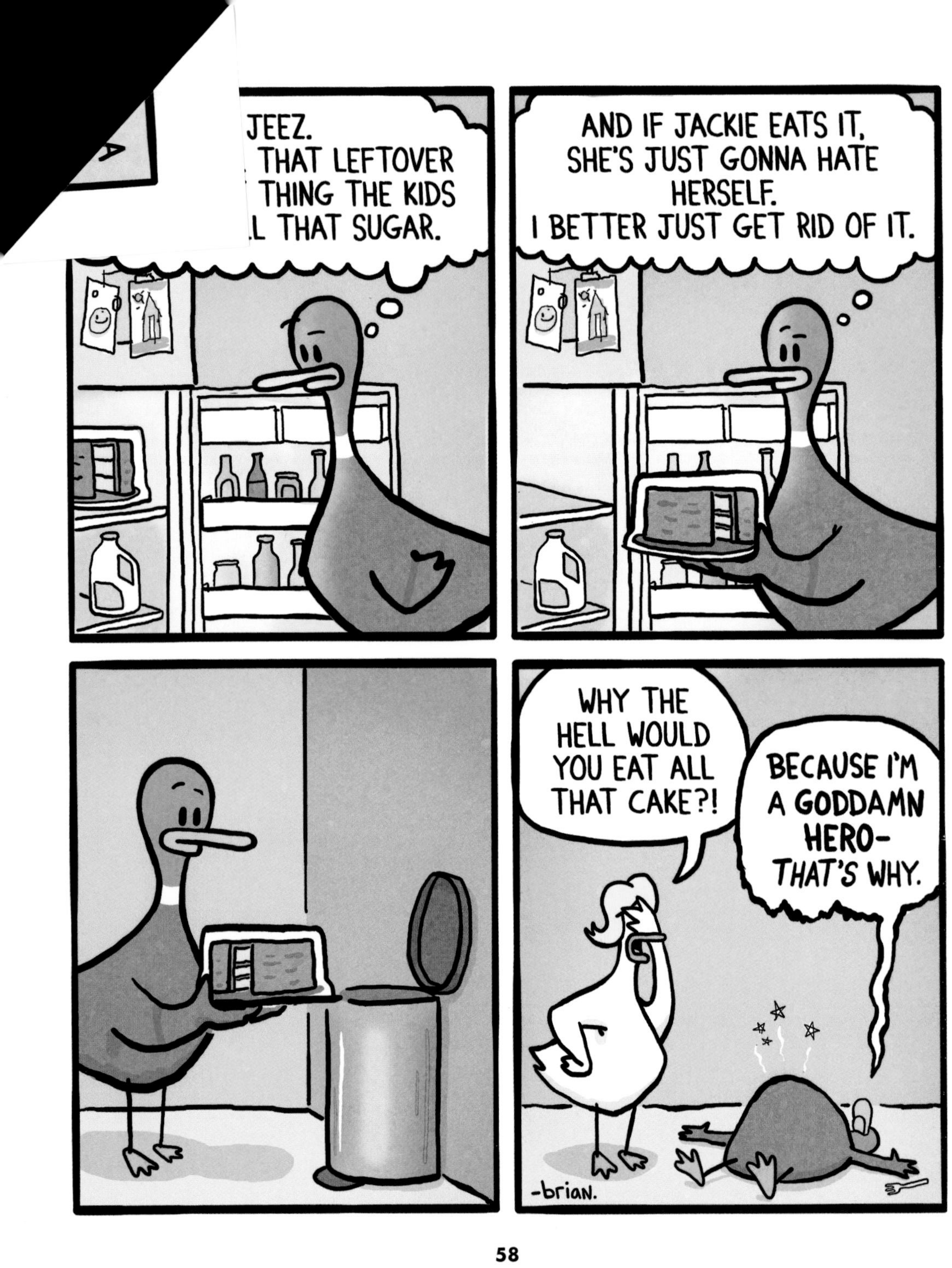
JEEZ.
THAT LEFTOVER
THING THE KIDS
L THAT SUGAR.
AND IF JACKIE EATS IT, SHE'S JUST GONNA HATE HERSELF. I BETTER JUST GET RID OF IT.
WHY THE HELL WOULD YOU EAT ALL THAT CAKE?!
BECAUSE I'M A GODDAMN HERO- THAT'S WHY.
-brian.

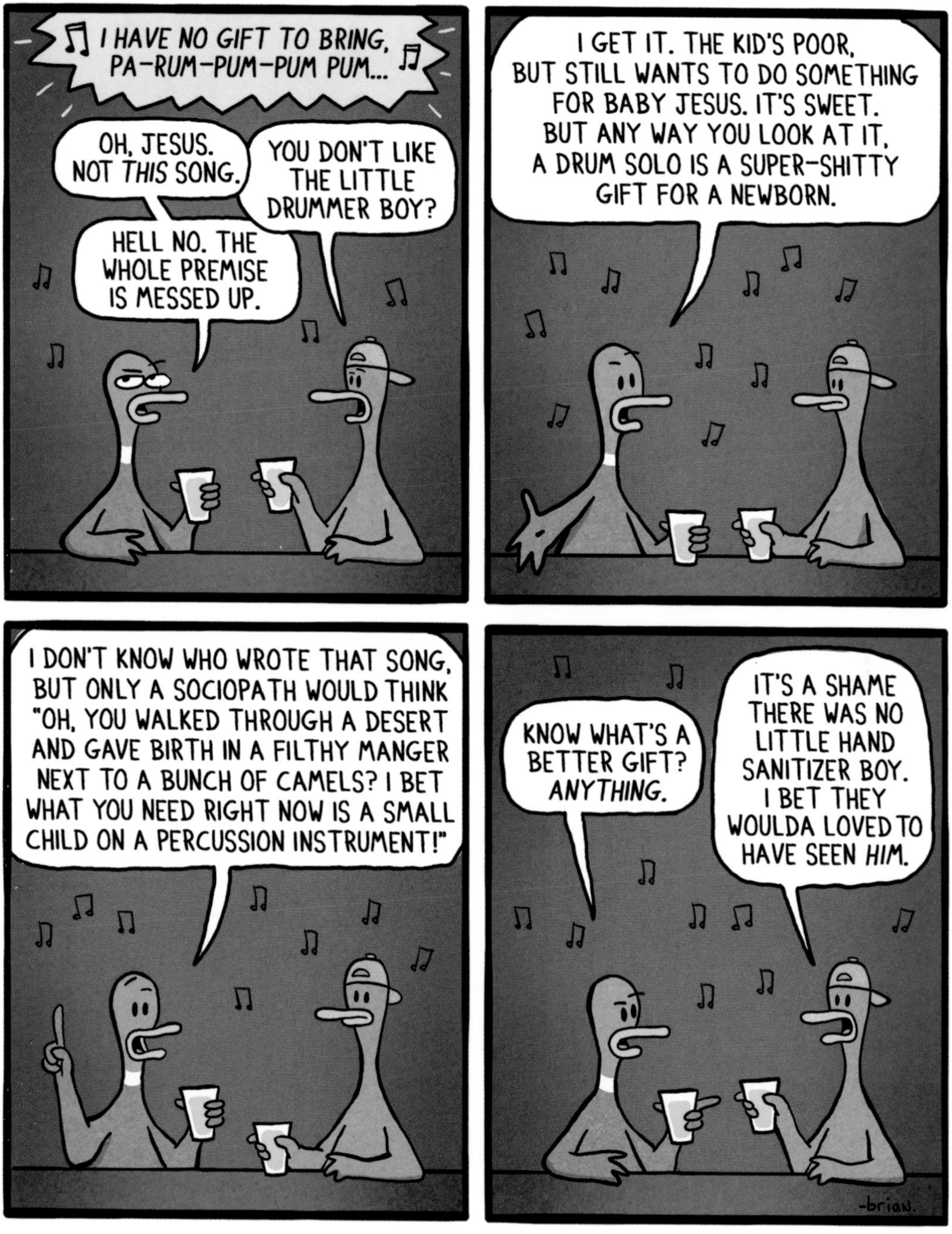
I HAVE NO GIFT TO BRING, PA-RUM-PUM-PUM PUM...
OH, JESUS. NOT *THIS* SONG.
YOU DON'T LIKE THE LITTLE DRUMMER BOY?
HELL NO. THE WHOLE PREMISE IS MESSED UP.
I GET IT. THE KID'S POOR, BUT STILL WANTS TO DO SOMETHING FOR BABY JESUS. IT'S SWEET. BUT ANY WAY YOU LOOK AT IT, A DRUM SOLO IS A SUPER-SHITTY GIFT FOR A NEWBORN.
I DON'T KNOW WHO WROTE THAT SONG, BUT ONLY A SOCIOPATH WOULD THINK "OH, YOU WALKED THROUGH A DESERT AND GAVE BIRTH IN A FILTHY MANGER NEXT TO A BUNCH OF CAMELS? I BET WHAT YOU NEED RIGHT NOW IS A SMALL CHILD ON A PERCUSSION INSTRUMENT!"
KNOW WHAT'S A BETTER GIFT? *ANYTHING.*
IT'S A SHAME THERE WAS NO LITTLE HAND SANITIZER BOY. I BET THEY WOULDA LOVED TO HAVE SEEN *HIM.*
-brian.

RETURNING TO WORK AFTER A
LONG WEEKEND

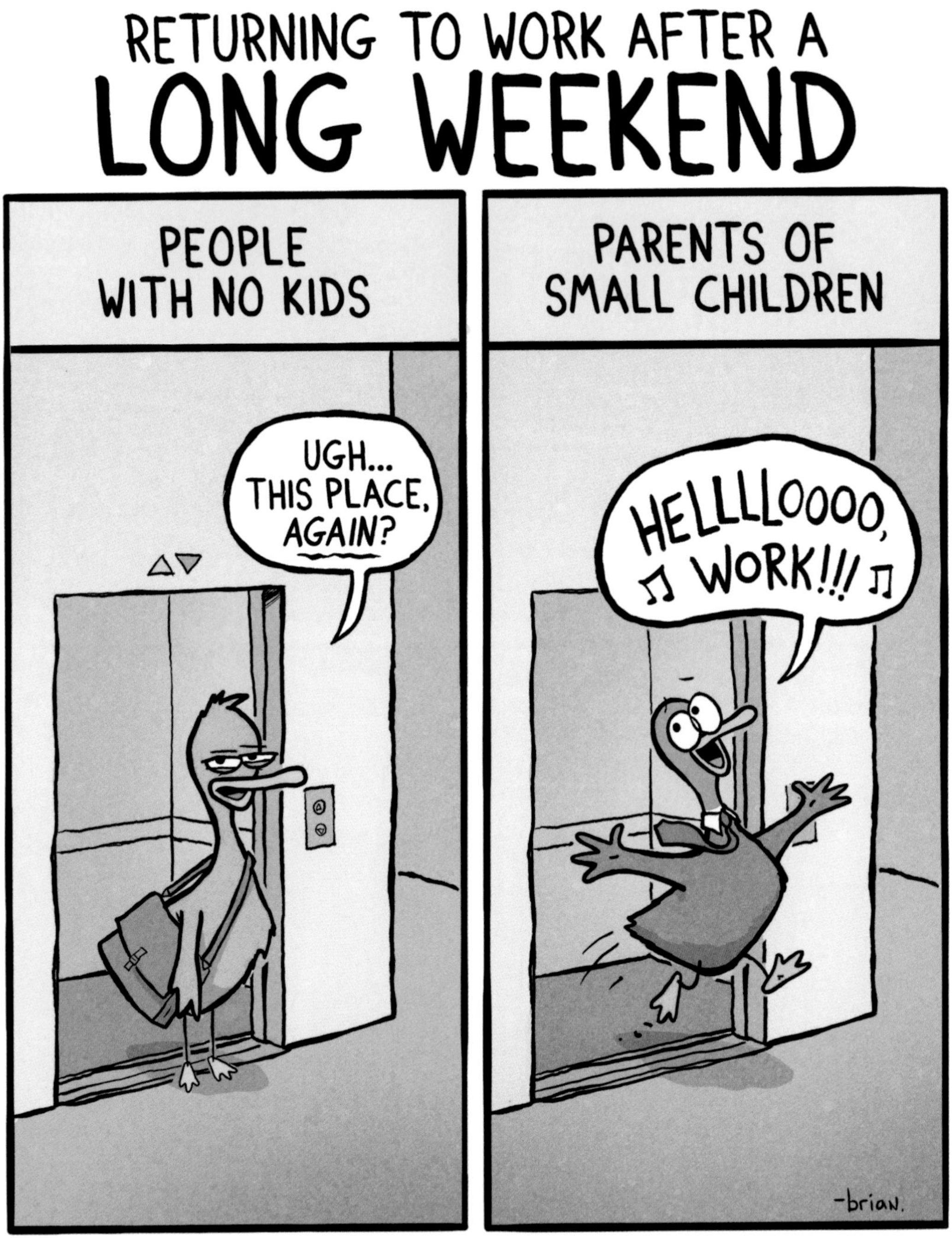
PEOPLE WITH NO KIDS
UGH... THIS PLACE, AGAIN?
PARENTS OF SMALL CHILDREN
HELLLLOOOO, ♫ WORK!!! ♫
-brian.

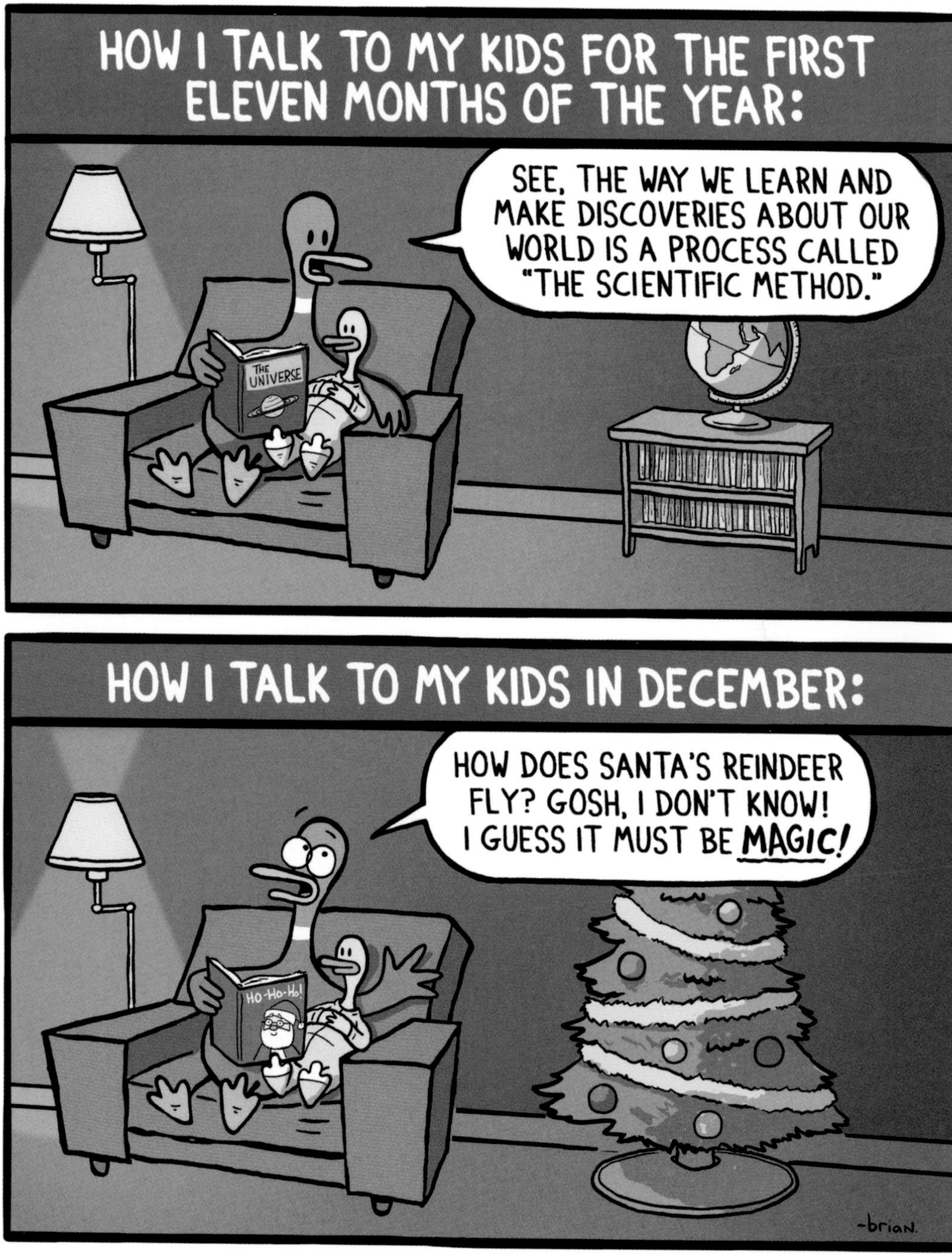

HOW I TALK TO MY KIDS FOR THE FIRST ELEVEN MONTHS OF THE YEAR:
SEE, THE WAY WE LEARN AND MAKE DISCOVERIES ABOUT OUR WORLD IS A PROCESS CALLED "THE SCIENTIFIC METHOD."
THE UNIVERSE
HOW I TALK TO MY KIDS IN DECEMBER:
HOW DOES SANTA'S REINDEER FLY? GOSH, I DON'T KNOW! I GUESS IT MUST BE MAGIC!
Ho-Ho-Ho!
-brian.

PLAYING MAKE PRETEND

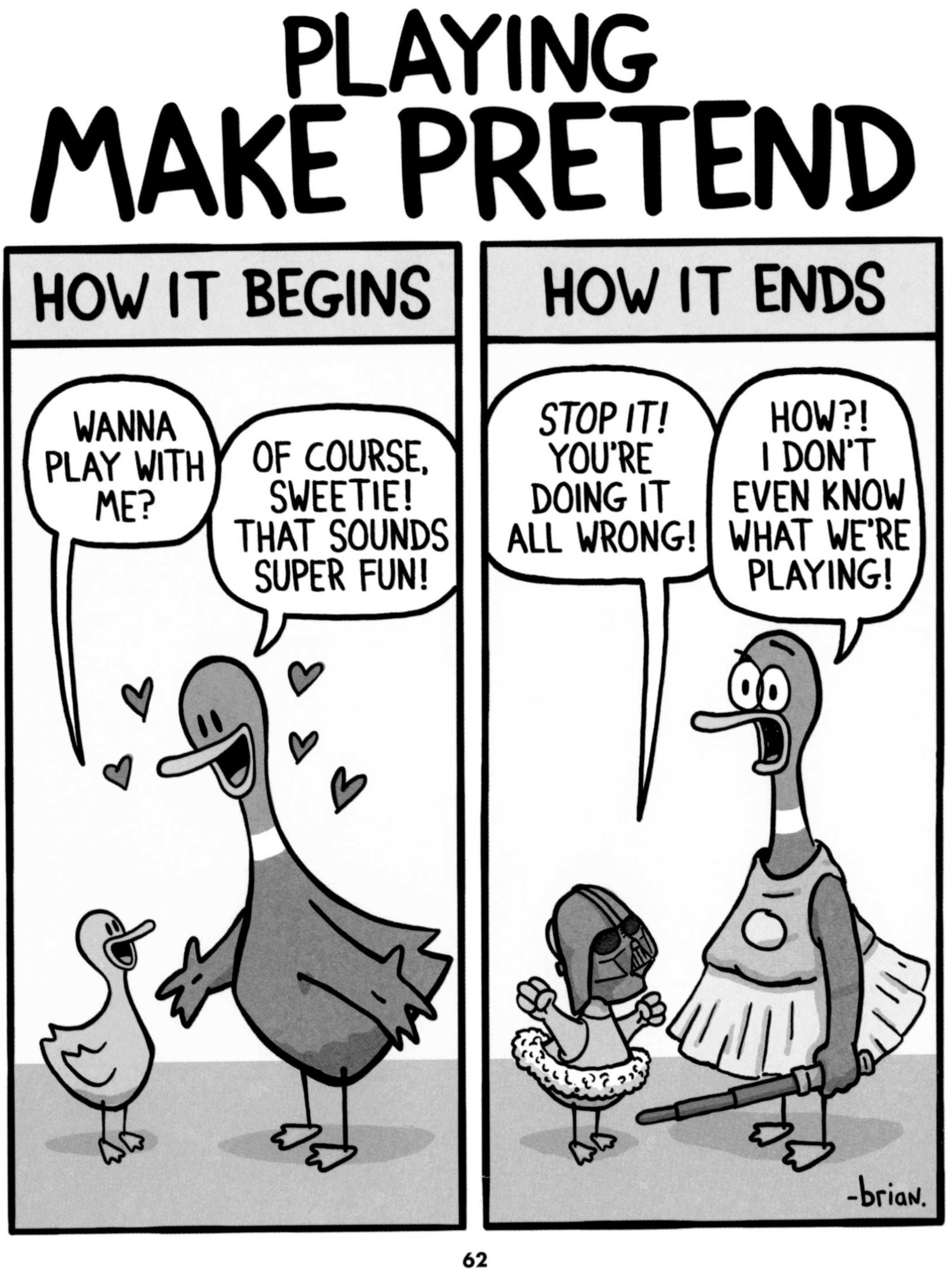
HOW IT BEGINS
WANNA PLAY WITH ME?
OF COURSE, SWEETIE! THAT SOUNDS SUPER FUN!
HOW IT ENDS
STOP IT! YOU'RE DOING IT ALL WRONG!
HOW?! I DON'T EVEN KNOW WHAT WE'RE PLAYING!
-brian.

ME-TIME

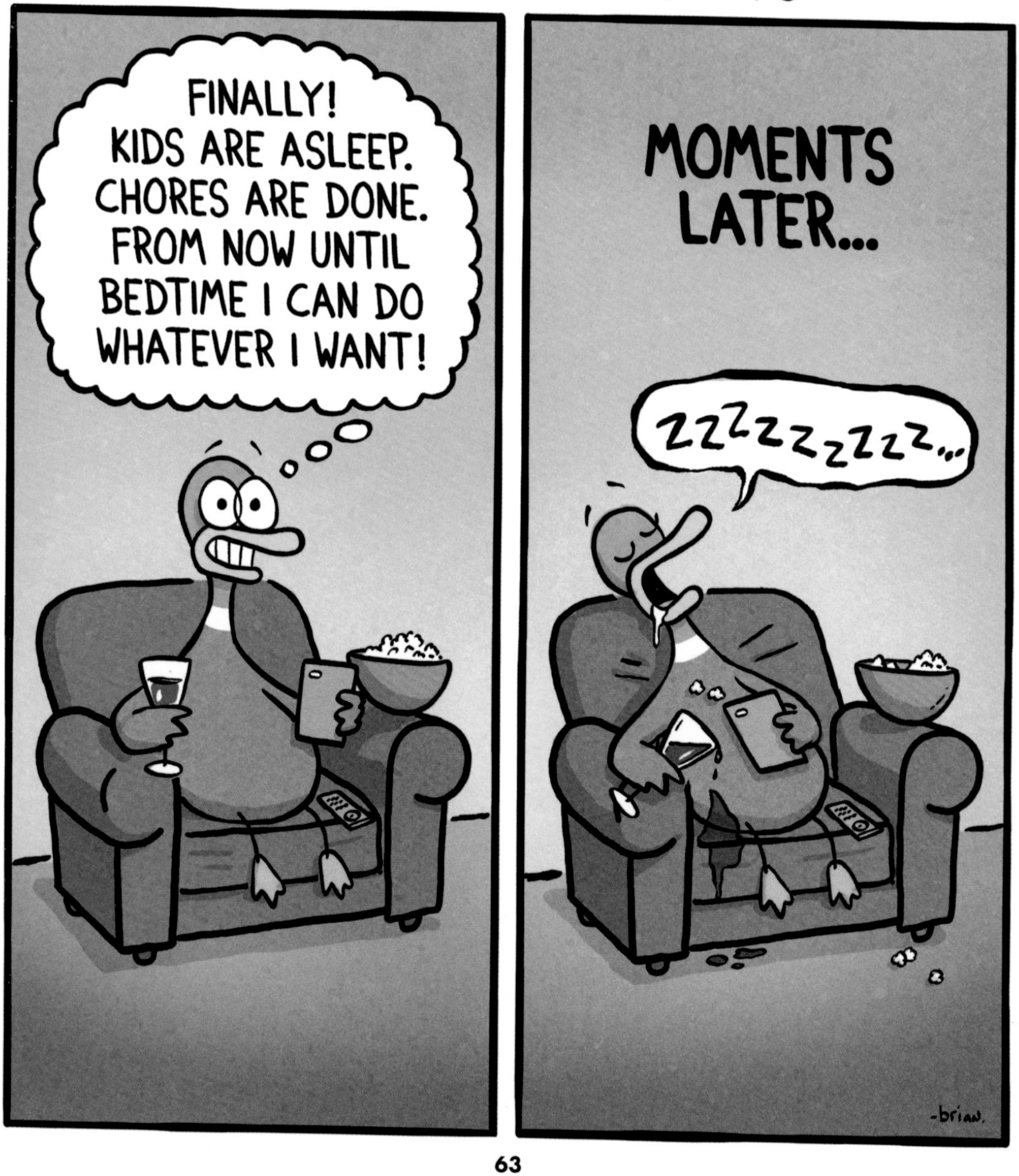

FINALLY! KIDS ARE ASLEEP. CHORES ARE DONE. FROM NOW UNTIL BEDTIME I CAN DO WHATEVER I WANT!
MOMENTS LATER...
ZZZZZZZZZZ...
-brian.

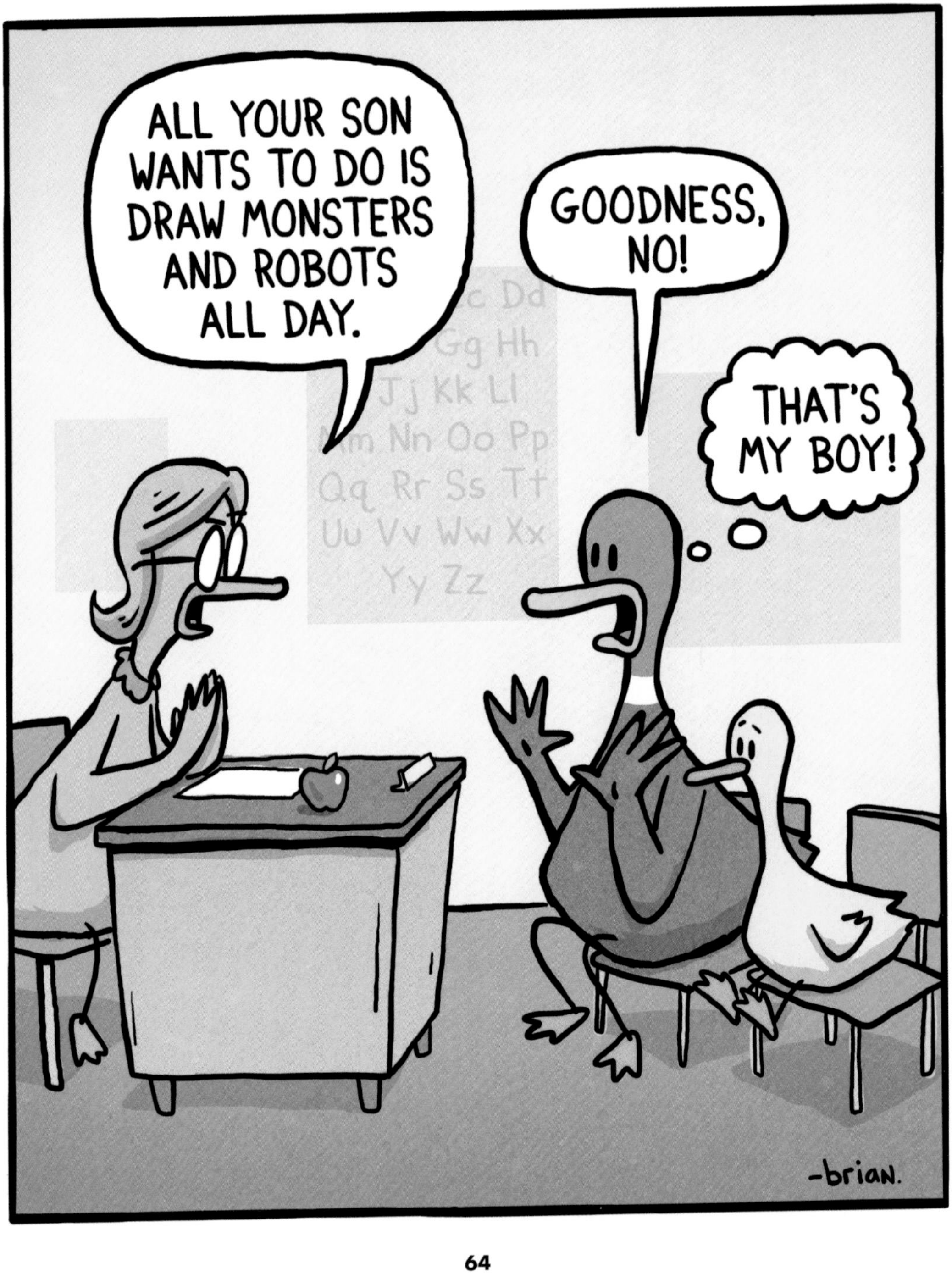
ALL YOUR SON WANTS TO DO IS DRAW MONSTERS AND ROBOTS ALL DAY.
GOODNESS, NO!
THAT'S MY BOY!
Aa Bb Cc Dd Ee Ff Gg Hh Ii Jj Kk Ll Mm Nn Oo Pp Qq Rr Ss Tt Uu Vv Ww Xx Yy Zz
-brian.

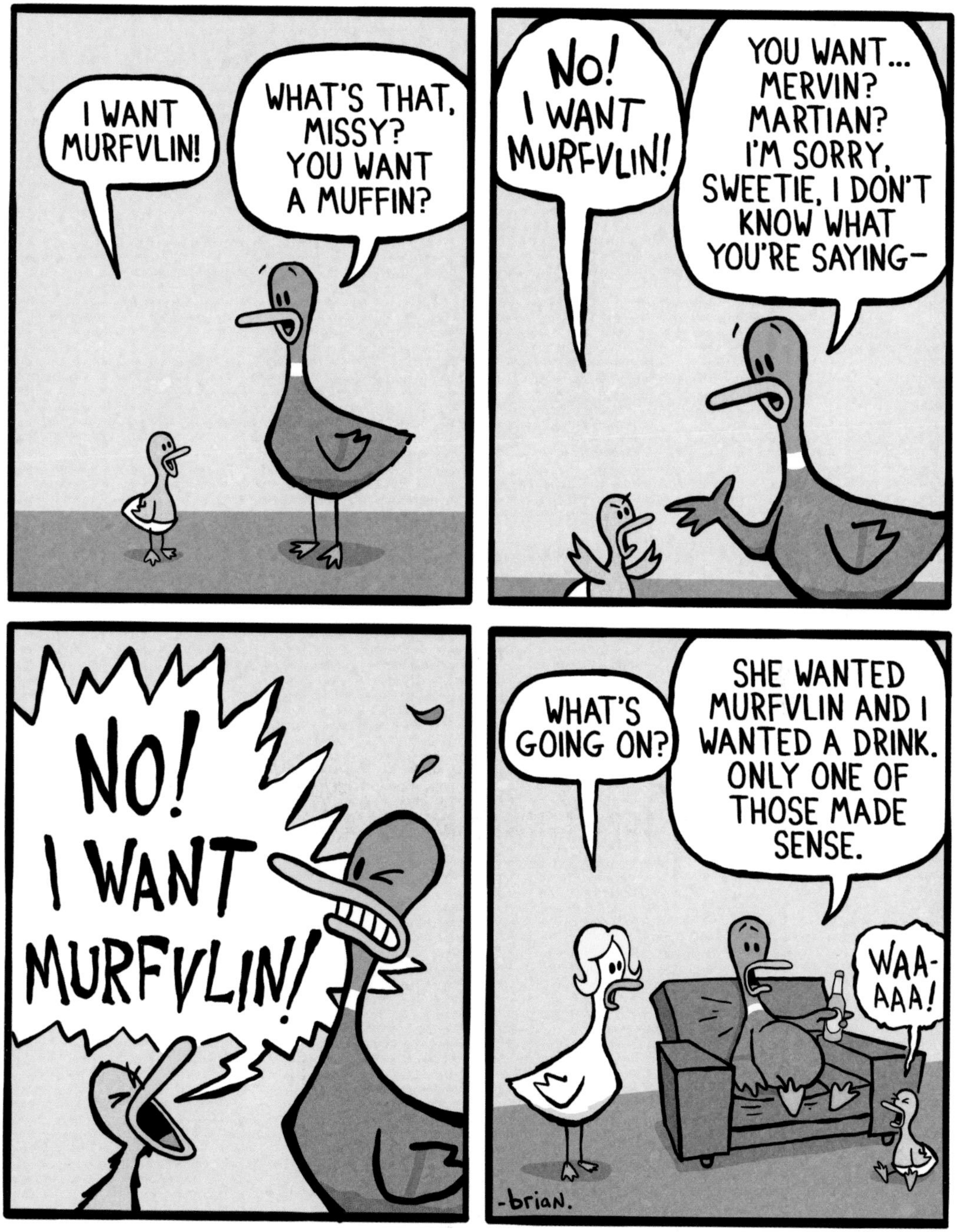
I WANT MURFVLIN!
WHAT'S THAT, MISSY? YOU WANT A MUFFIN?
NO! I WANT MURFVLIN!
YOU WANT... MERVIN? MARTIAN? I'M SORRY, SWEETIE, I DON'T KNOW WHAT YOU'RE SAYING—
NO! I WANT MURFVLIN!
WHAT'S GOING ON?
SHE WANTED MURFVLIN AND I WANTED A DRINK. ONLY ONE OF THOSE MADE SENSE.
WAA-AAA!
-brian.

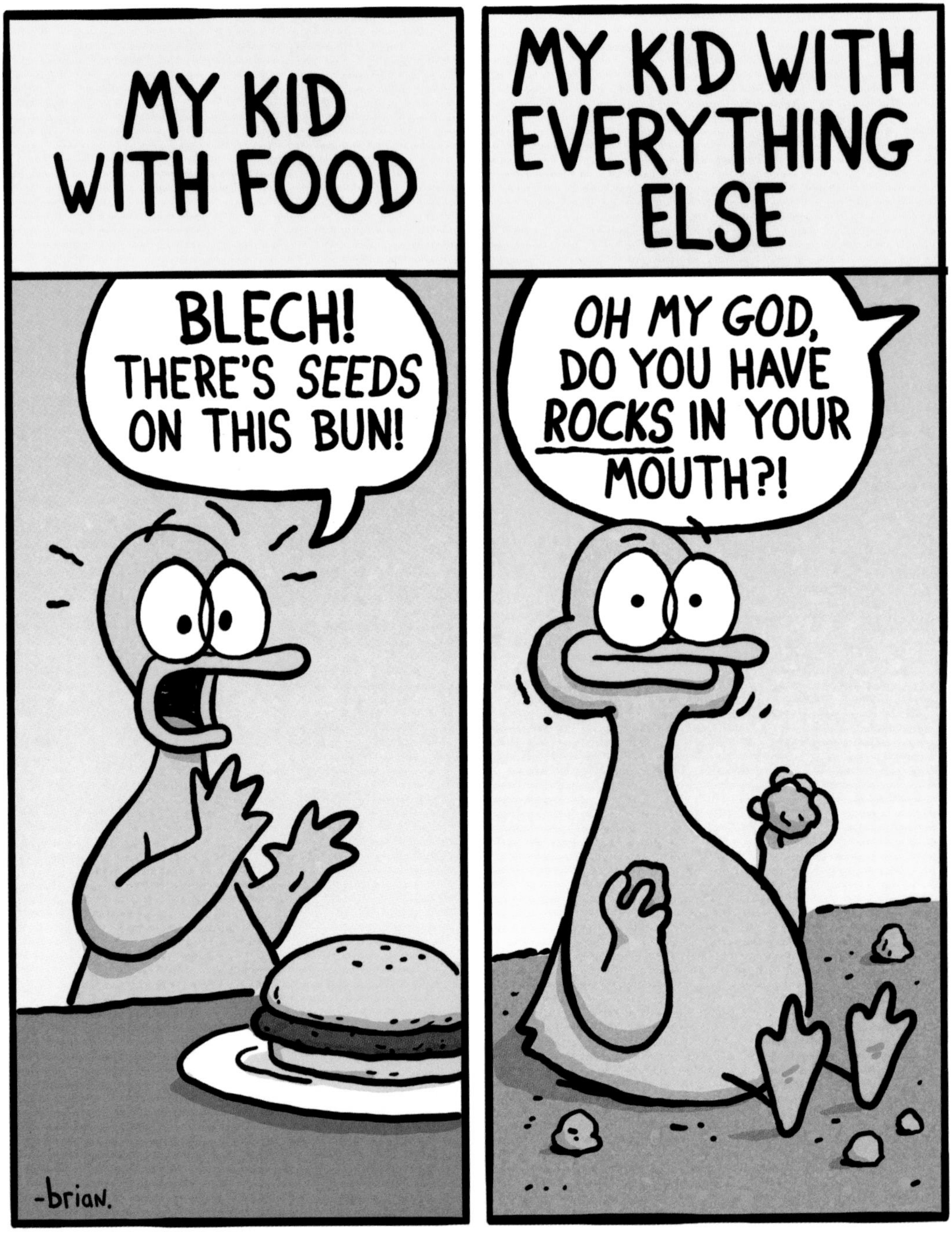
MY KID WITH FOOD
BLECH! THERE'S SEEDS ON THIS BUN!
-brian.
MY KID WITH EVERYTHING ELSE
OH MY GOD, DO YOU HAVE ROCKS IN YOUR MOUTH?!

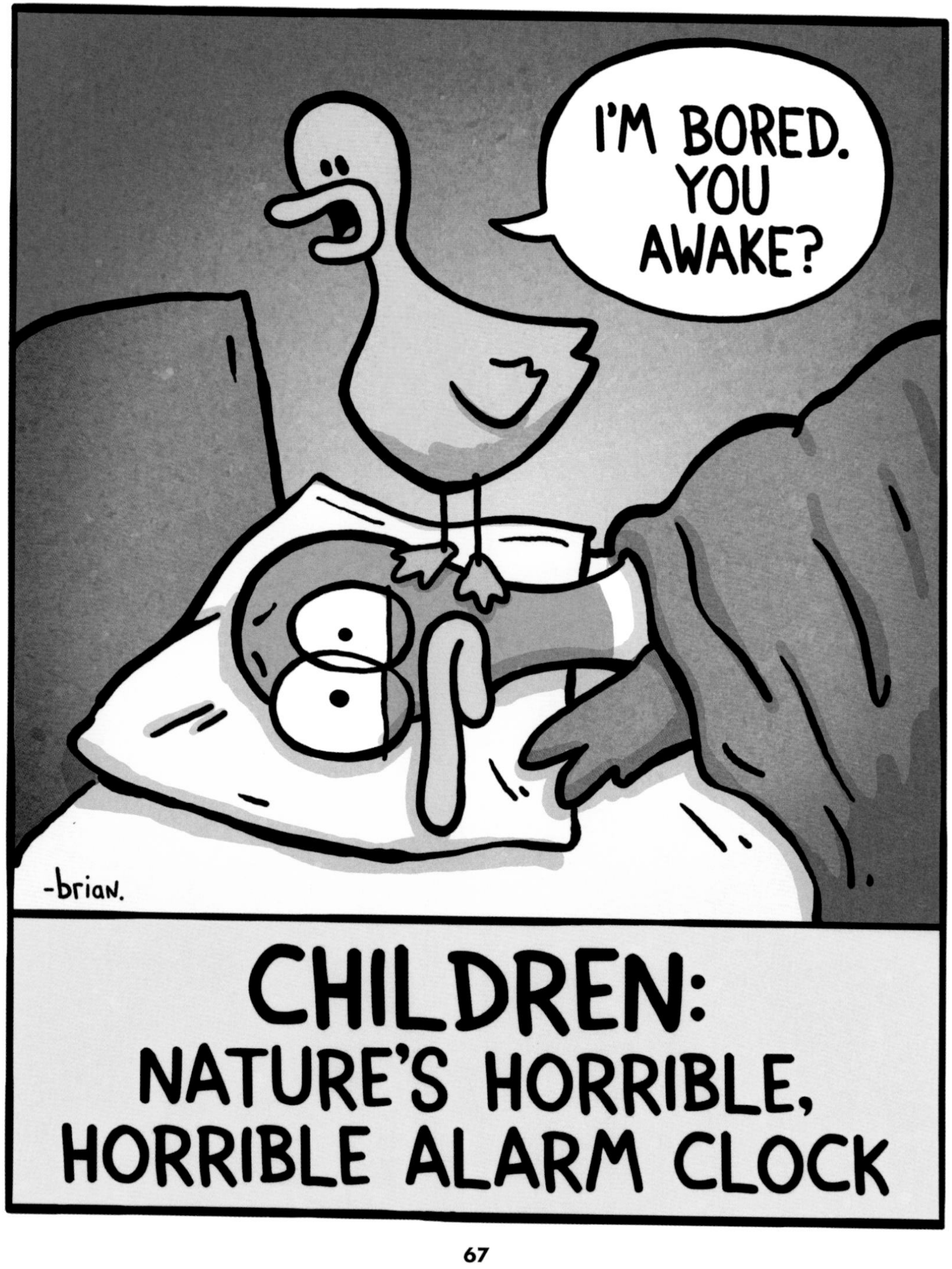
I'M BORED. YOU AWAKE?
-brian.

CHILDREN:
NATURE'S HORRIBLE,
HORRIBLE ALARM CLOCK

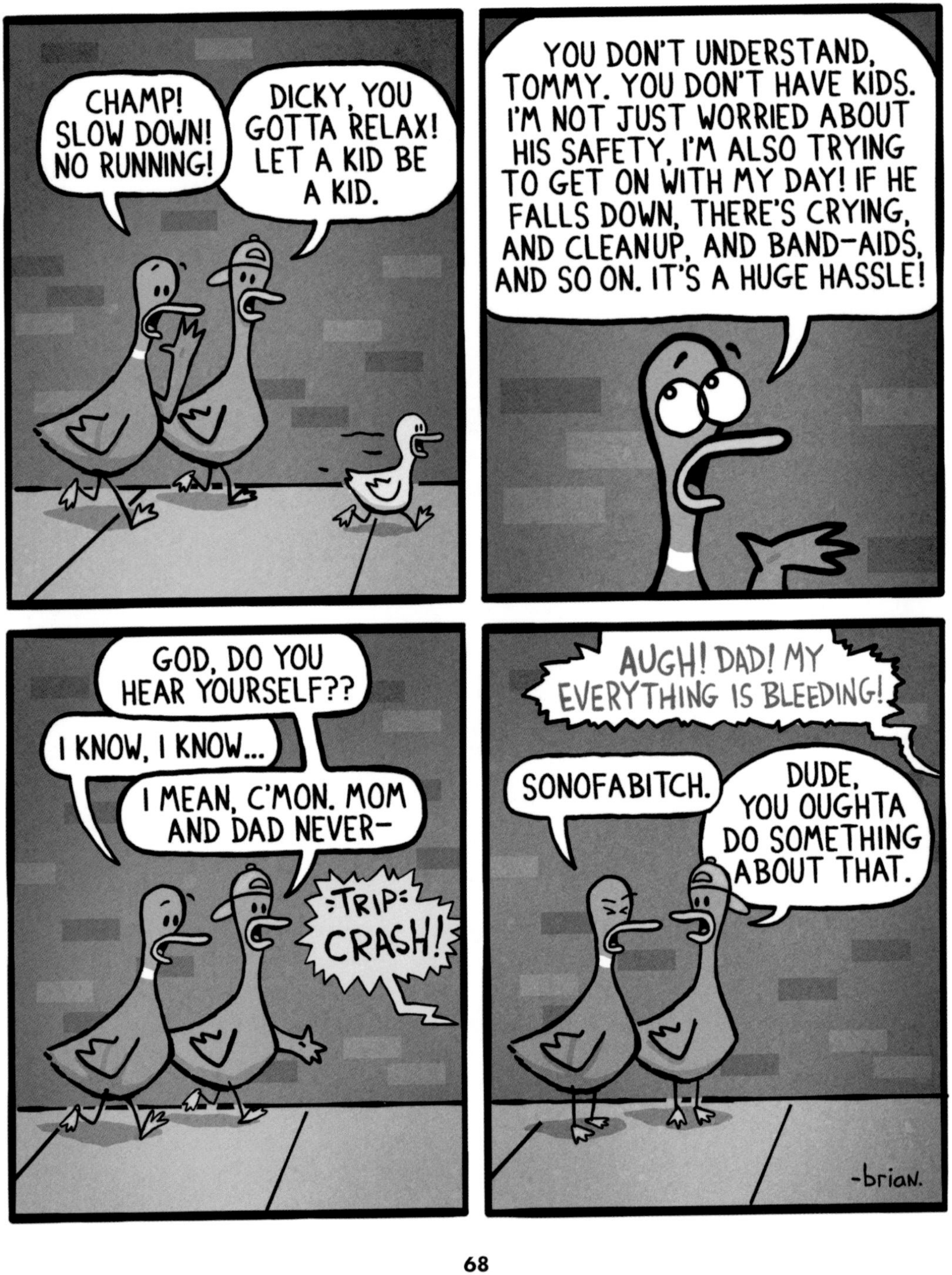
CHAMP! SLOW DOWN! NO RUNNING!
DICKY, YOU GOTTA RELAX! LET A KID BE A KID.
YOU DON'T UNDERSTAND, TOMMY. YOU DON'T HAVE KIDS. I'M NOT JUST WORRIED ABOUT HIS SAFETY, I'M ALSO TRYING TO GET ON WITH MY DAY! IF HE FALLS DOWN, THERE'S CRYING, AND CLEANUP, AND BAND-AIDS, AND SO ON. IT'S A HUGE HASSLE!
GOD, DO YOU HEAR YOURSELF??
I KNOW, I KNOW...
I MEAN, C'MON. MOM AND DAD NEVER—
TRIP
CRASH!
AUGH! DAD! MY EVERYTHING IS BLEEDING!
SONOFABITCH.
DUDE, YOU OUGHTA DO SOMETHING ABOUT THAT.
-brian.

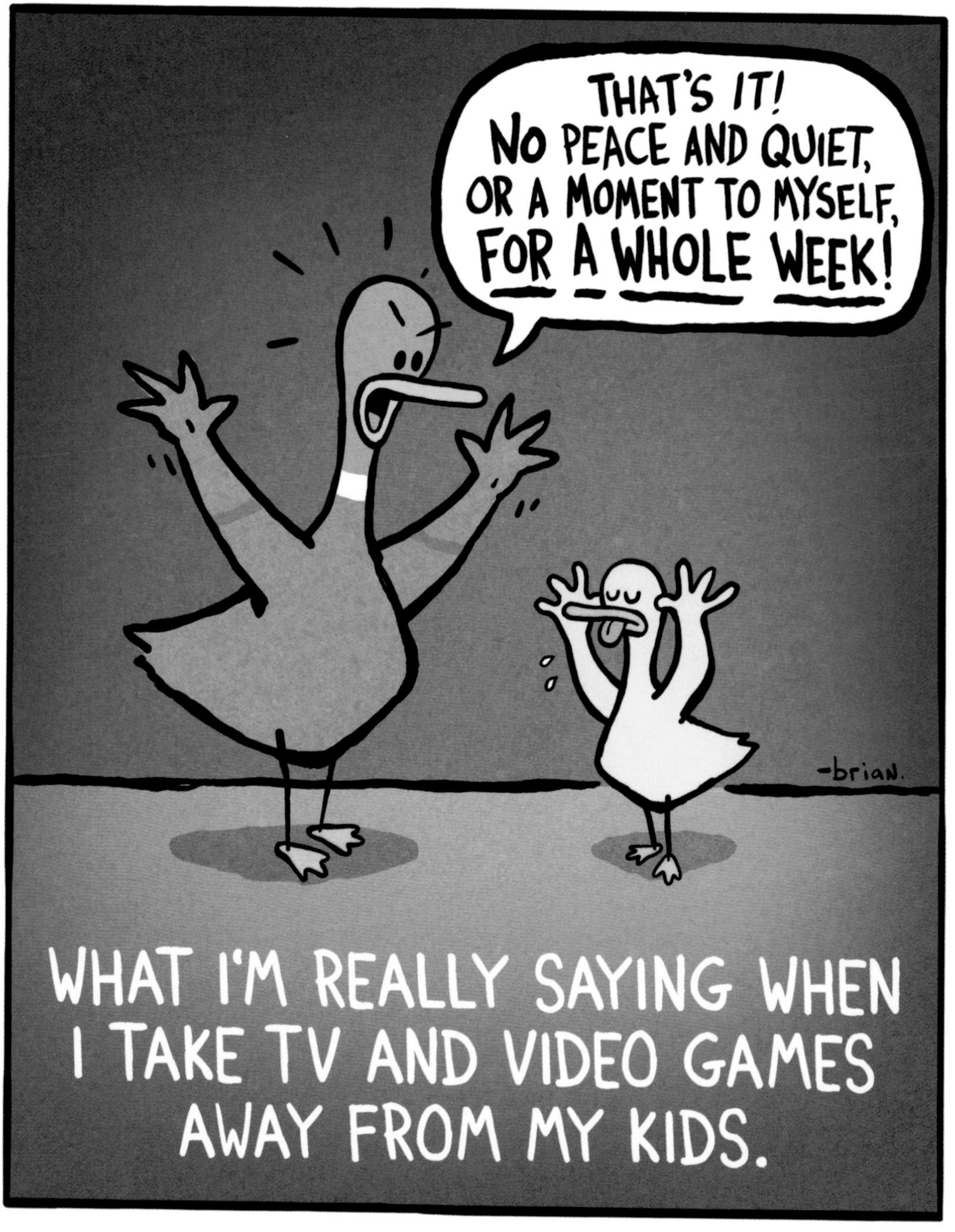
THAT'S IT! NO PEACE AND QUIET, OR A MOMENT TO MYSELF, FOR A WHOLE WEEK!
-brian.
WHAT I'M REALLY SAYING WHEN I TAKE TV AND VIDEO GAMES AWAY FROM MY KIDS.

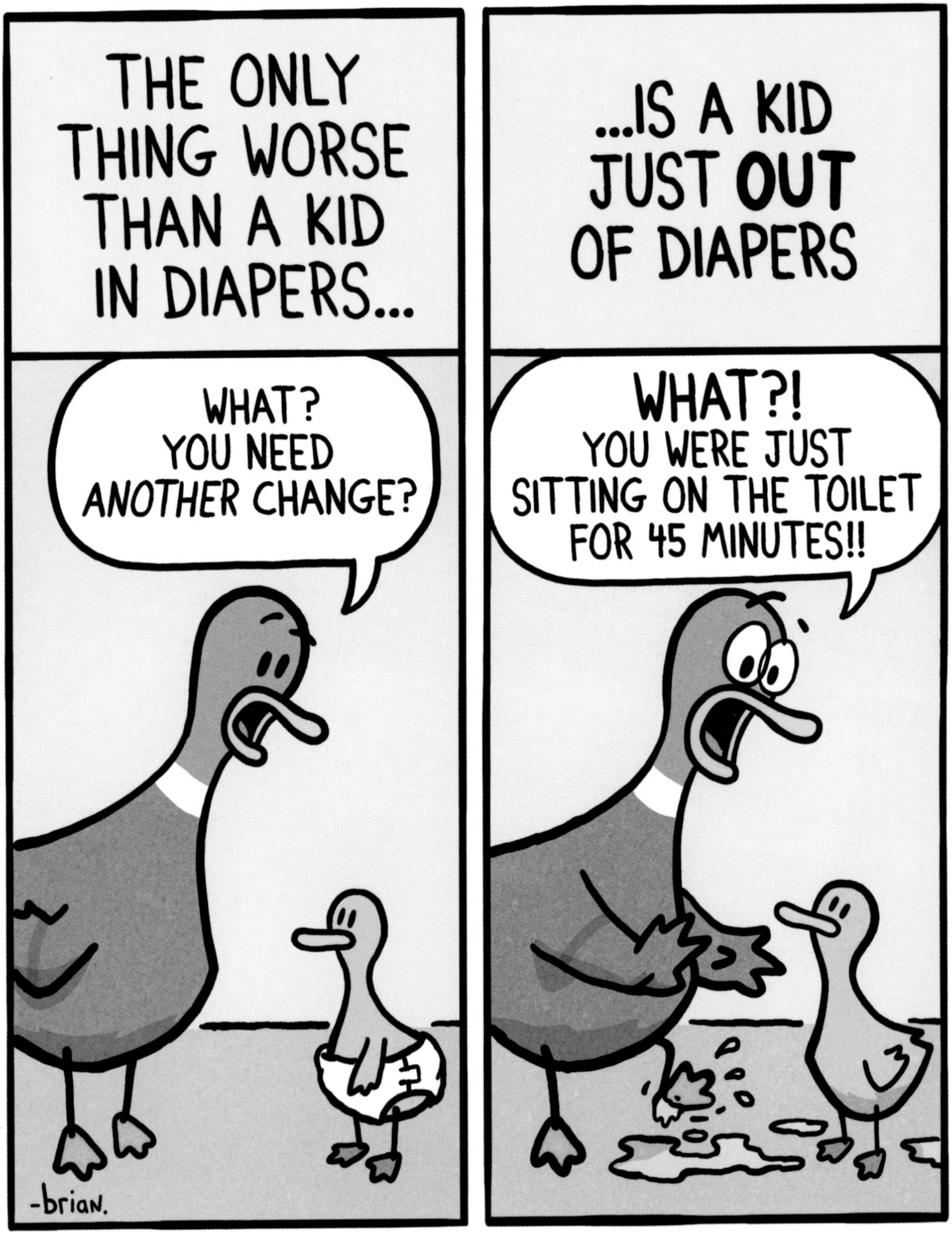
THE ONLY THING WORSE THAN A KID IN DIAPERS...
WHAT? YOU NEED ANOTHER CHANGE?
-brian.
...IS A KID JUST **OUT** OF DIAPERS
WHAT?! YOU WERE JUST SITTING ON THE TOILET FOR 45 MINUTES!!

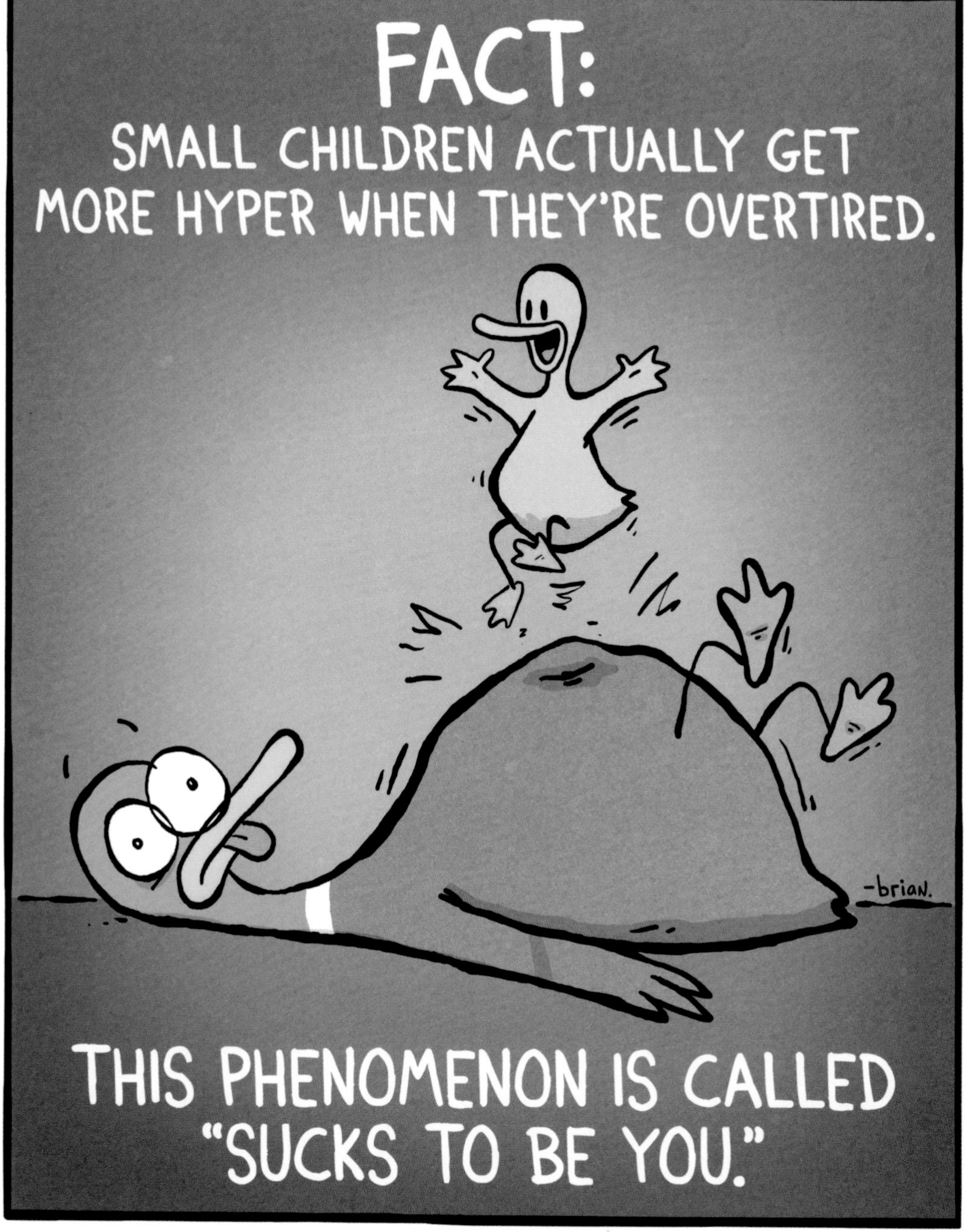
FACT:
SMALL CHILDREN ACTUALLY GET MORE HYPER WHEN THEY'RE OVERTIRED.
-brian.
THIS PHENOMENON IS CALLED "SUCKS TO BE YOU."

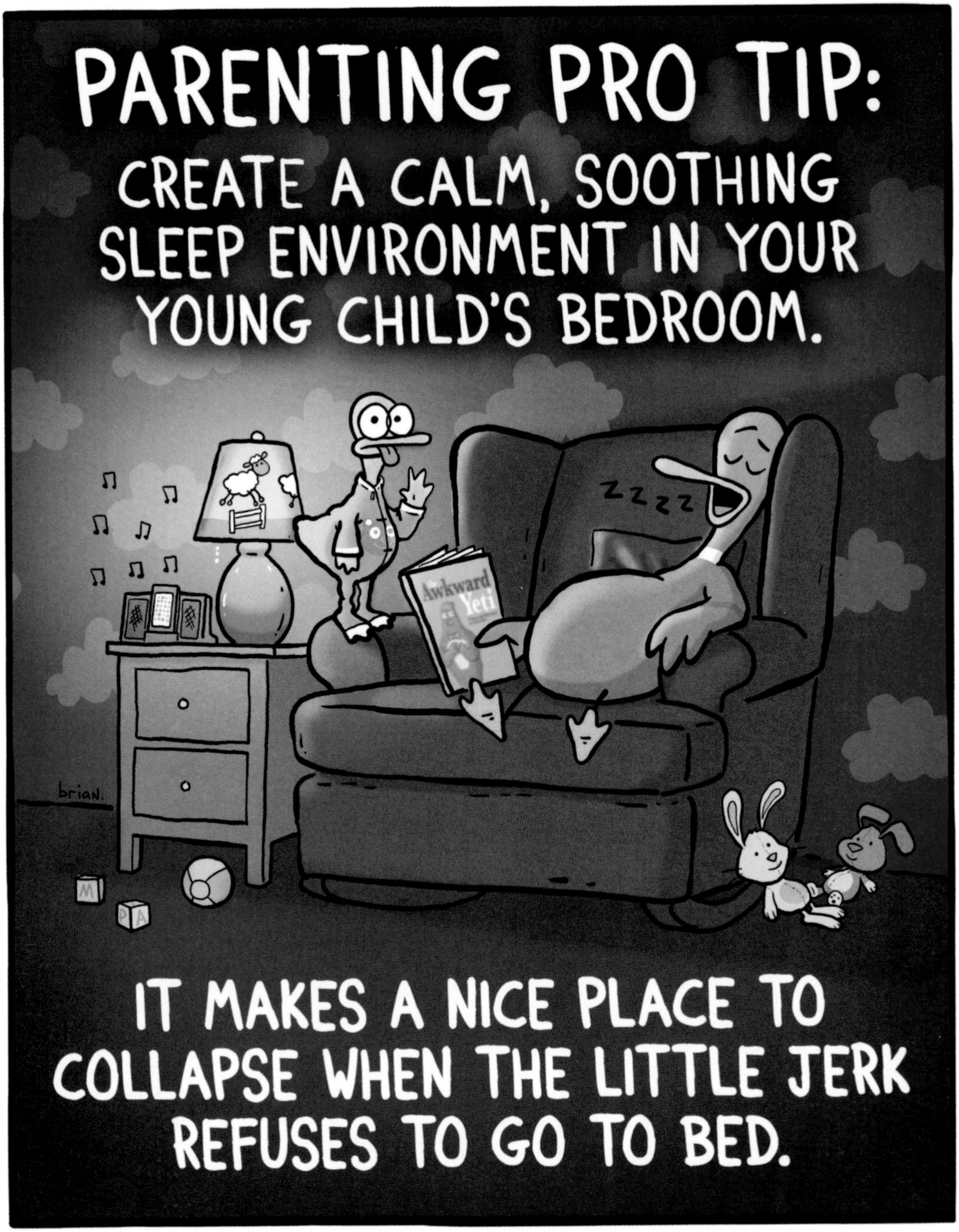
PARENTING PRO TIP:
CREATE A CALM, SOOTHING SLEEP ENVIRONMENT IN YOUR YOUNG CHILD'S BEDROOM.
ZZZZ
Awkward Yeti
brian.
IT MAKES A NICE PLACE TO COLLAPSE WHEN THE LITTLE JERK REFUSES TO GO TO BED.

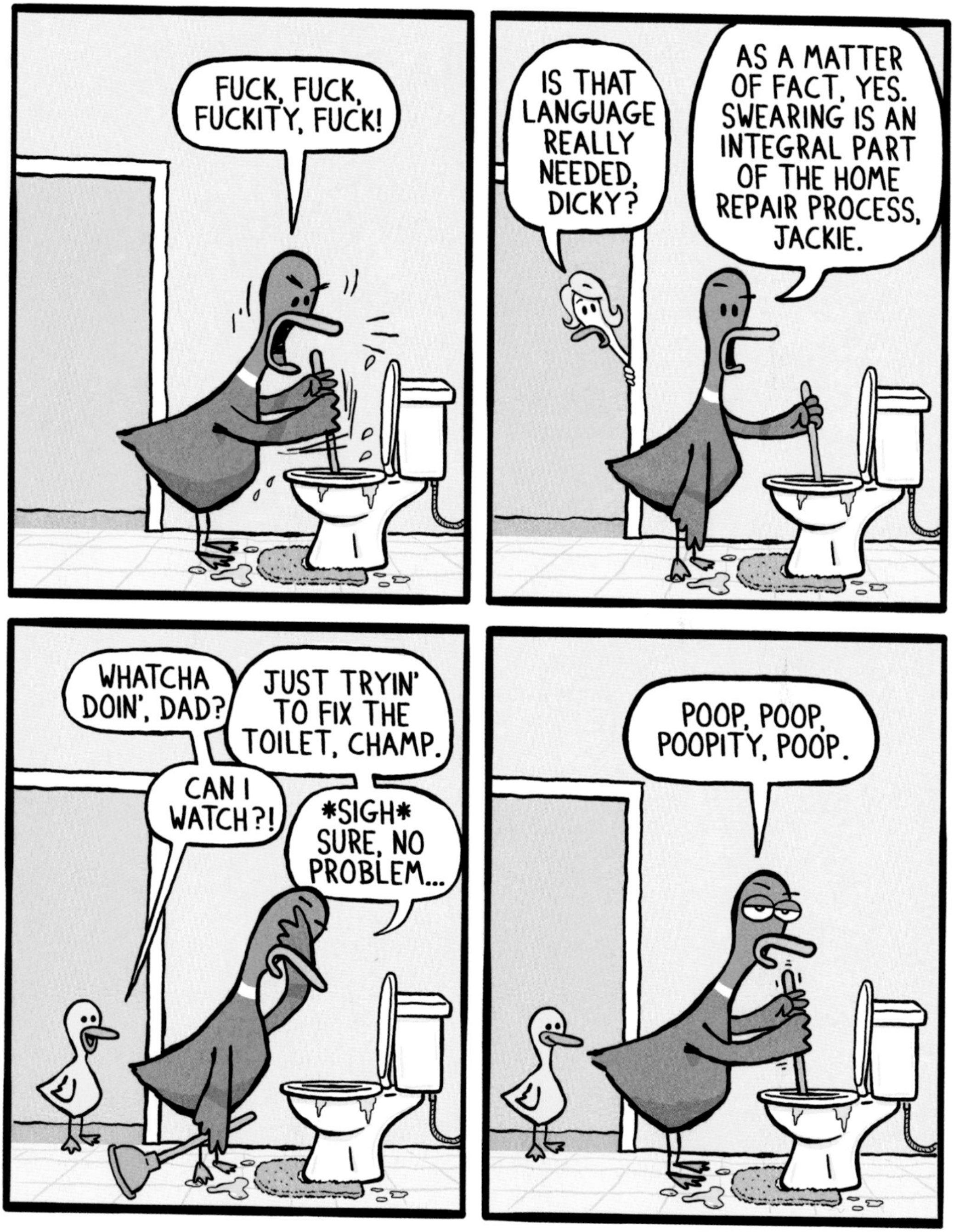
FUCK, FUCK, FUCKITY, FUCK!
IS THAT LANGUAGE REALLY NEEDED, DICKY?
AS A MATTER OF FACT, YES. SWEARING IS AN INTEGRAL PART OF THE HOME REPAIR PROCESS, JACKIE.
WHATCHA DOIN', DAD?
JUST TRYIN' TO FIX THE TOILET, CHAMP.
CAN I WATCH?!
SIGH SURE, NO PROBLEM...
POOP, POOP, POOPITY, POOP.

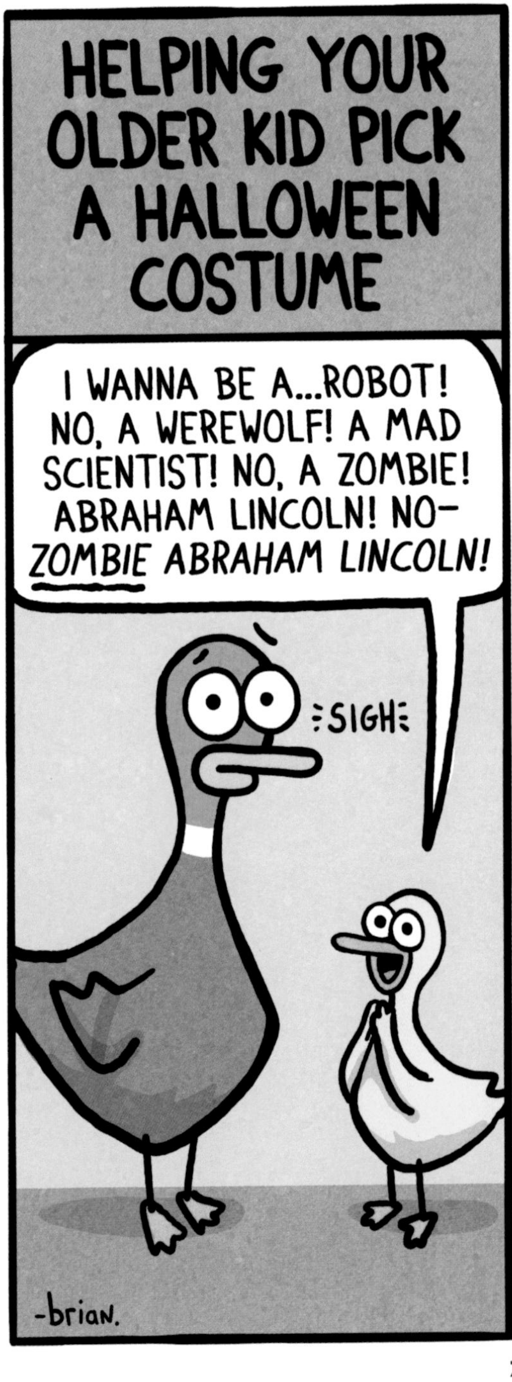
HELPING YOUR OLDER KID PICK A HALLOWEEN COSTUME
I WANNA BE A...ROBOT! NO, A WEREWOLF! A MAD SCIENTIST! NO, A ZOMBIE! ABRAHAM LINCOLN! NO— ZOMBIE ABRAHAM LINCOLN!
SIGH
-brian.

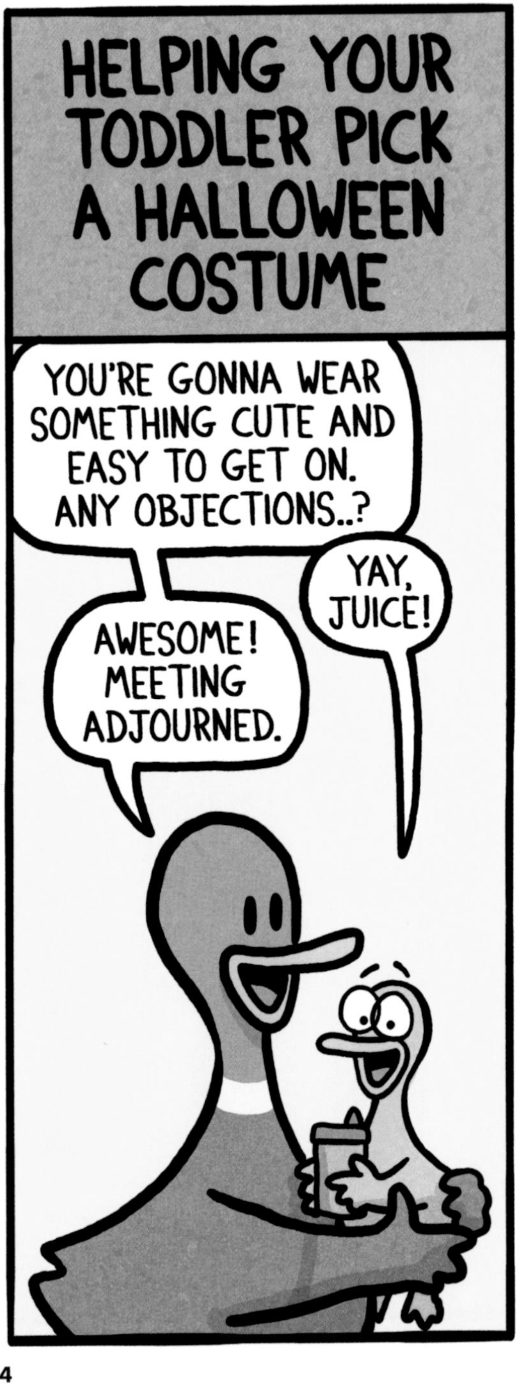
HELPING YOUR TODDLER PICK A HALLOWEEN COSTUME
YOU'RE GONNA WEAR SOMETHING CUTE AND EASY TO GET ON. ANY OBJECTIONS..?
YAY, JUICE!
AWESOME! MEETING ADJOURNED.

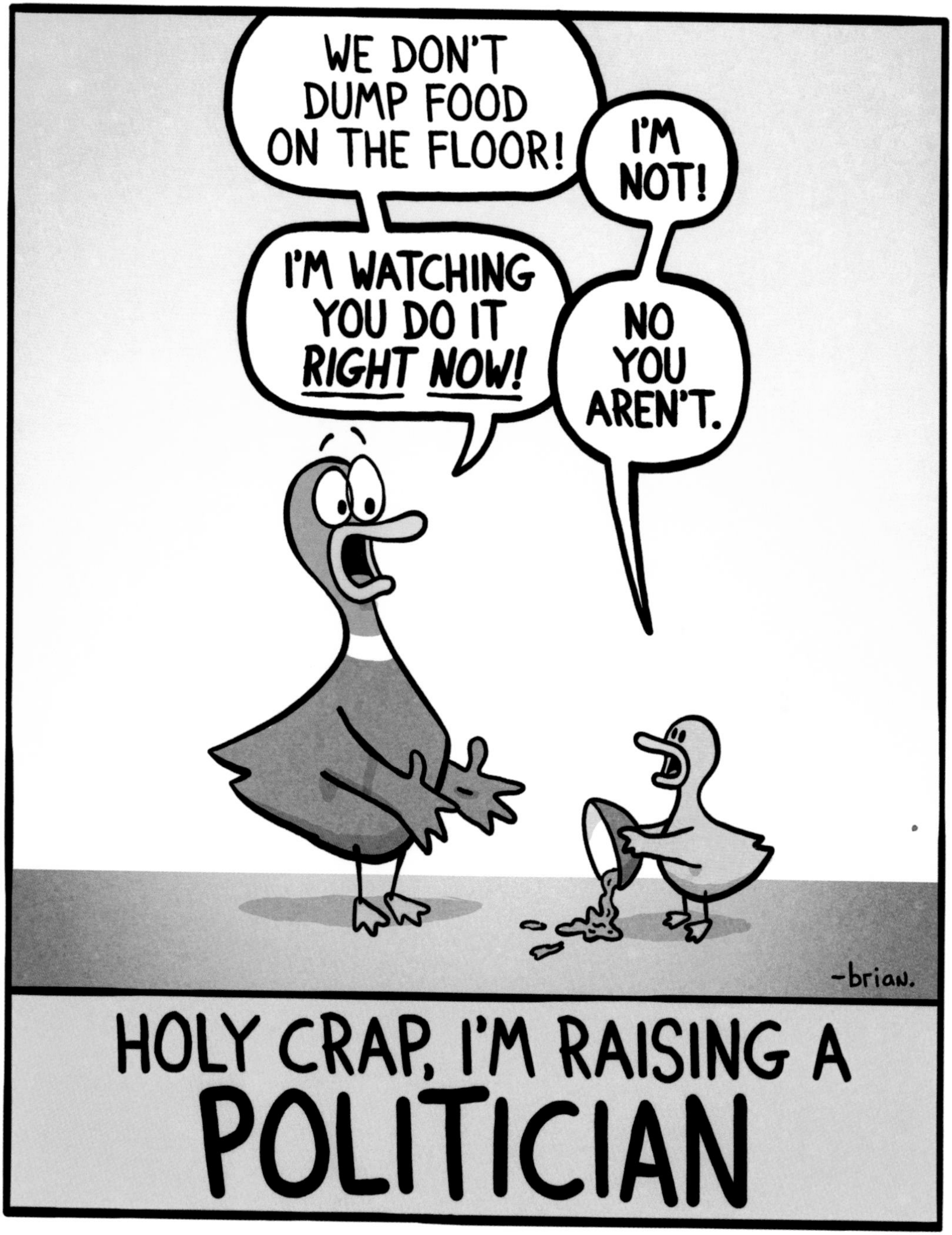
WE DON'T DUMP FOOD ON THE FLOOR!
I'M NOT!
I'M WATCHING YOU DO IT RIGHT NOW!
NO YOU AREN'T.
-brian.
HOLY CRAP, I'M RAISING A POLITICIAN

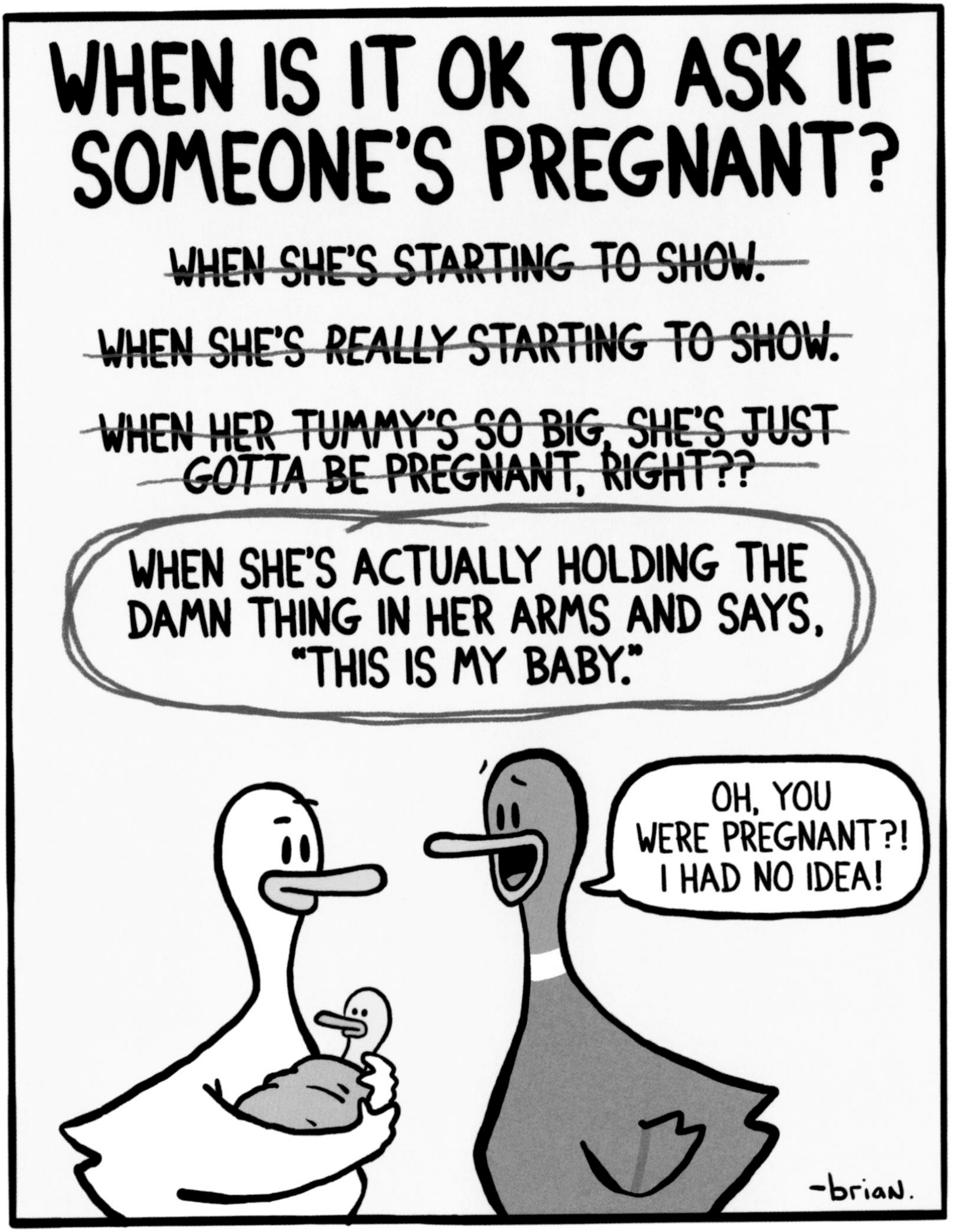
WHEN IS IT OK TO ASK IF SOMEONE'S PREGNANT?
~~WHEN SHE'S STARTING TO SHOW.~~
~~WHEN SHE'S *REALLY* STARTING TO SHOW.~~
~~WHEN HER TUMMY'S SO BIG, SHE'S JUST *GOTTA* BE PREGNANT, RIGHT??~~
WHEN SHE'S ACTUALLY HOLDING THE DAMN THING IN HER ARMS AND SAYS, "THIS IS MY BABY."
OH, YOU WERE PREGNANT?! I HAD NO IDEA!
-brian.

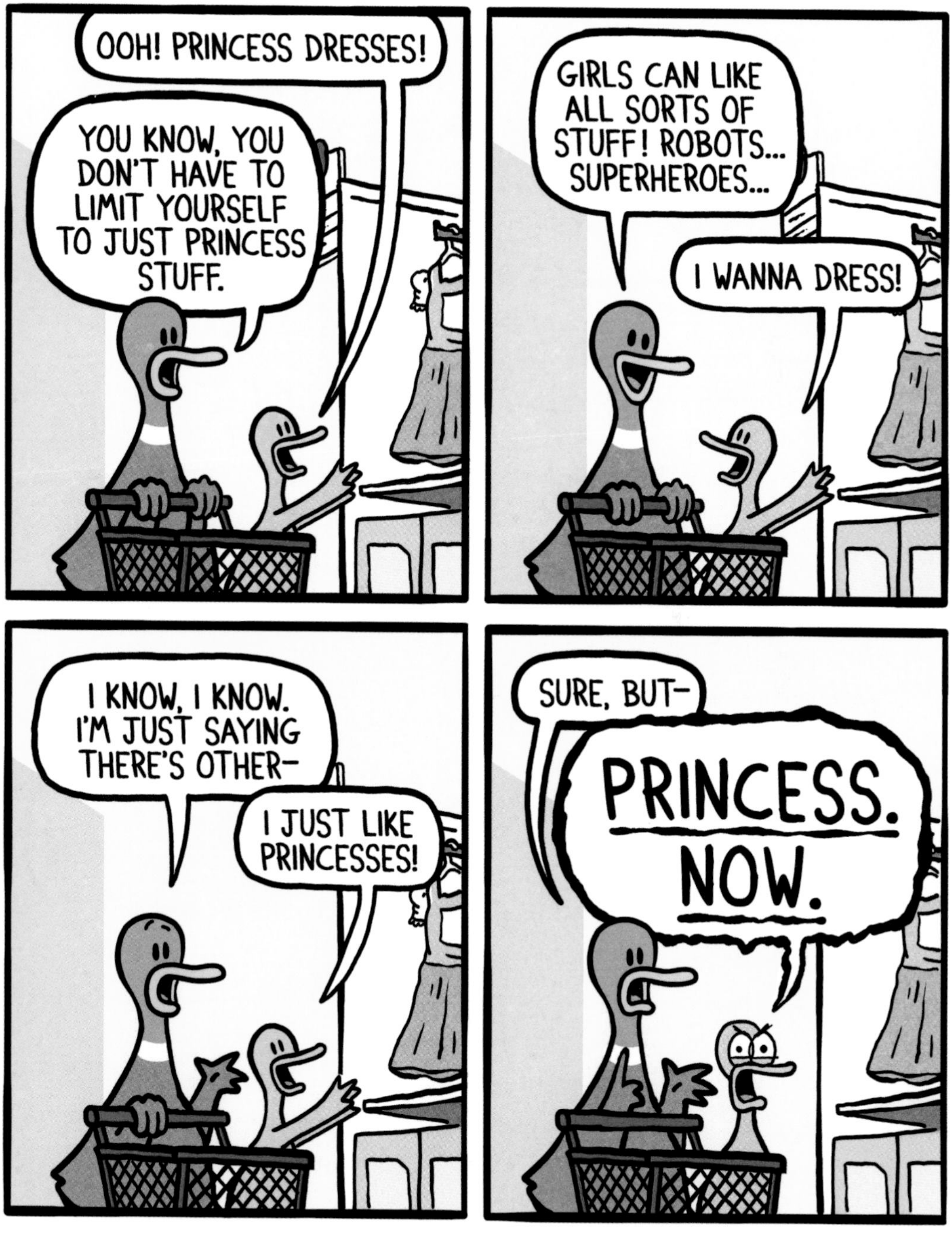
OOH! PRINCESS DRESSES!
YOU KNOW, YOU DON'T HAVE TO LIMIT YOURSELF TO JUST PRINCESS STUFF.
GIRLS CAN LIKE ALL SORTS OF STUFF! ROBOTS... SUPERHEROES...
I WANNA DRESS!
I KNOW, I KNOW. I'M JUST SAYING THERE'S OTHER-
I JUST LIKE PRINCESSES!
SURE, BUT-
PRINCESS. NOW.

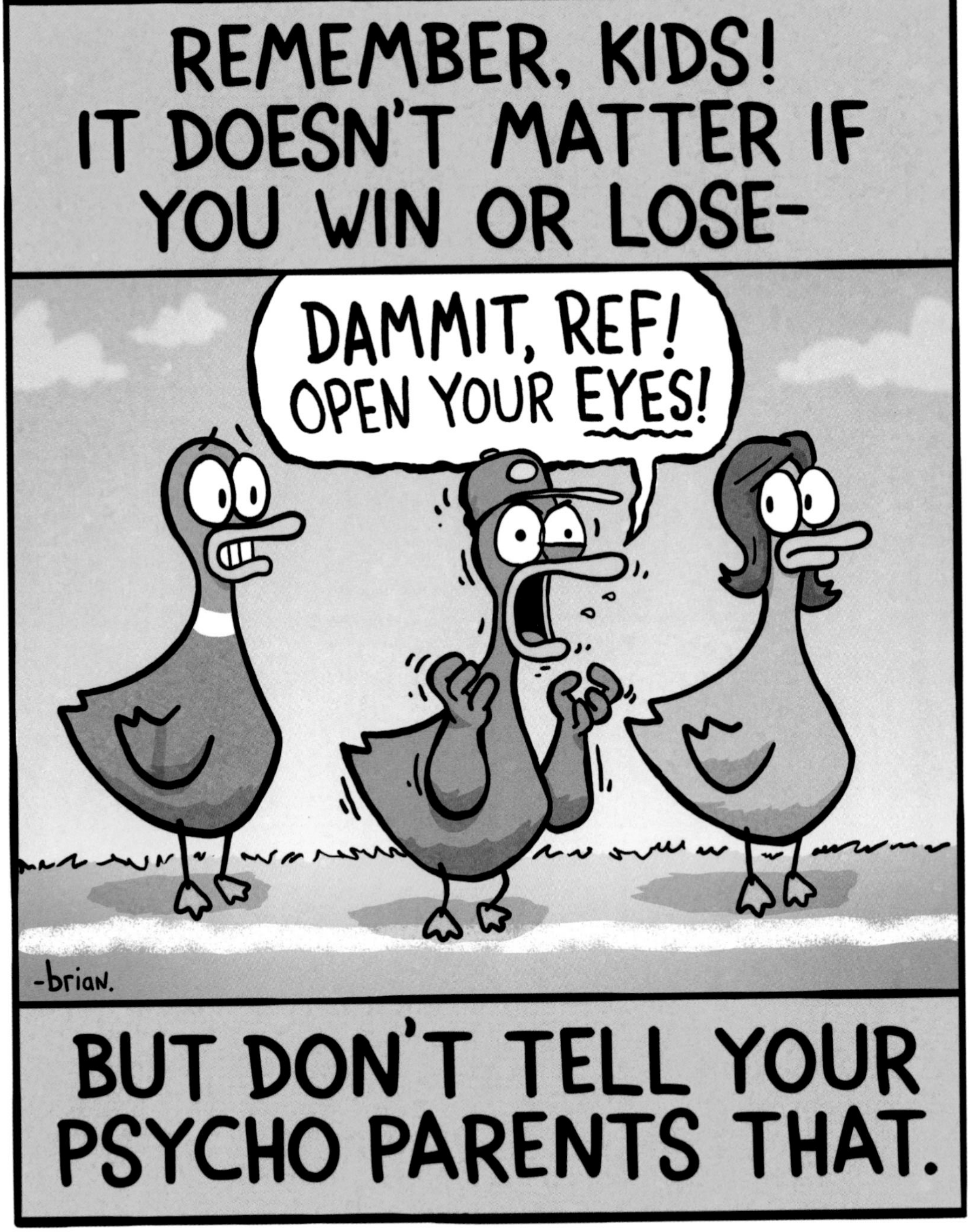

REMEMBER, KIDS! IT DOESN'T MATTER IF YOU WIN OR LOSE-
DAMMIT, REF! OPEN YOUR EYES!
-brian.
BUT DON'T TELL YOUR PSYCHO PARENTS THAT.

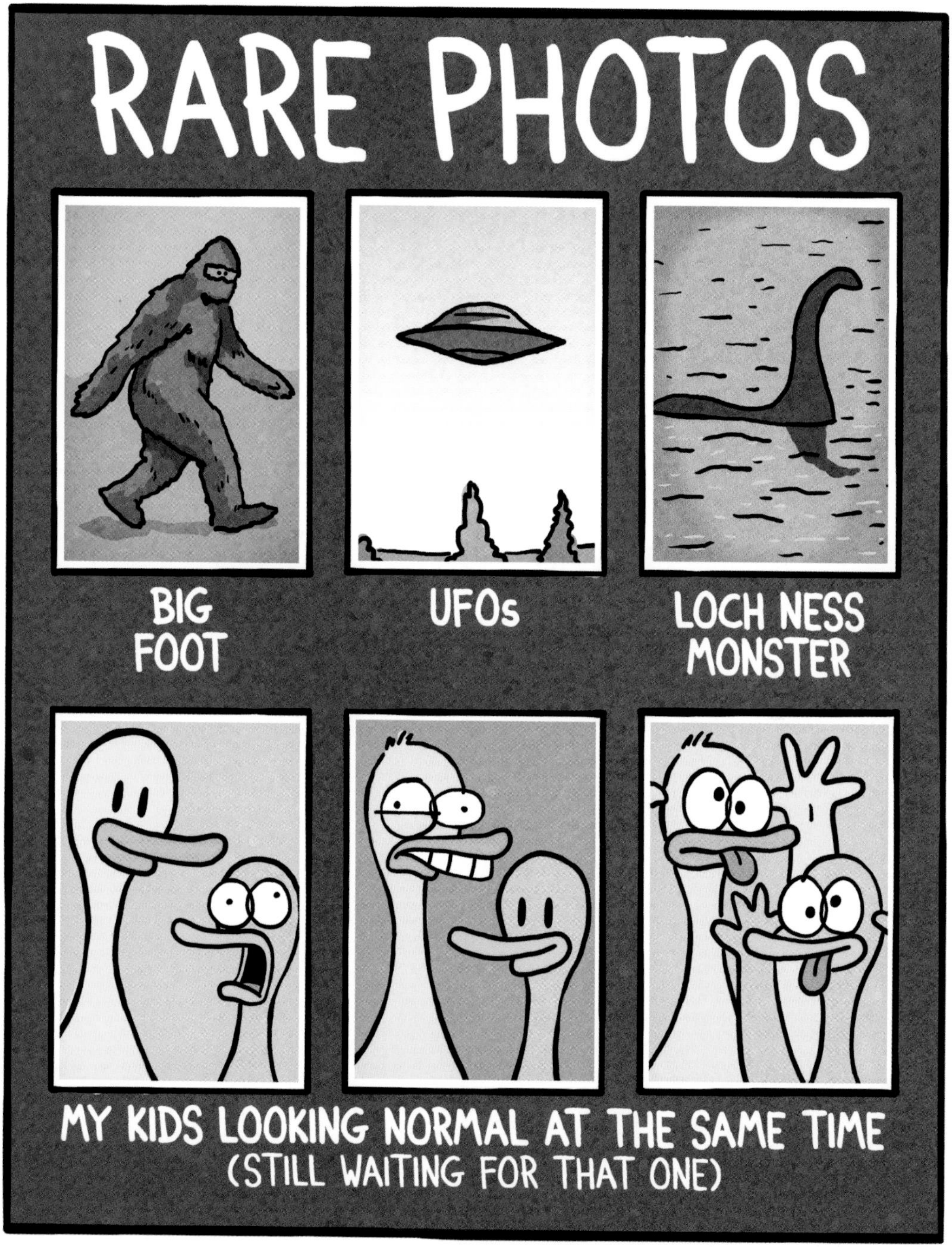
RARE PHOTOS
BIG FOOT
UFOs
LOCH NESS MONSTER
MY KIDS LOOKING NORMAL AT THE SAME TIME
(STILL WAITING FOR THAT ONE)

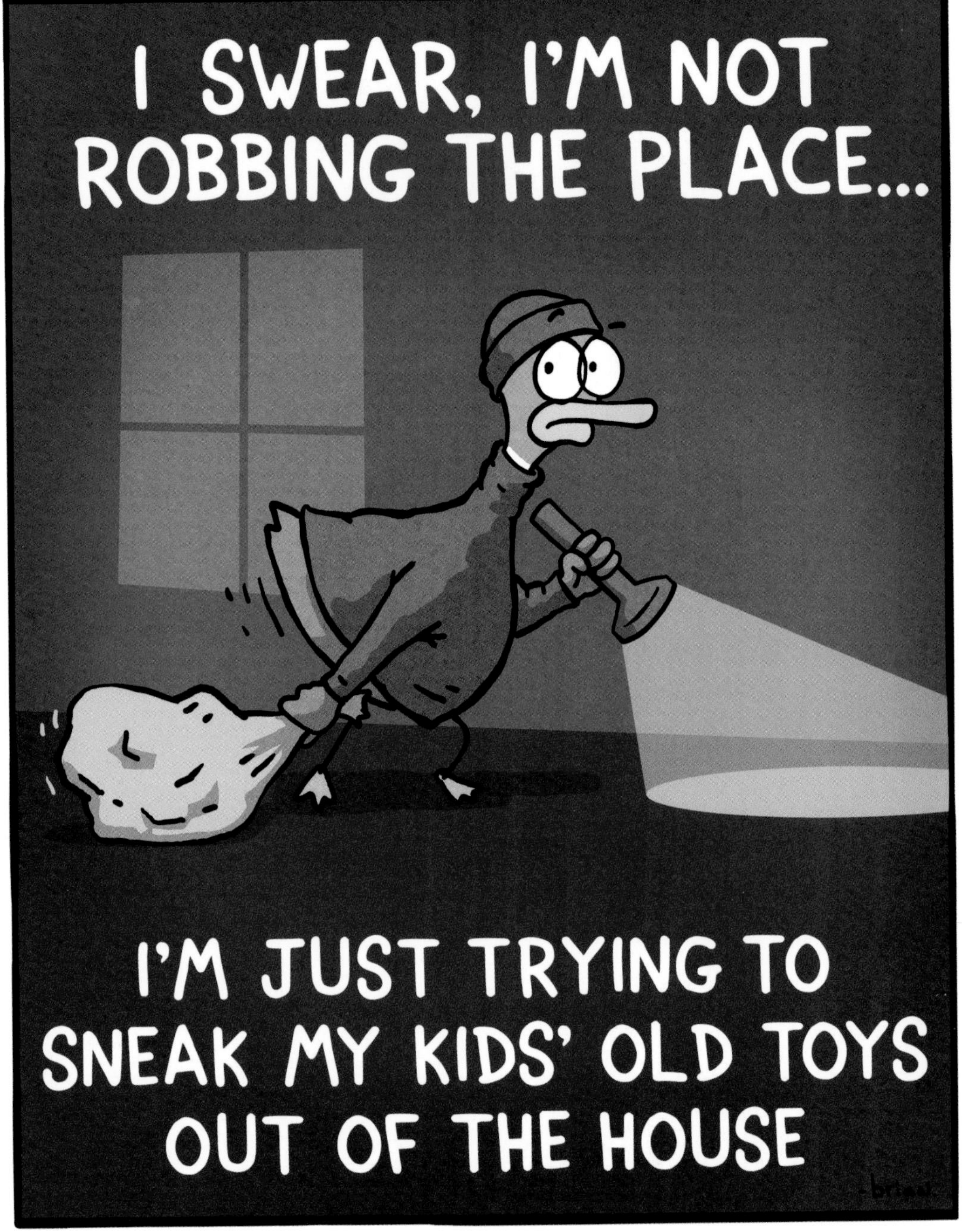
I SWEAR, I'M NOT ROBBING THE PLACE...
I'M JUST TRYING TO SNEAK MY KIDS' OLD TOYS OUT OF THE HOUSE

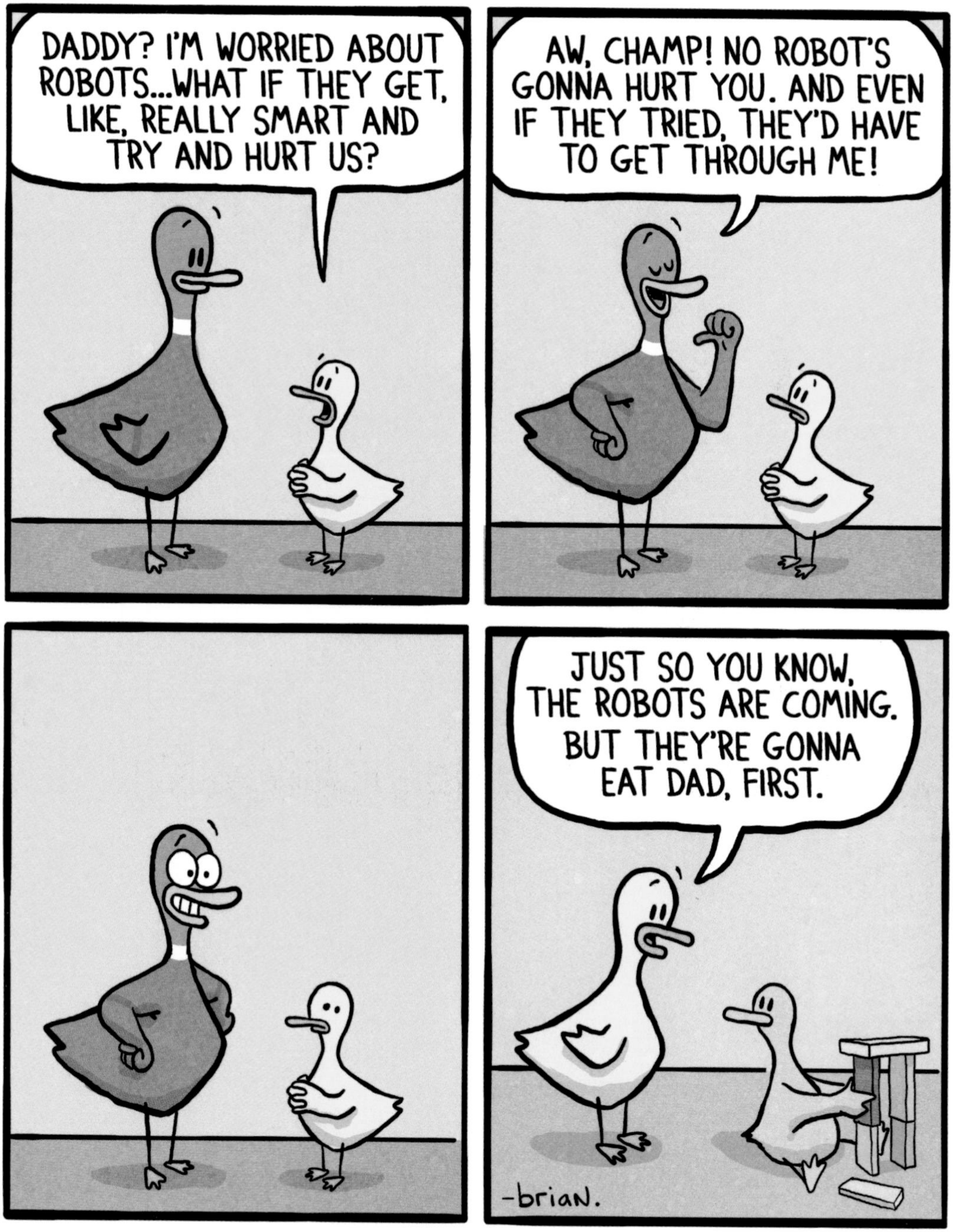
DADDY? I'M WORRIED ABOUT ROBOTS...WHAT IF THEY GET, LIKE, REALLY SMART AND TRY AND HURT US?
AW, CHAMP! NO ROBOT'S GONNA HURT YOU. AND EVEN IF THEY TRIED, THEY'D HAVE TO GET THROUGH ME!
JUST SO YOU KNOW, THE ROBOTS ARE COMING. BUT THEY'RE GONNA EAT DAD, FIRST.
-brian.

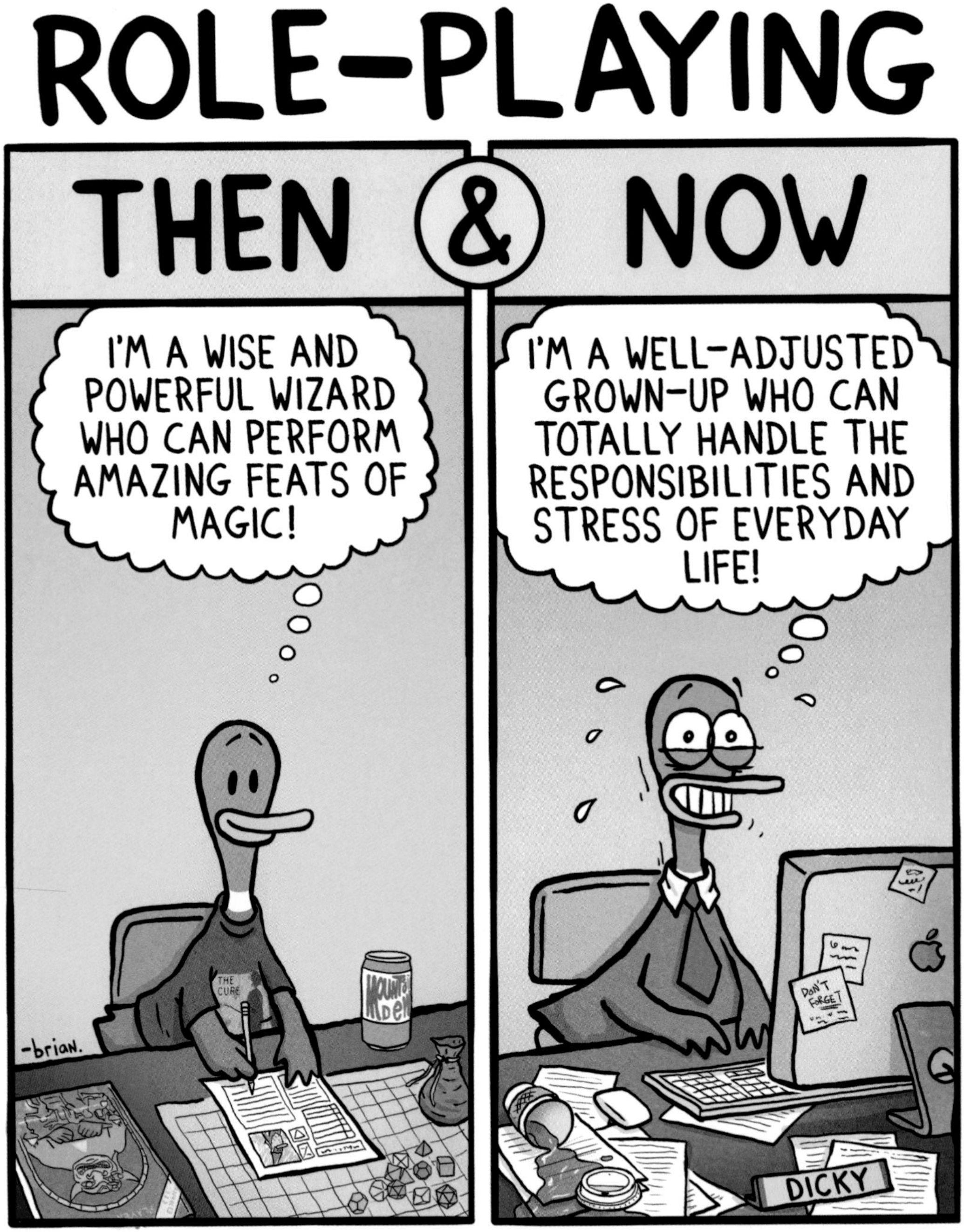

ROLE-PLAYING
THEN & NOW
I'M A WISE AND POWERFUL WIZARD WHO CAN PERFORM AMAZING FEATS OF MAGIC!
THE CURE
-brian.
I'M A WELL-ADJUSTED GROWN-UP WHO CAN TOTALLY HANDLE THE RESPONSIBILITIES AND STRESS OF EVERYDAY LIFE!
DON'T FORGET
DICKY

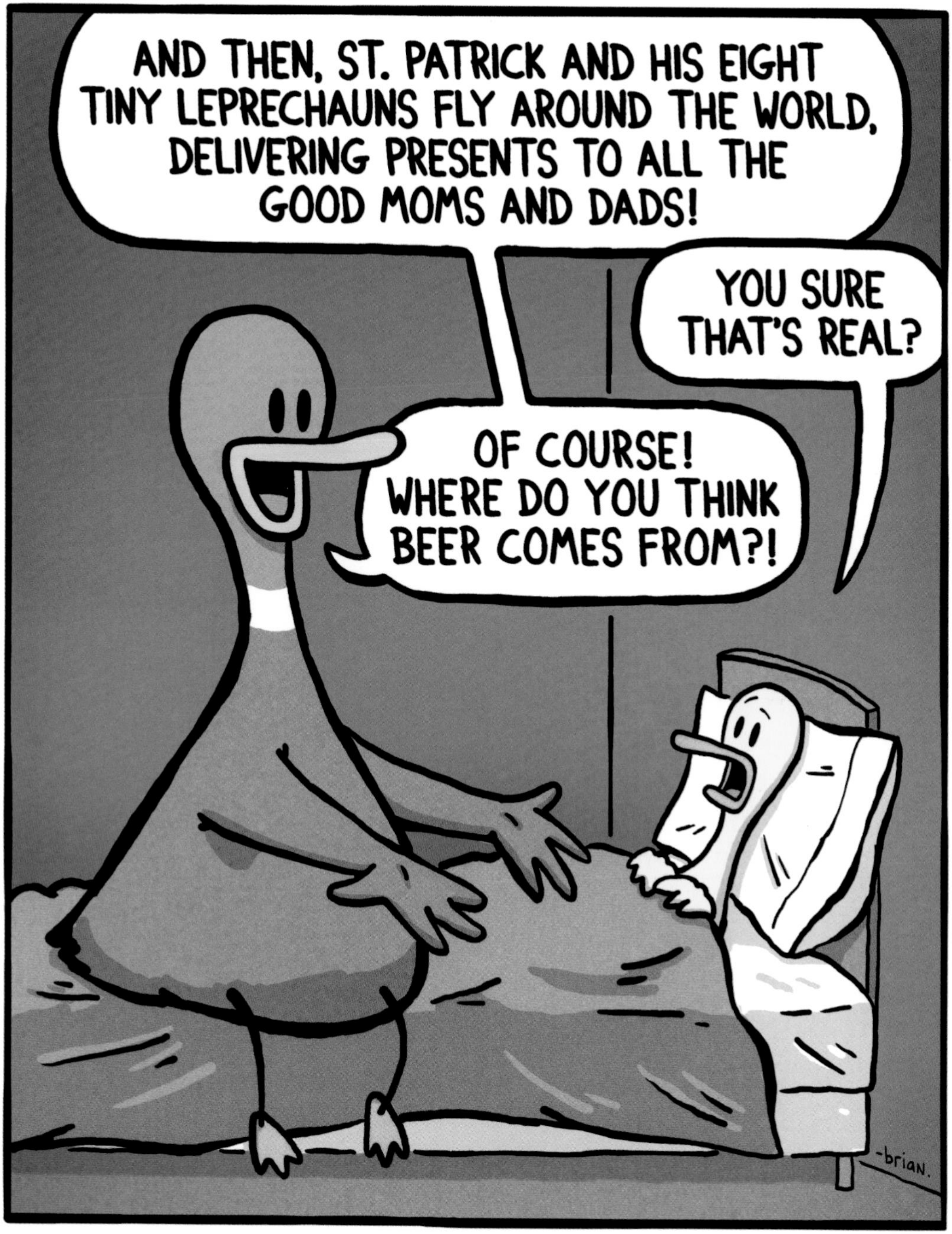
AND THEN, ST. PATRICK AND HIS EIGHT TINY LEPRECHAUNS FLY AROUND THE WORLD, DELIVERING PRESENTS TO ALL THE GOOD MOMS AND DADS!
YOU SURE THAT'S REAL?
OF COURSE! WHERE DO YOU THINK BEER COMES FROM?!
-brian.

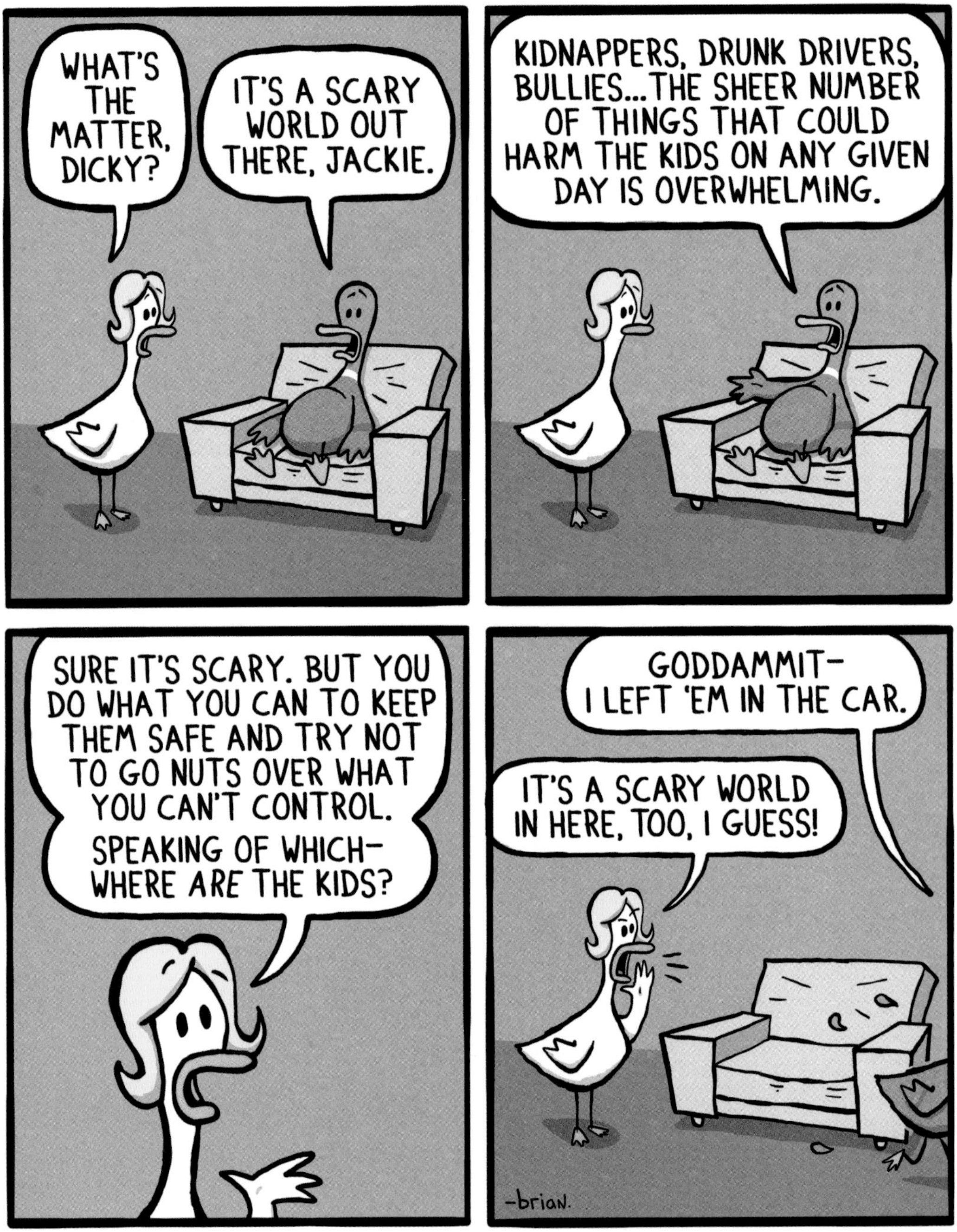
WHAT'S THE MATTER, DICKY?
IT'S A SCARY WORLD OUT THERE, JACKIE.
KIDNAPPERS, DRUNK DRIVERS, BULLIES...THE SHEER NUMBER OF THINGS THAT COULD HARM THE KIDS ON ANY GIVEN DAY IS OVERWHELMING.
SURE IT'S SCARY. BUT YOU DO WHAT YOU CAN TO KEEP THEM SAFE AND TRY NOT TO GO NUTS OVER WHAT YOU CAN'T CONTROL.
SPEAKING OF WHICH– WHERE ARE THE KIDS?
GODDAMMIT– I LEFT 'EM IN THE CAR.
IT'S A SCARY WORLD IN HERE, TOO, I GUESS!
-brian.

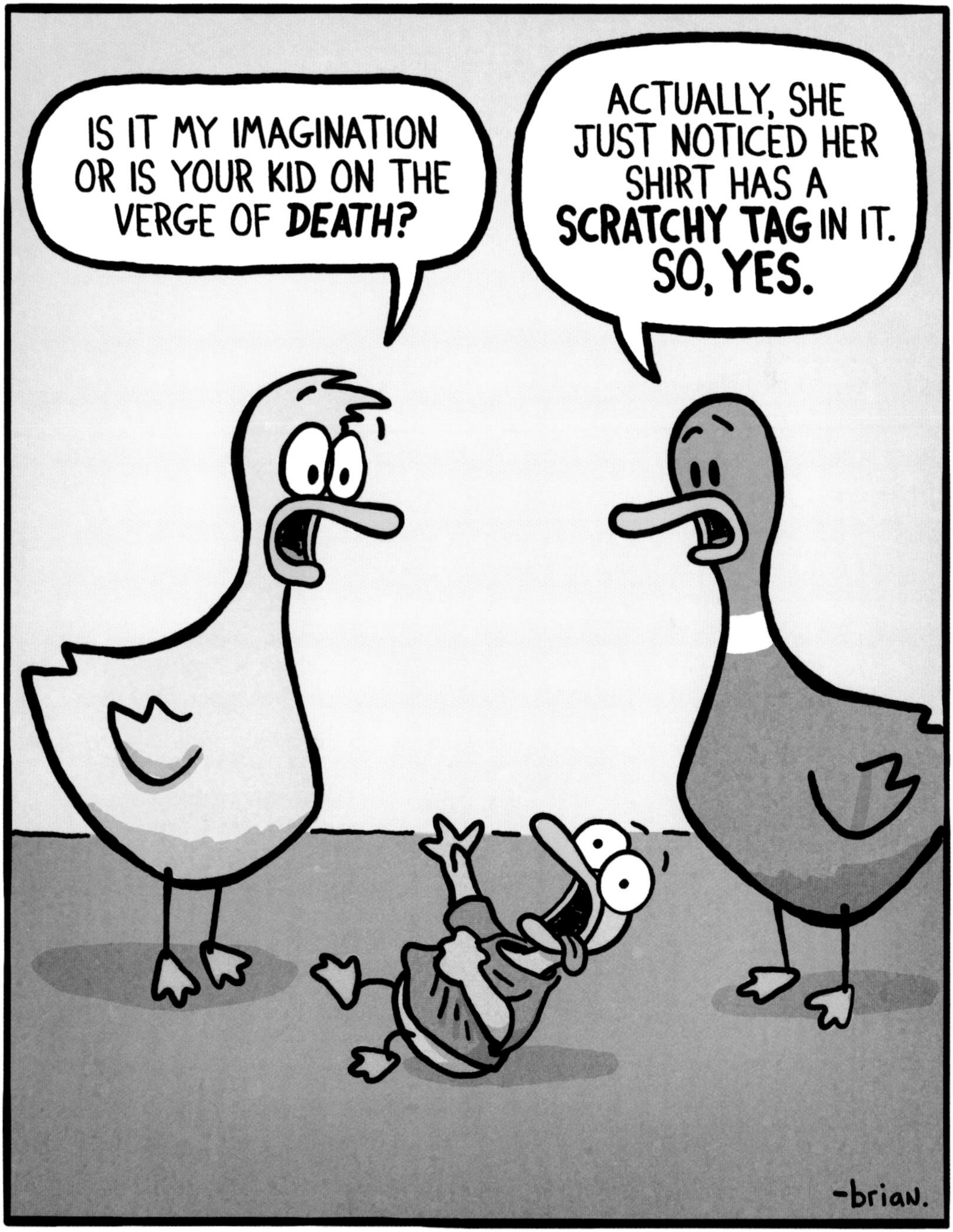
IS IT MY IMAGINATION OR IS YOUR KID ON THE VERGE OF **DEATH?**
ACTUALLY, SHE JUST NOTICED HER SHIRT HAS A **SCRATCHY TAG** IN IT. SO, **YES.**
-brian.

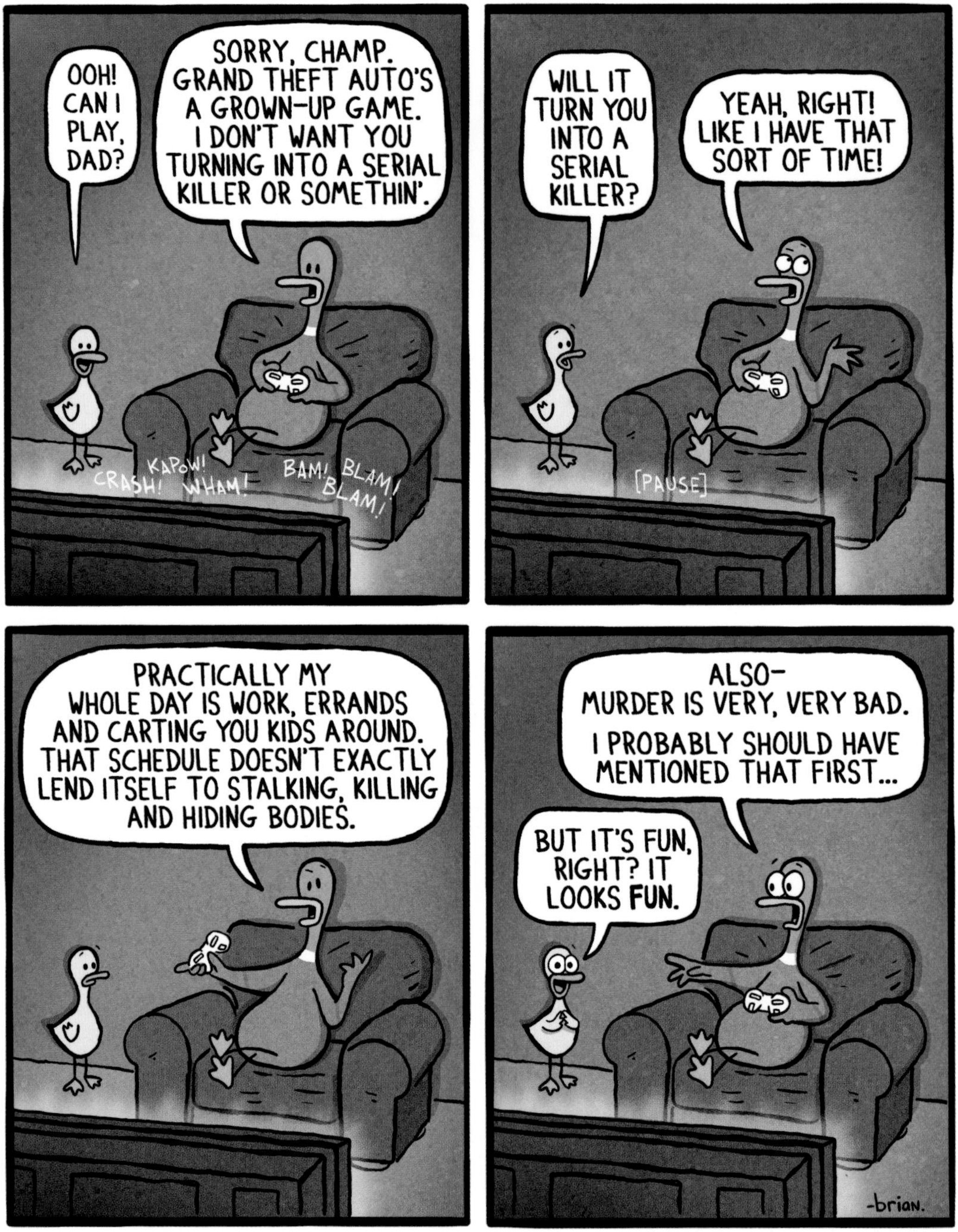
OOH! CAN I PLAY, DAD?
SORRY, CHAMP. GRAND THEFT AUTO'S A GROWN-UP GAME. I DON'T WANT YOU TURNING INTO A SERIAL KILLER OR SOMETHIN'.
KAPOW! CRASH! WHAM! BAM! BLAM! BLAM!
WILL IT TURN YOU INTO A SERIAL KILLER?
YEAH, RIGHT! LIKE I HAVE THAT SORT OF TIME!
[PAUSE]
PRACTICALLY MY WHOLE DAY IS WORK, ERRANDS AND CARTING YOU KIDS AROUND. THAT SCHEDULE DOESN'T EXACTLY LEND ITSELF TO STALKING, KILLING AND HIDING BODIES.
ALSO— MURDER IS VERY, VERY BAD.
I PROBABLY SHOULD HAVE MENTIONED THAT FIRST...
BUT IT'S FUN, RIGHT? IT LOOKS FUN.
-brian.

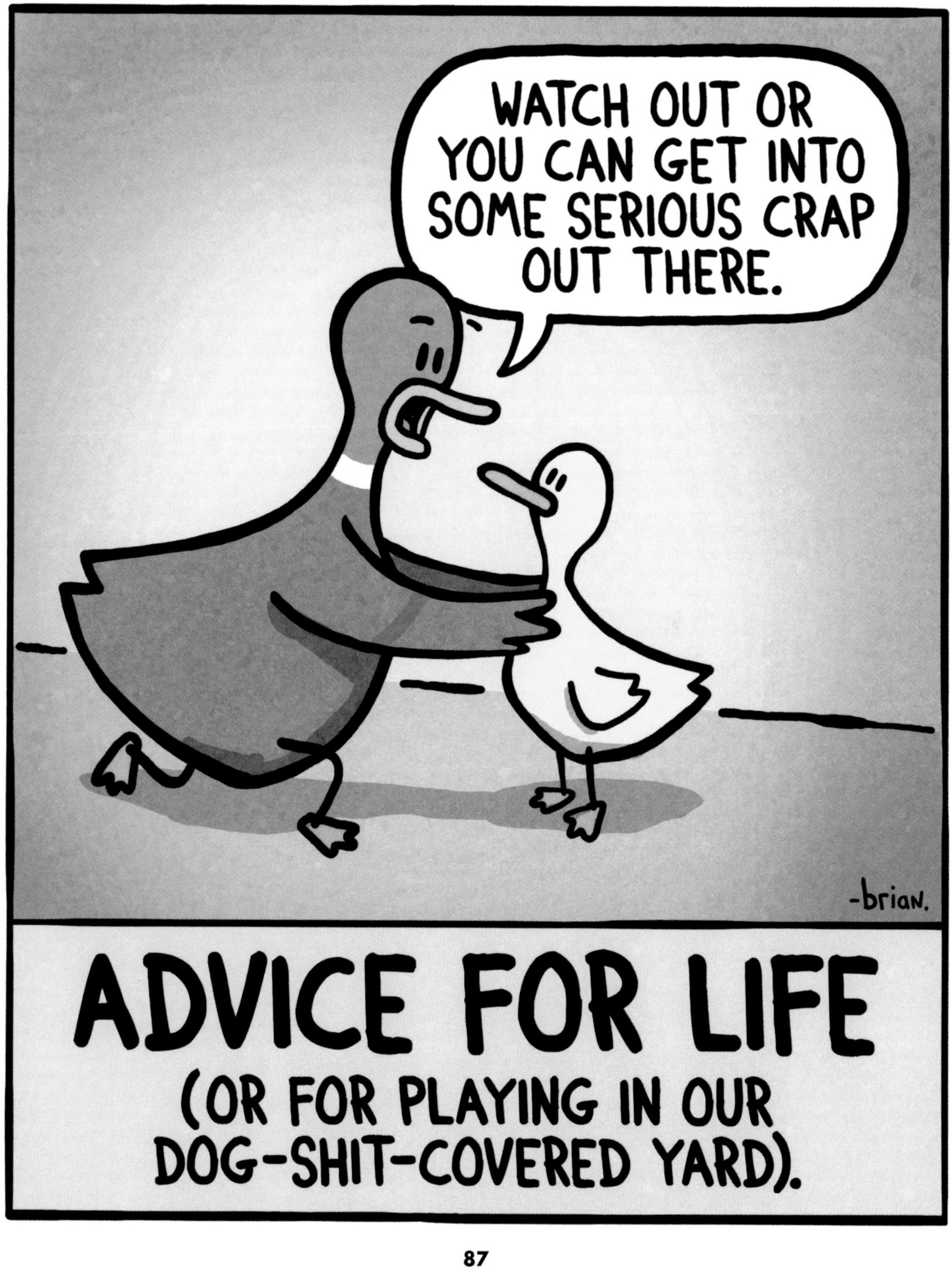
WATCH OUT OR YOU CAN GET INTO SOME SERIOUS CRAP OUT THERE.
-brian.

ADVICE FOR LIFE

(OR FOR PLAYING IN OUR DOG-SHIT-COVERED YARD).

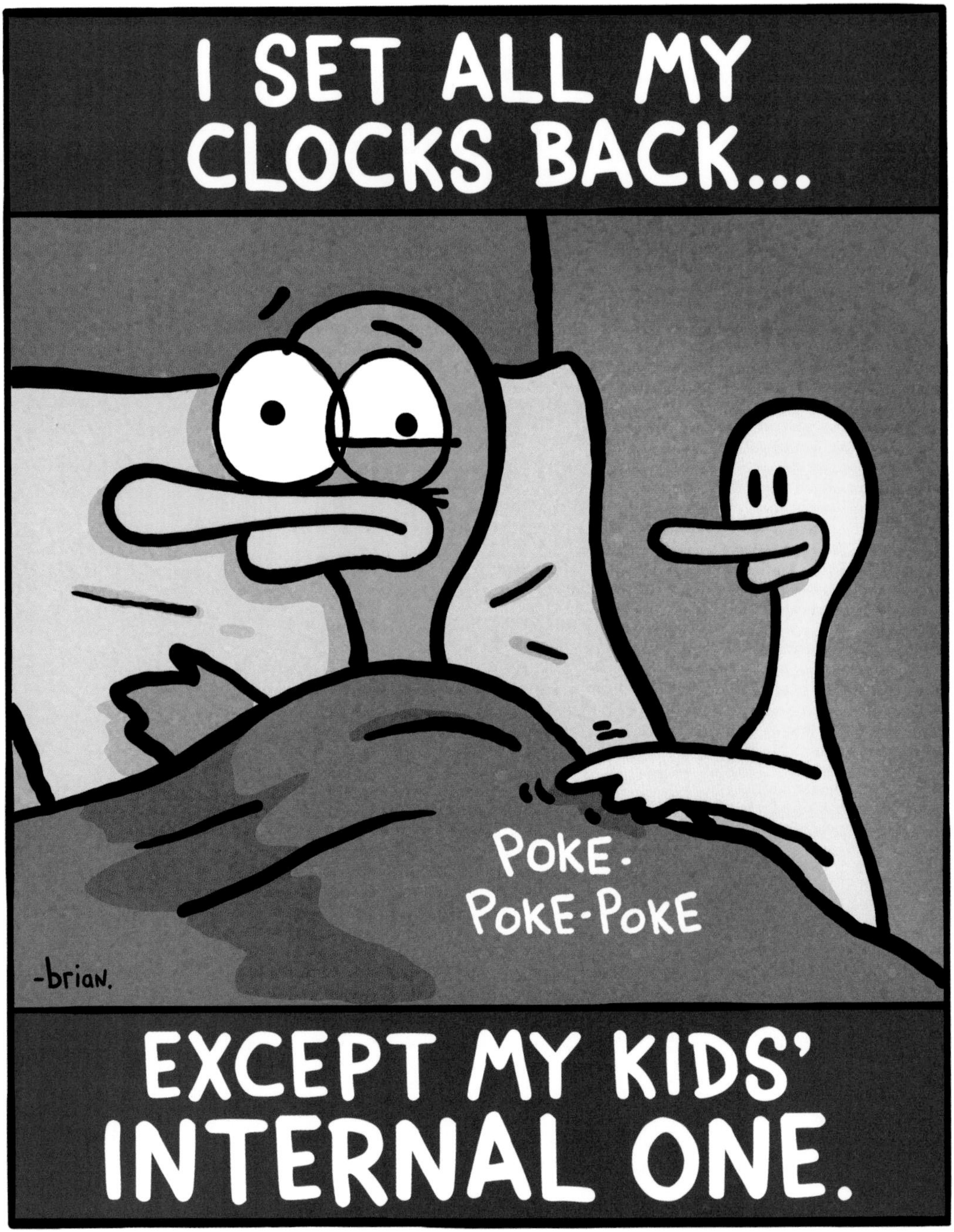

I SET ALL MY CLOCKS BACK...
POKE.
POKE-POKE
-brian.
EXCEPT MY KIDS' INTERNAL ONE.

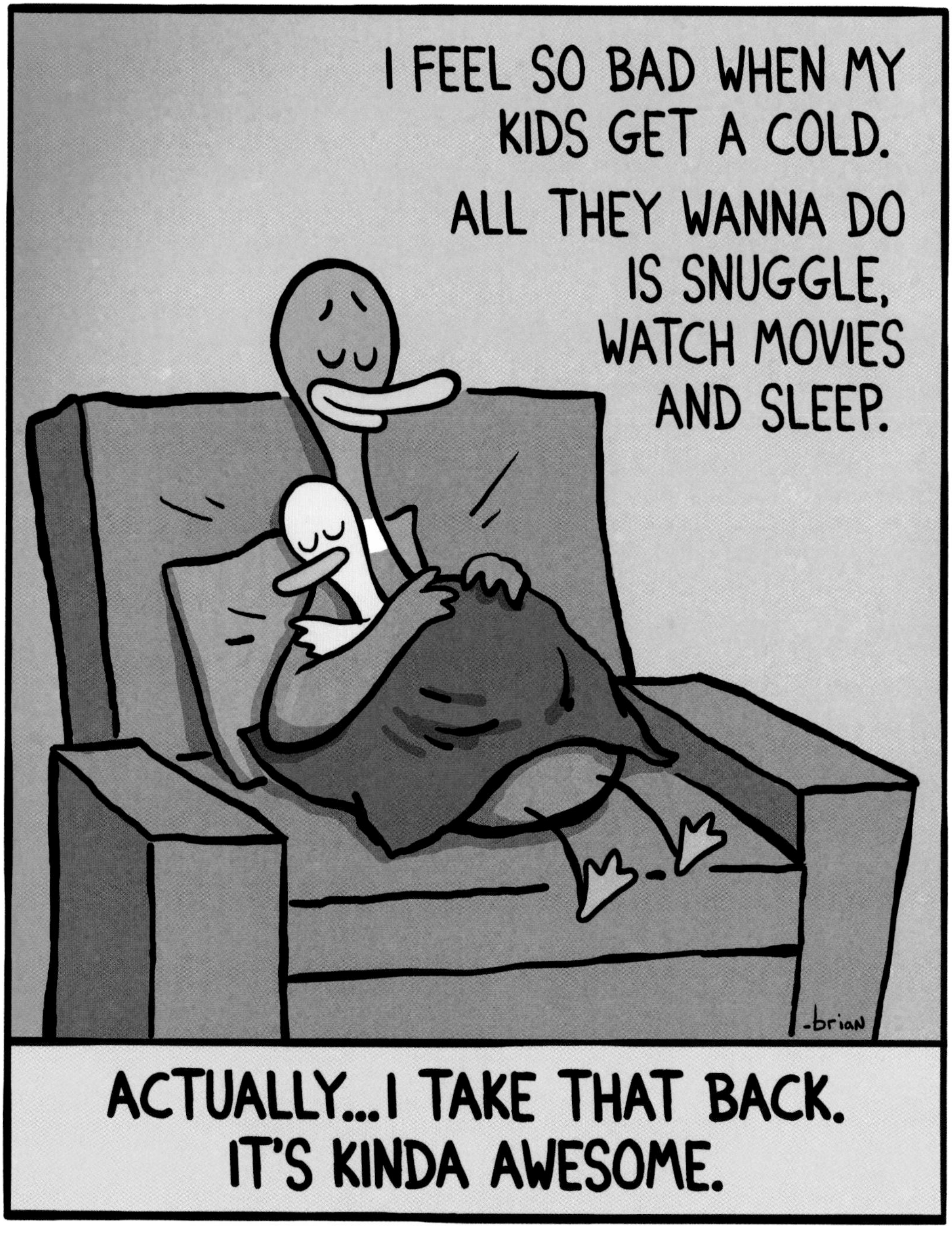
I FEEL SO BAD WHEN MY KIDS GET A COLD.
ALL THEY WANNA DO IS SNUGGLE, WATCH MOVIES AND SLEEP.
-brian
ACTUALLY...I TAKE THAT BACK. IT'S KINDA AWESOME.

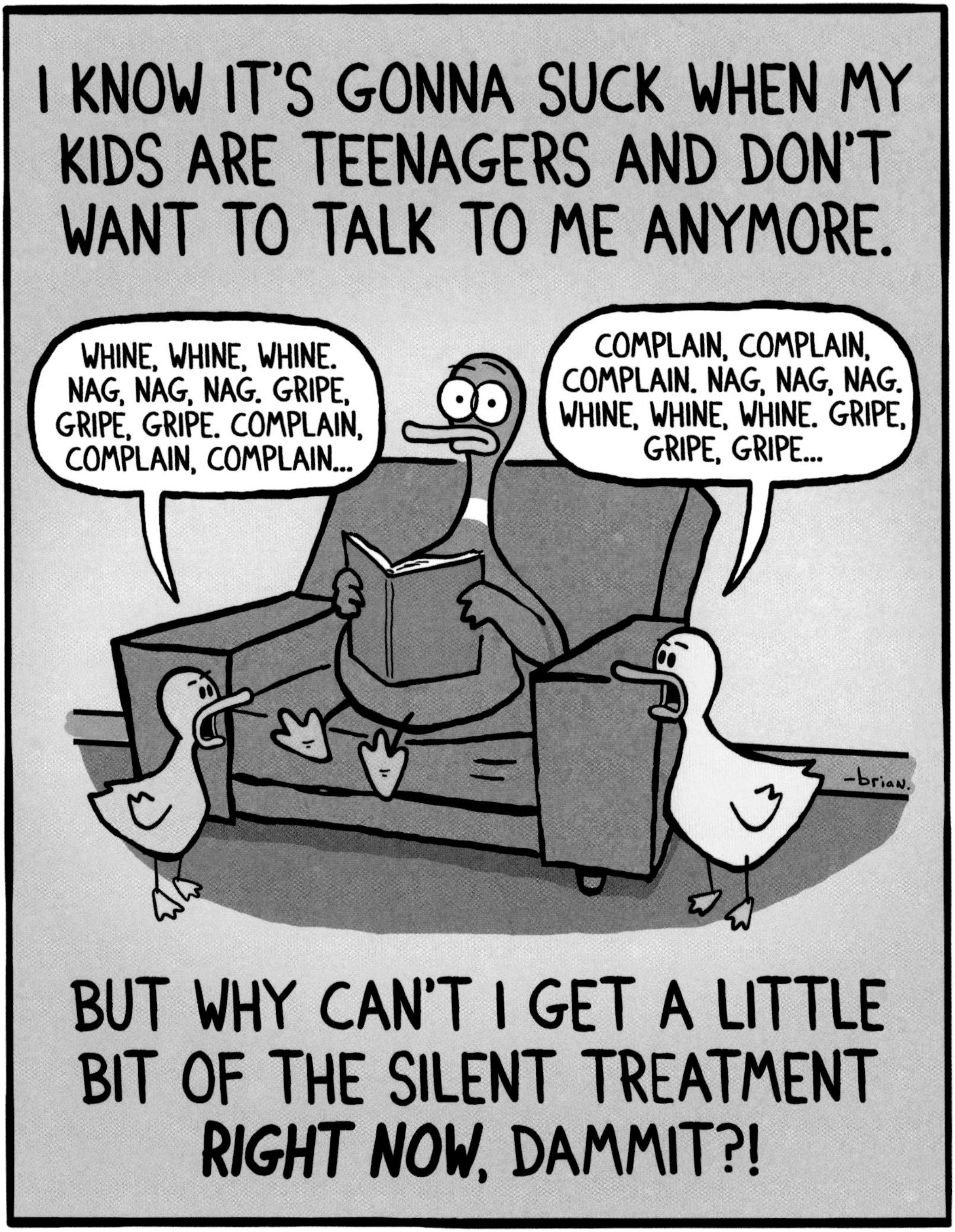
I KNOW IT'S GONNA SUCK WHEN MY KIDS ARE TEENAGERS AND DON'T WANT TO TALK TO ME ANYMORE.
WHINE, WHINE, WHINE. NAG, NAG, NAG. GRIPE, GRIPE, GRIPE. COMPLAIN, COMPLAIN, COMPLAIN...
COMPLAIN, COMPLAIN, COMPLAIN. NAG, NAG, NAG. WHINE, WHINE, WHINE. GRIPE, GRIPE, GRIPE...
-brian.
BUT WHY CAN'T I GET A LITTLE BIT OF THE SILENT TREATMENT *RIGHT NOW*, DAMMIT?!

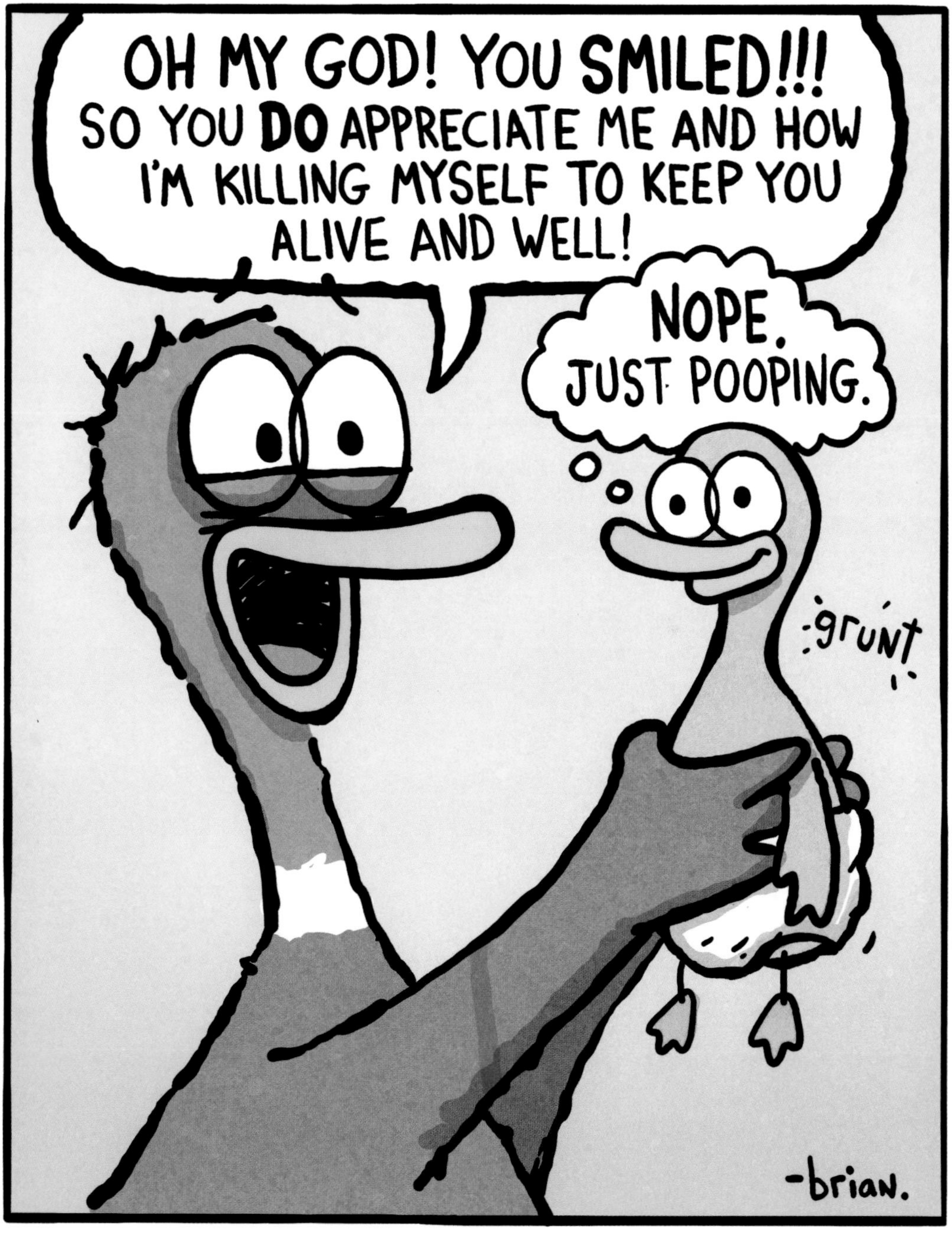
OH MY GOD! YOU SMILED!!! SO YOU DO APPRECIATE ME AND HOW I'M KILLING MYSELF TO KEEP YOU ALIVE AND WELL!
NOPE. JUST POOPING.
grunt
-brian.

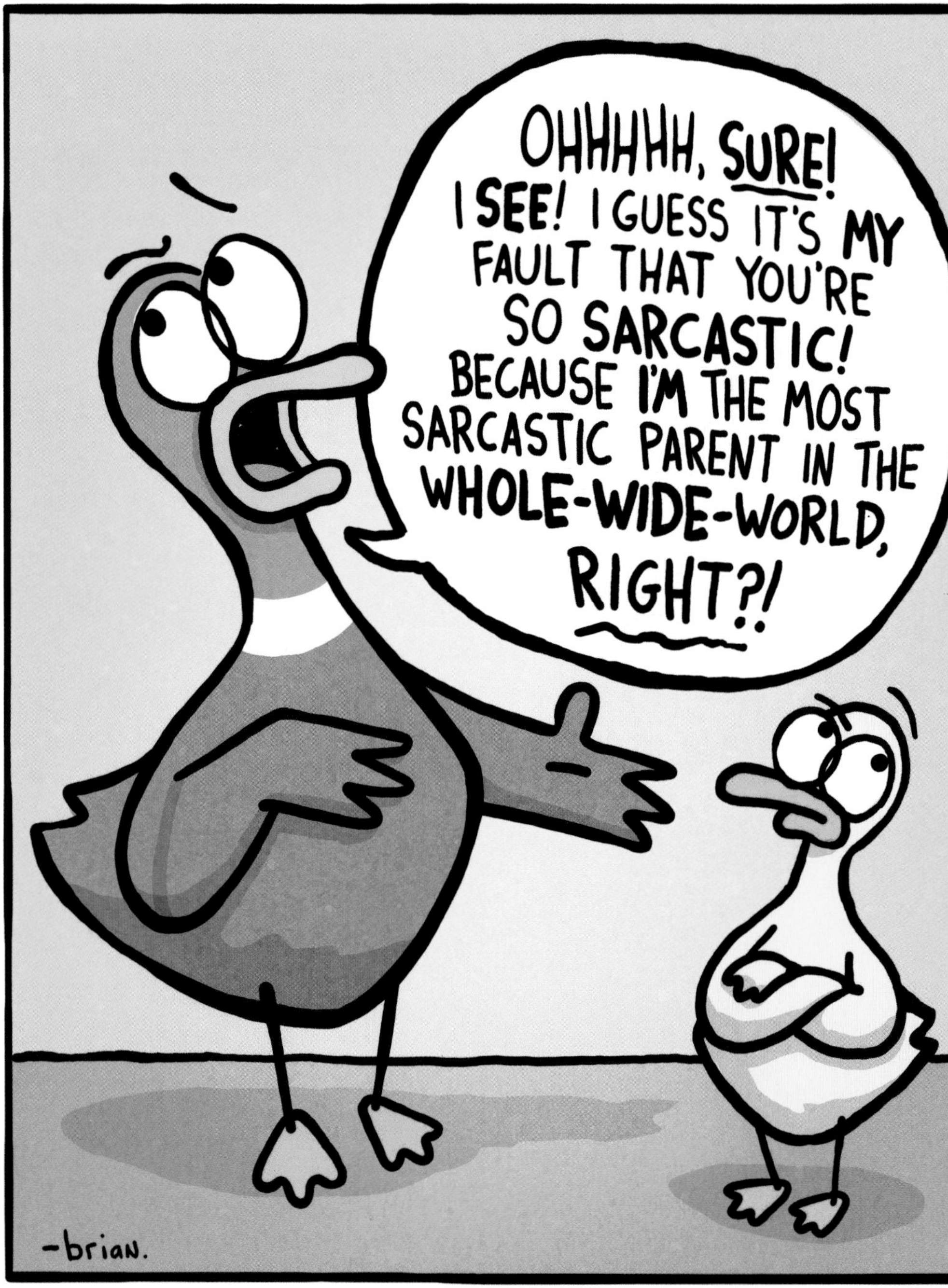
OHHHHH, SURE! I SEE! I GUESS IT'S MY FAULT THAT YOU'RE SO SARCASTIC! BECAUSE I'M THE MOST SARCASTIC PARENT IN THE WHOLE-WIDE-WORLD, RIGHT?!
-brian.

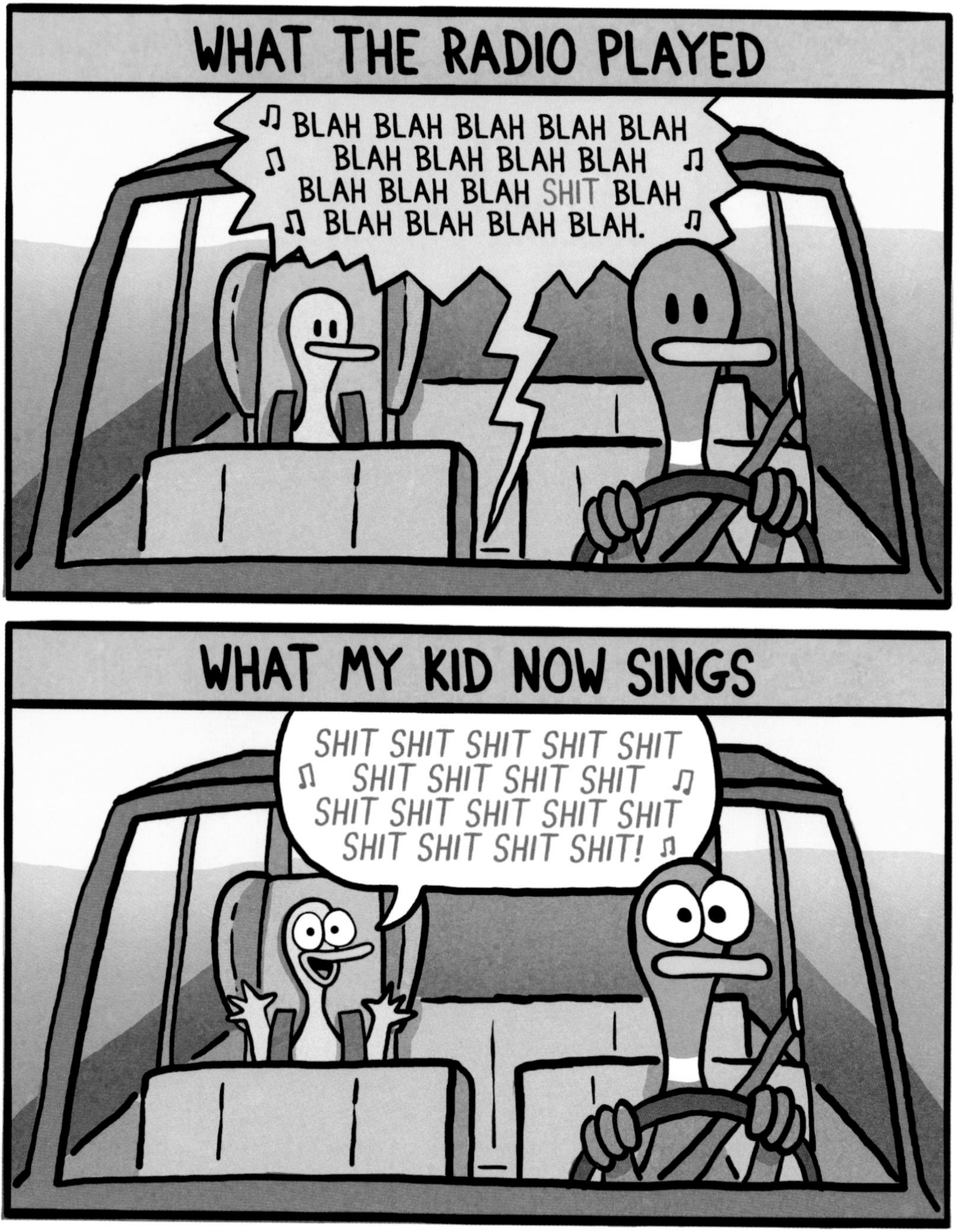
WHAT THE RADIO PLAYED
BLAH BLAH BLAH BLAH BLAH BLAH BLAH BLAH BLAH BLAH BLAH BLAH SHIT BLAH BLAH BLAH BLAH BLAH.
WHAT MY KID NOW SINGS
SHIT SHIT SHIT SHIT SHIT SHIT SHIT SHIT SHIT SHIT SHIT SHIT SHIT SHIT SHIT SHIT SHIT SHIT!

HOW TO SPEAK LITTLE GIRL

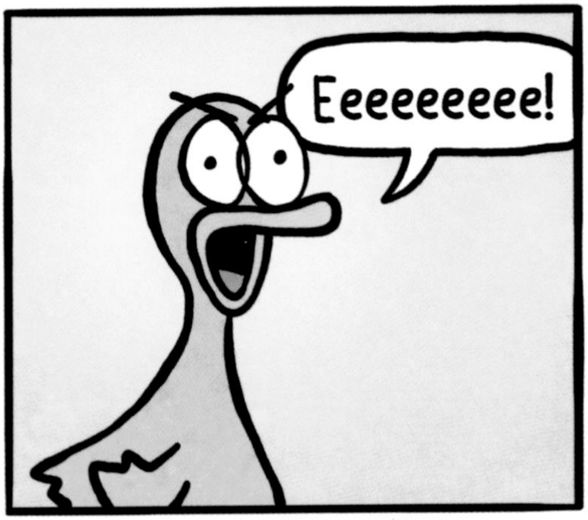
Eeeeeeeee!

"I AM UPSET."

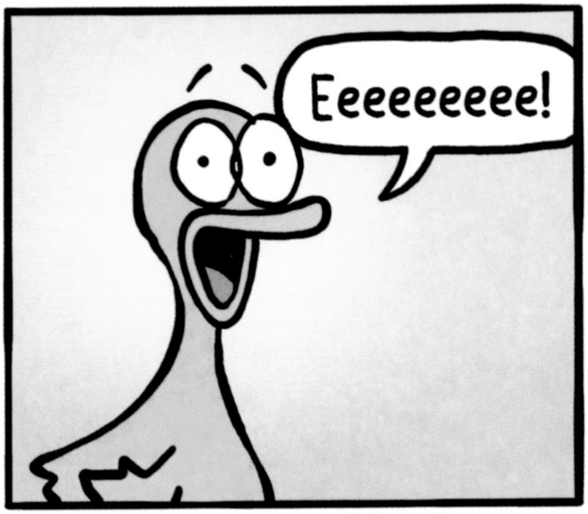
Eeeeeeeee!

"I AM HAPPY."

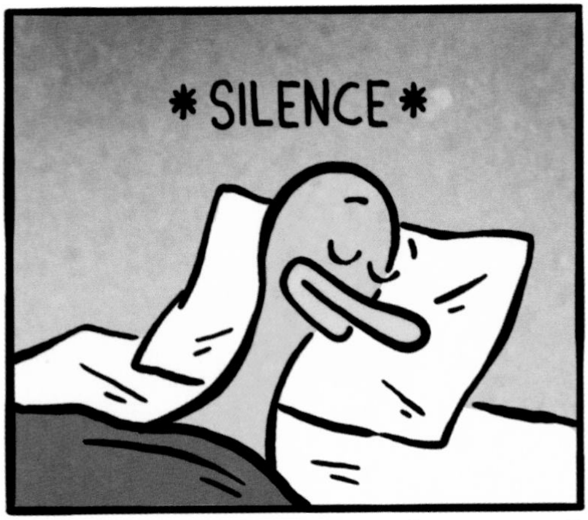
SILENCE

"I AM RESTING (BRIEFLY)."

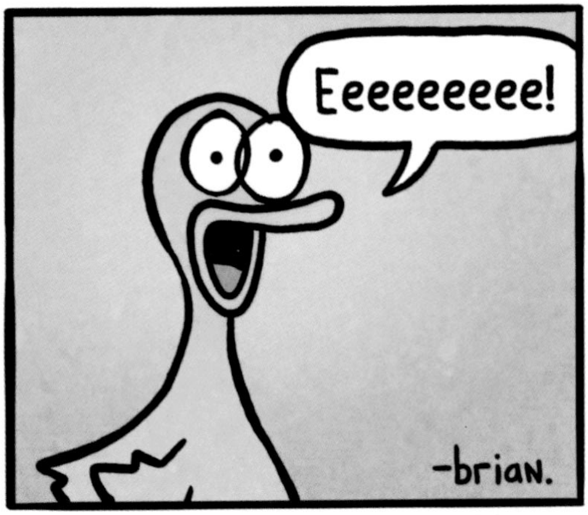
Eeeeeeeee!
-brian.

"I AM AWAKE AGAIN. WHY ARE YOU CRYING?"

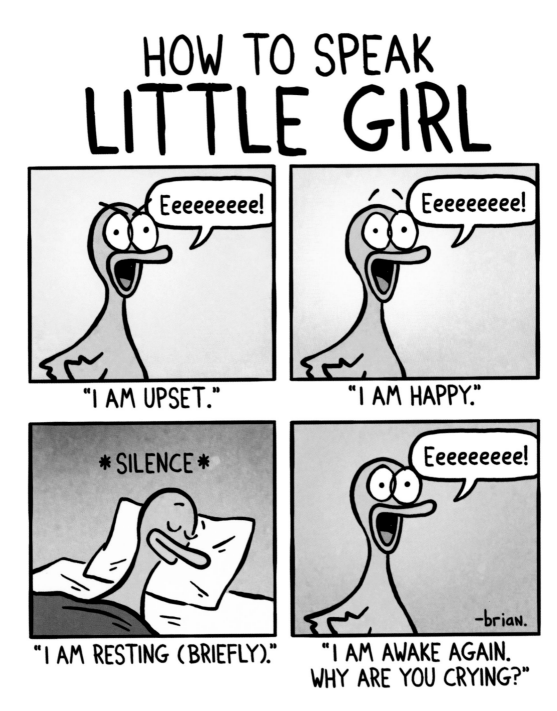

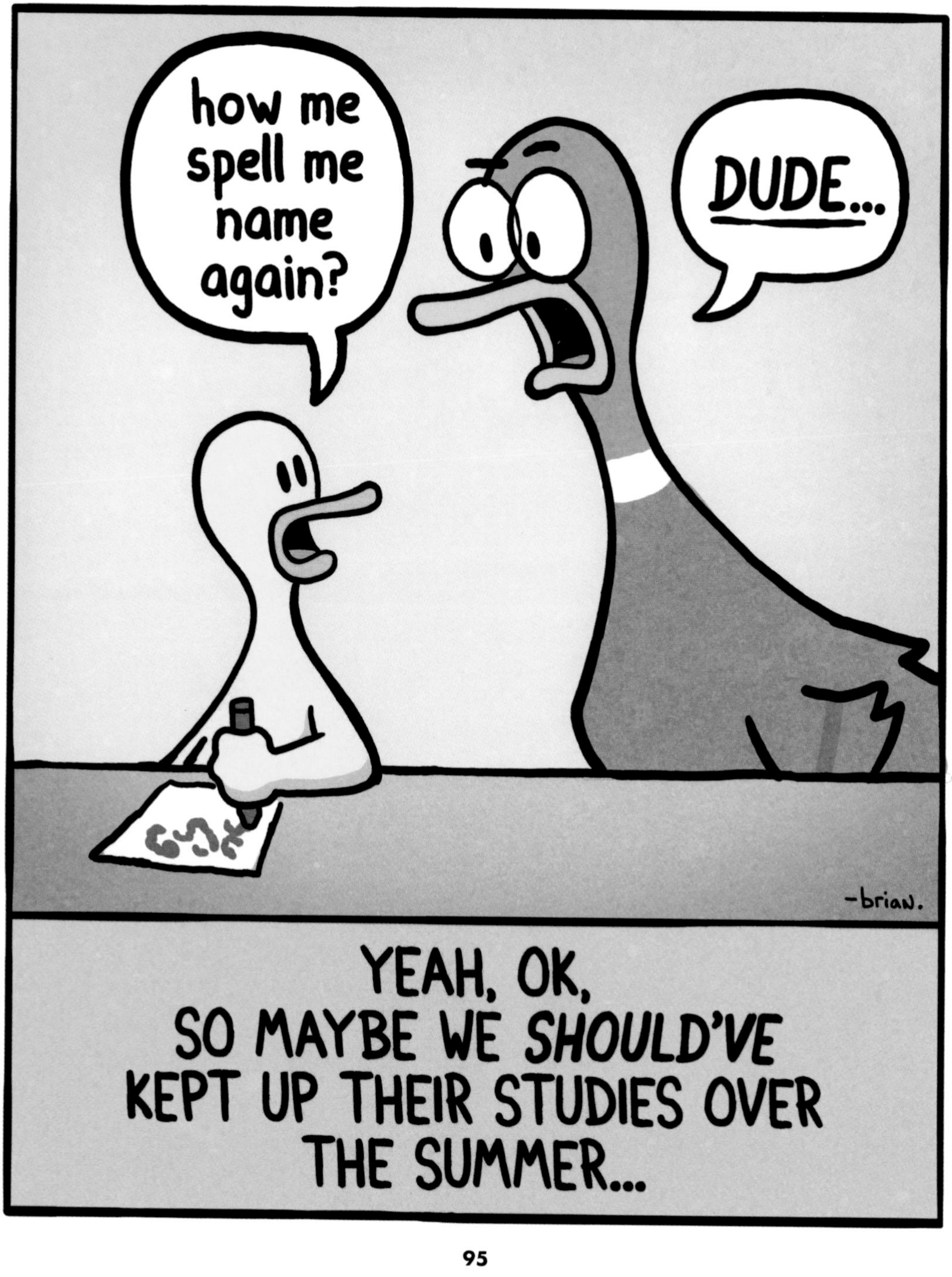
how me spell me name again?
DUDE...
-brian.
YEAH, OK, SO MAYBE WE *SHOULD'VE* KEPT UP THEIR STUDIES OVER THE SUMMER...

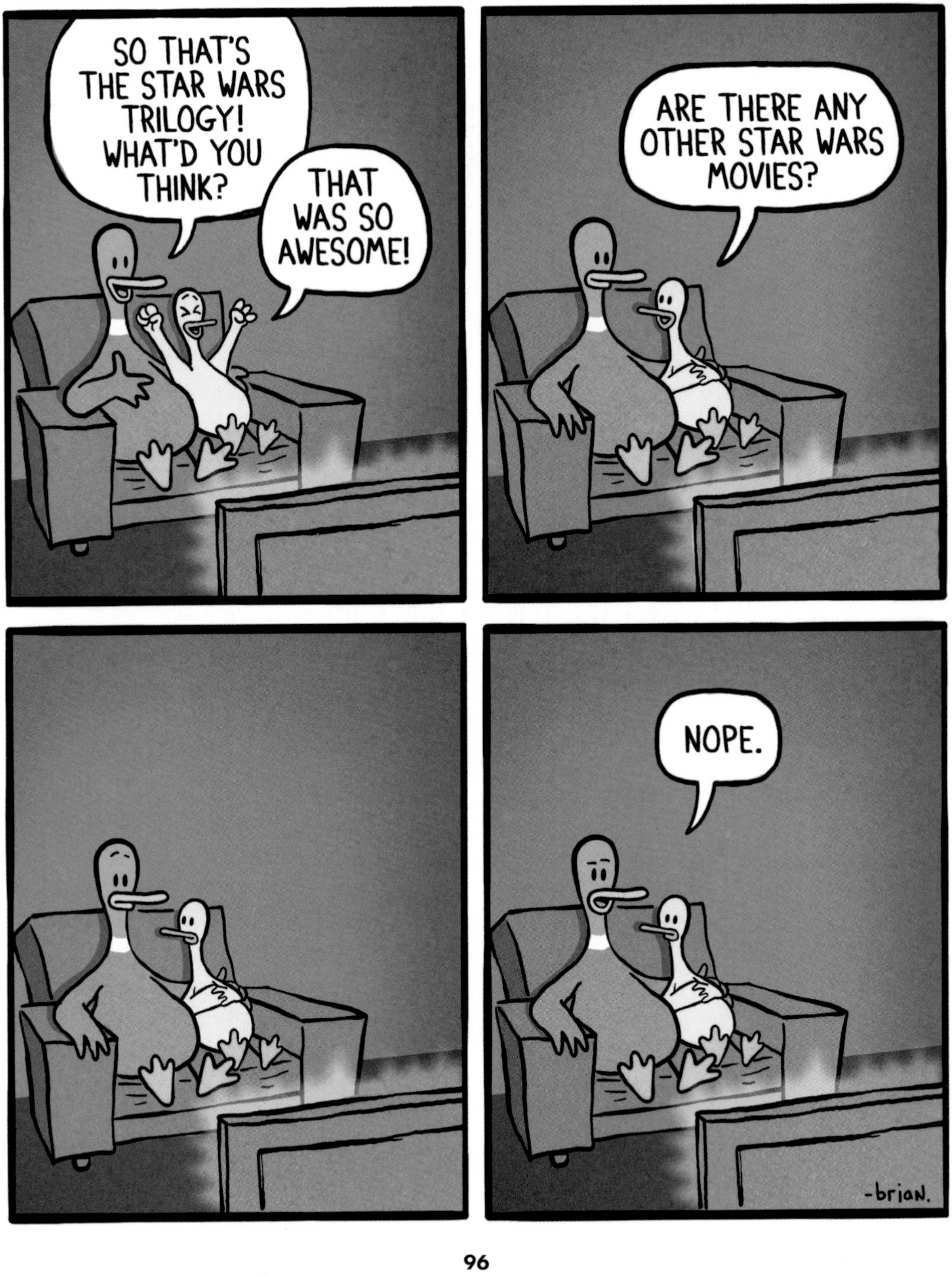
SO THAT'S THE STAR WARS TRILOGY! WHAT'D YOU THINK?
THAT WAS SO AWESOME!
ARE THERE ANY OTHER STAR WARS MOVIES?
NOPE.
-brian.

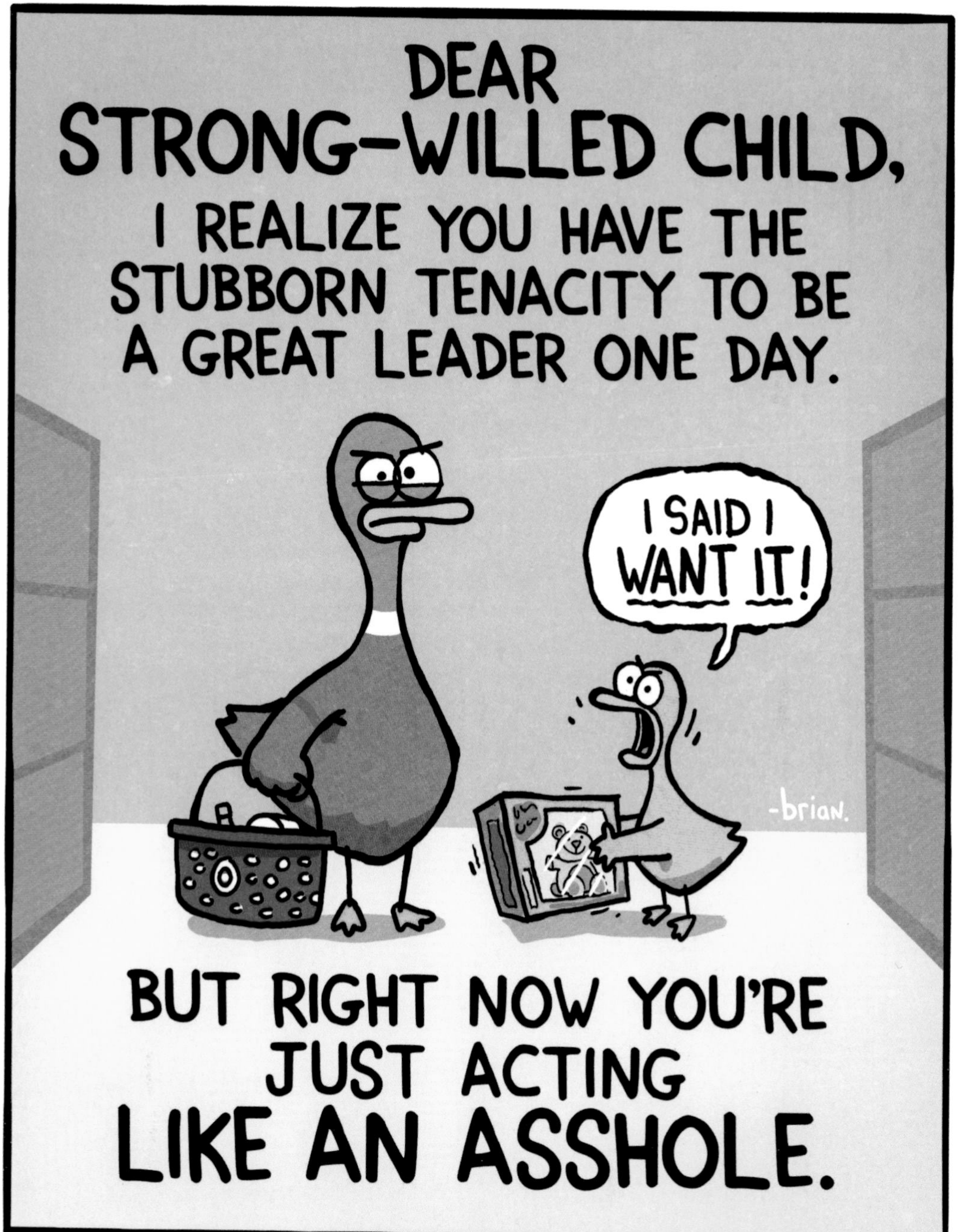
DEAR
STRONG-WILLED CHILD,
I REALIZE YOU HAVE THE
STUBBORN TENACITY TO BE
A GREAT LEADER ONE DAY.
I SAID I
WANT IT!
-brian.
BUT RIGHT NOW YOU'RE
JUST ACTING
LIKE AN ASSHOLE.

THE STUDENT BECOMES THE MASTER

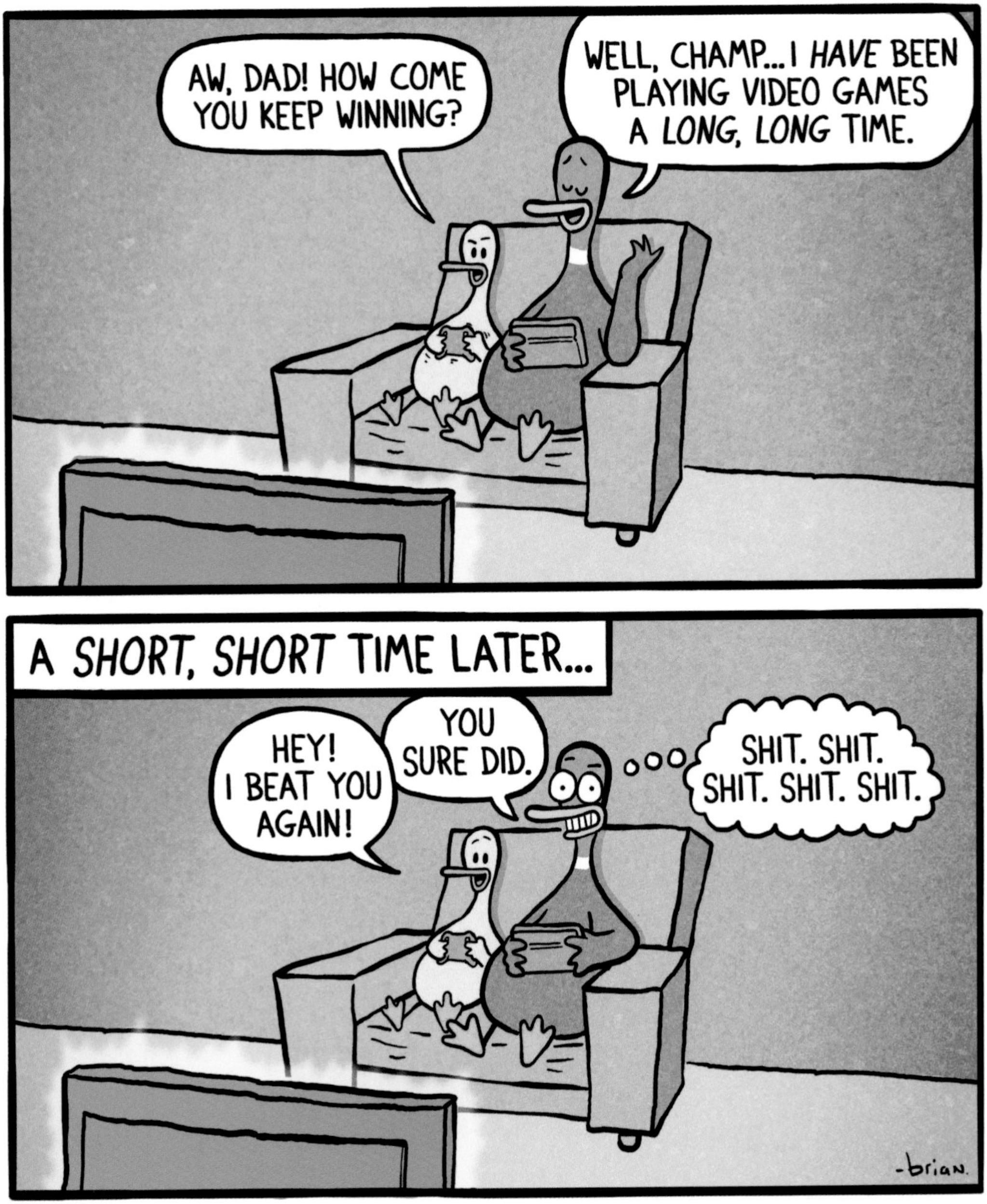
AW, DAD! HOW COME YOU KEEP WINNING?
WELL, CHAMP...I *HAVE* BEEN PLAYING VIDEO GAMES A *LONG, LONG* TIME.
A *SHORT, SHORT* TIME LATER...
HEY! I BEAT YOU AGAIN!
YOU SURE DID.
SHIT. SHIT. SHIT. SHIT. SHIT.
-brian.

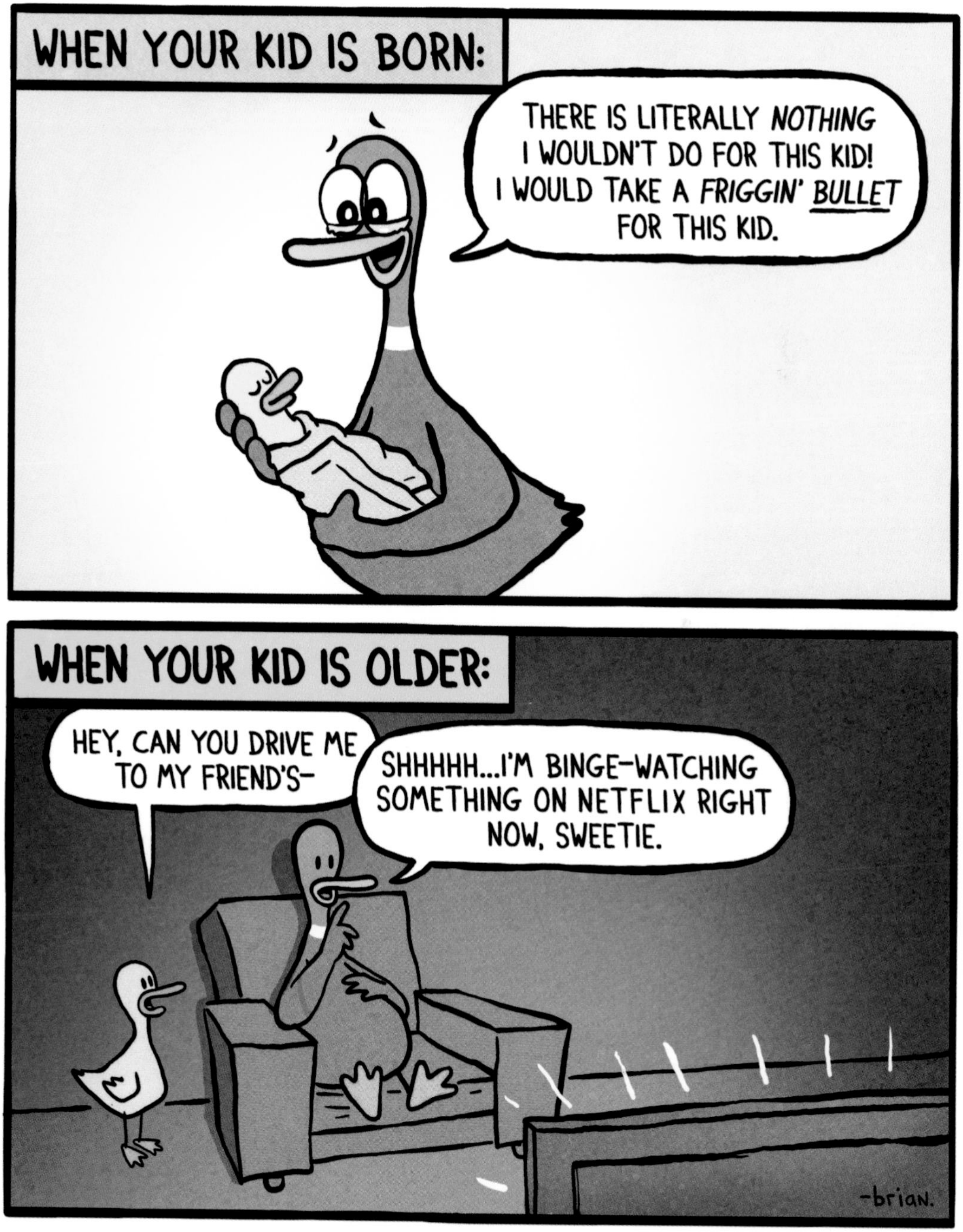

WHEN YOUR KID IS BORN:
THERE IS LITERALLY NOTHING I WOULDN'T DO FOR THIS KID! I WOULD TAKE A FRIGGIN' BULLET FOR THIS KID.
WHEN YOUR KID IS OLDER:
HEY, CAN YOU DRIVE ME TO MY FRIEND'S–
SHHHHH...I'M BINGE-WATCHING SOMETHING ON NETFLIX RIGHT NOW, SWEETIE.
-brian.

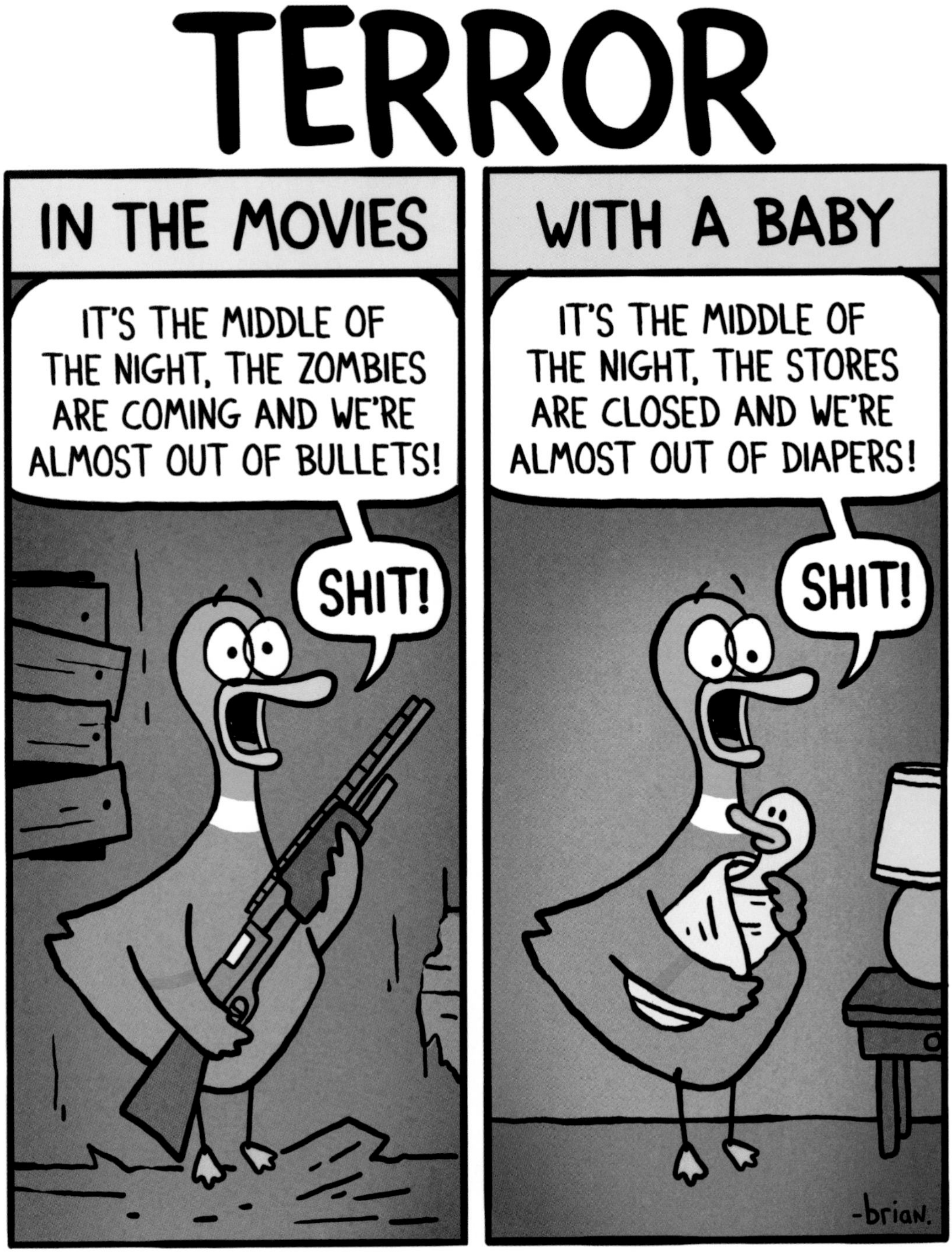
TERROR
IN THE MOVIES
IT'S THE MIDDLE OF THE NIGHT, THE ZOMBIES ARE COMING AND WE'RE ALMOST OUT OF BULLETS!
SHIT!
WITH A BABY
IT'S THE MIDDLE OF THE NIGHT, THE STORES ARE CLOSED AND WE'RE ALMOST OUT OF DIAPERS!
SHIT!
-brian.

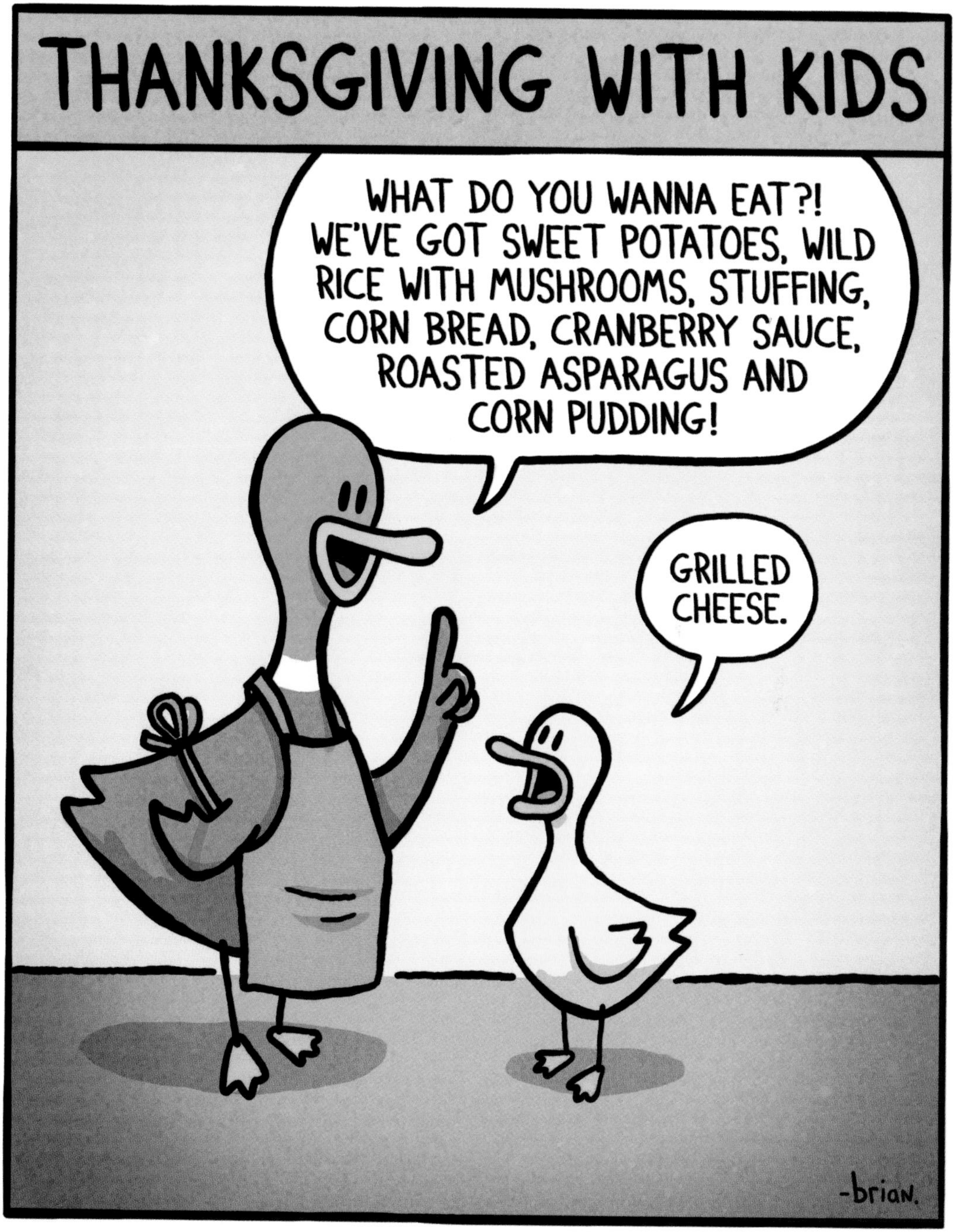
THANKSGIVING WITH KIDS
WHAT DO YOU WANNA EAT?! WE'VE GOT SWEET POTATOES, WILD RICE WITH MUSHROOMS, STUFFING, CORN BREAD, CRANBERRY SAUCE, ROASTED ASPARAGUS AND CORN PUDDING!
GRILLED CHEESE.
-brian.

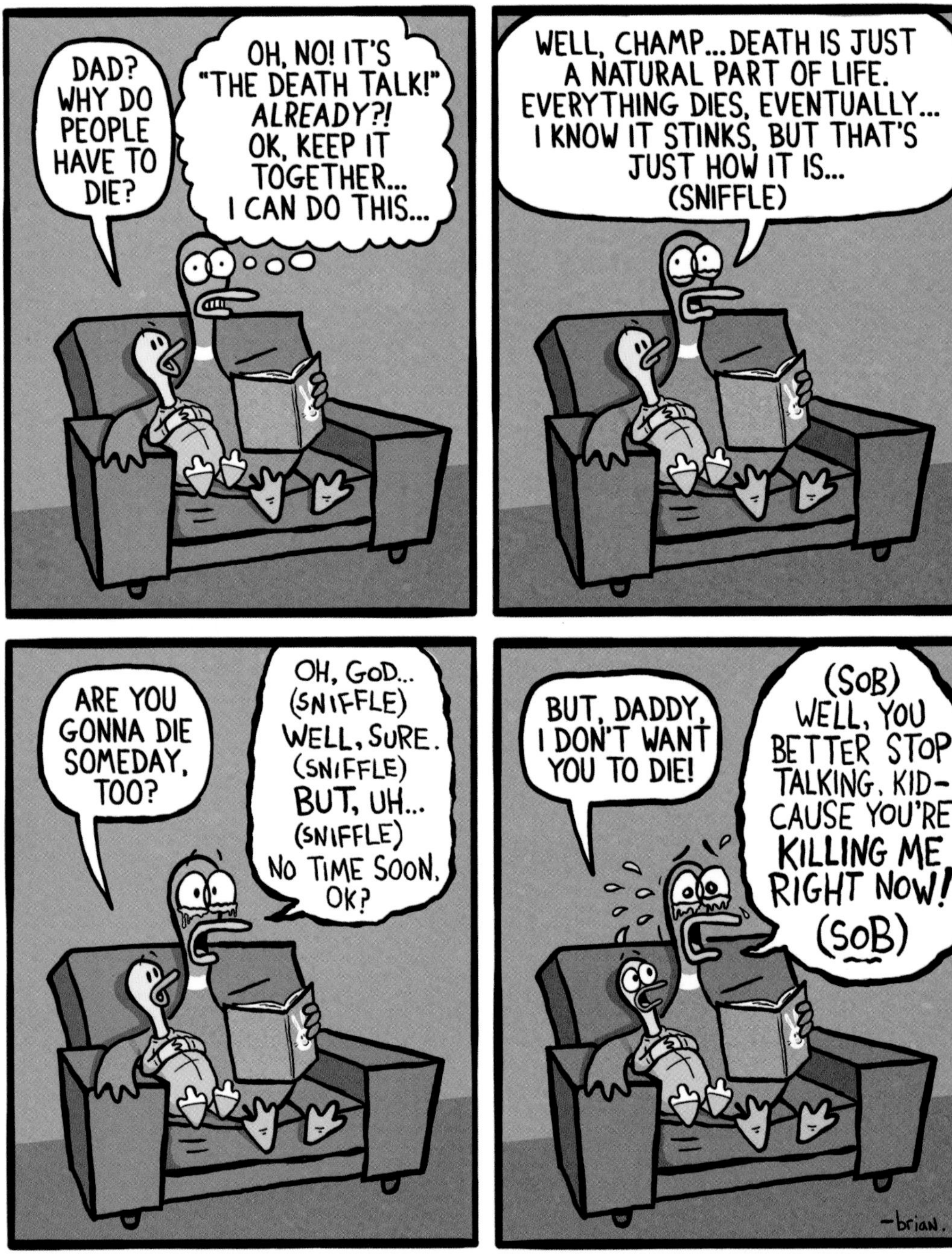
DAD? WHY DO PEOPLE HAVE TO DIE?
OH, NO! IT'S "THE DEATH TALK!" ALREADY?! OK, KEEP IT TOGETHER... I CAN DO THIS...
WELL, CHAMP... DEATH IS JUST A NATURAL PART OF LIFE. EVERYTHING DIES, EVENTUALLY... I KNOW IT STINKS, BUT THAT'S JUST HOW IT IS... (SNIFFLE)
ARE YOU GONNA DIE SOMEDAY, TOO?
OH, GOD... (SNIFFLE) WELL, SURE. (SNIFFLE) BUT, UH... (SNIFFLE) NO TIME SOON, OK?
BUT, DADDY, I DON'T WANT YOU TO DIE!
(SOB) WELL, YOU BETTER STOP TALKING, KID- CAUSE YOU'RE KILLING ME RIGHT NOW! (SOB)
-brian.

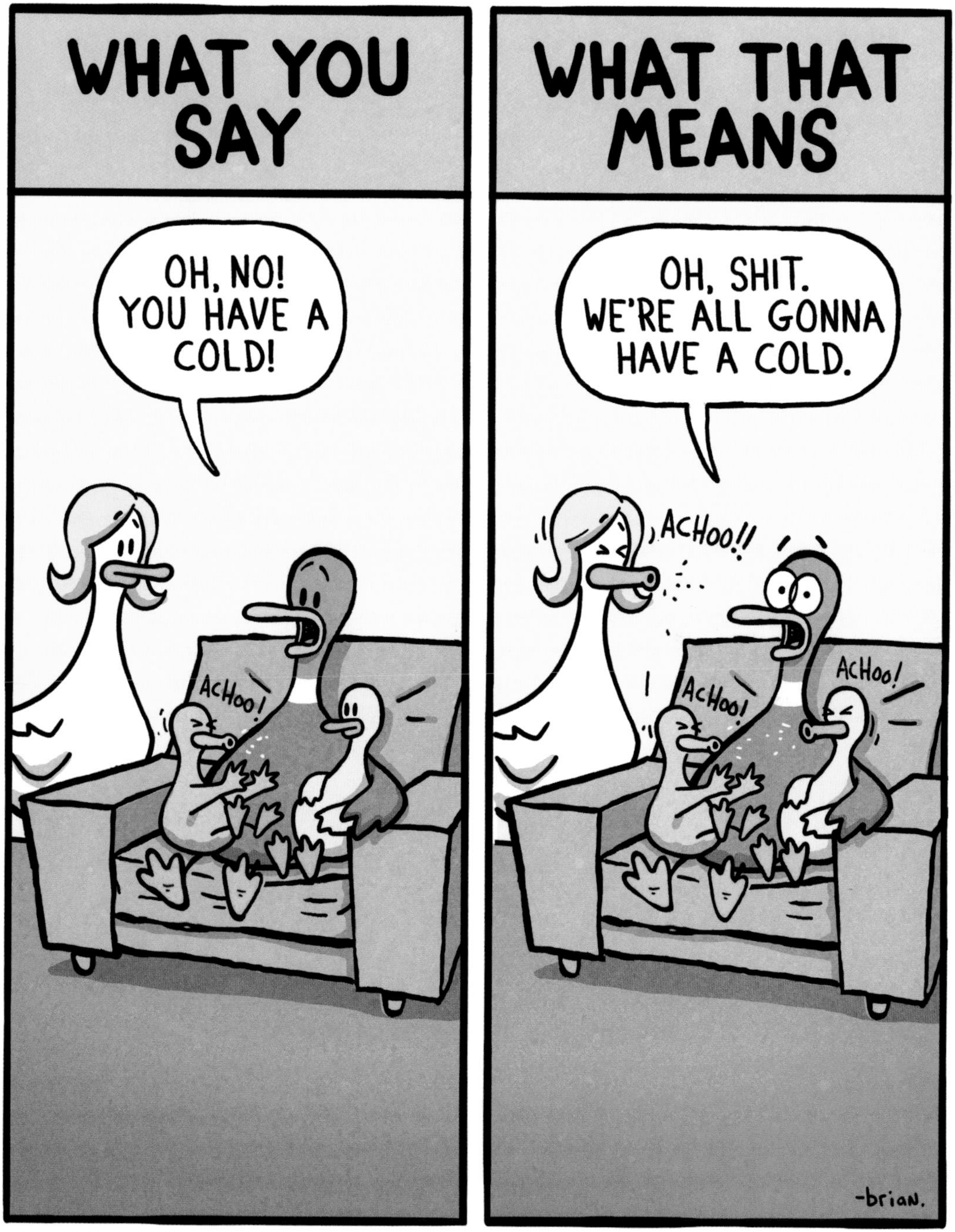
WHAT YOU SAY
OH, NO! YOU HAVE A COLD!
ACHOO!
WHAT THAT MEANS
OH, SHIT. WE'RE ALL GONNA HAVE A COLD.
ACHOO!!
ACHOO!
ACHOO!
-brian.

THE THREE STAGES OF PUMPKIN CARVING

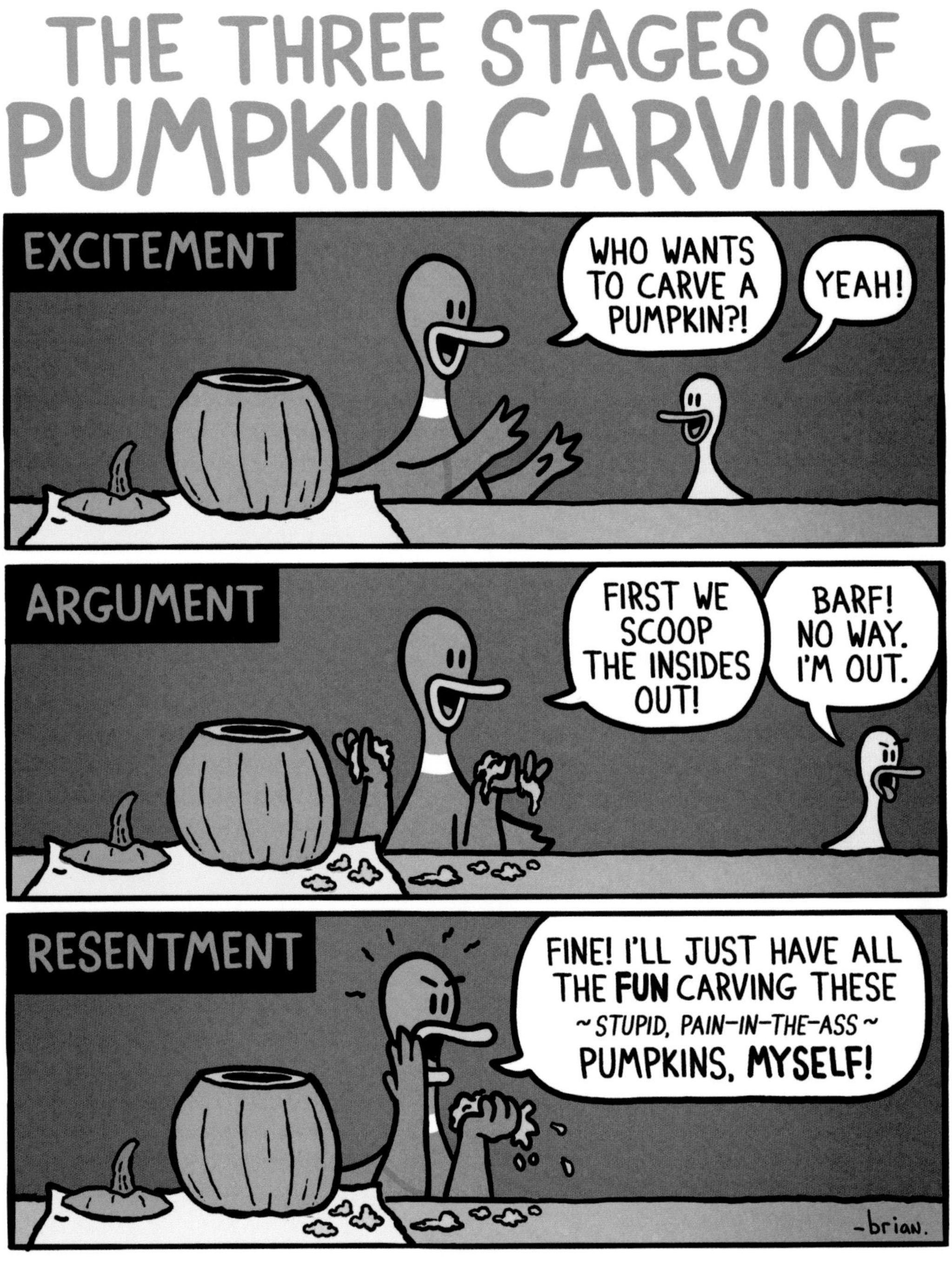

EXCITEMENT
WHO WANTS TO CARVE A PUMPKIN?!
YEAH!
ARGUMENT
FIRST WE SCOOP THE INSIDES OUT!
BARF! NO WAY. I'M OUT.
RESENTMENT
FINE! I'LL JUST HAVE ALL THE **FUN** CARVING THESE ~STUPID, PAIN-IN-THE-ASS~ PUMPKINS, **MYSELF!**
-brian.

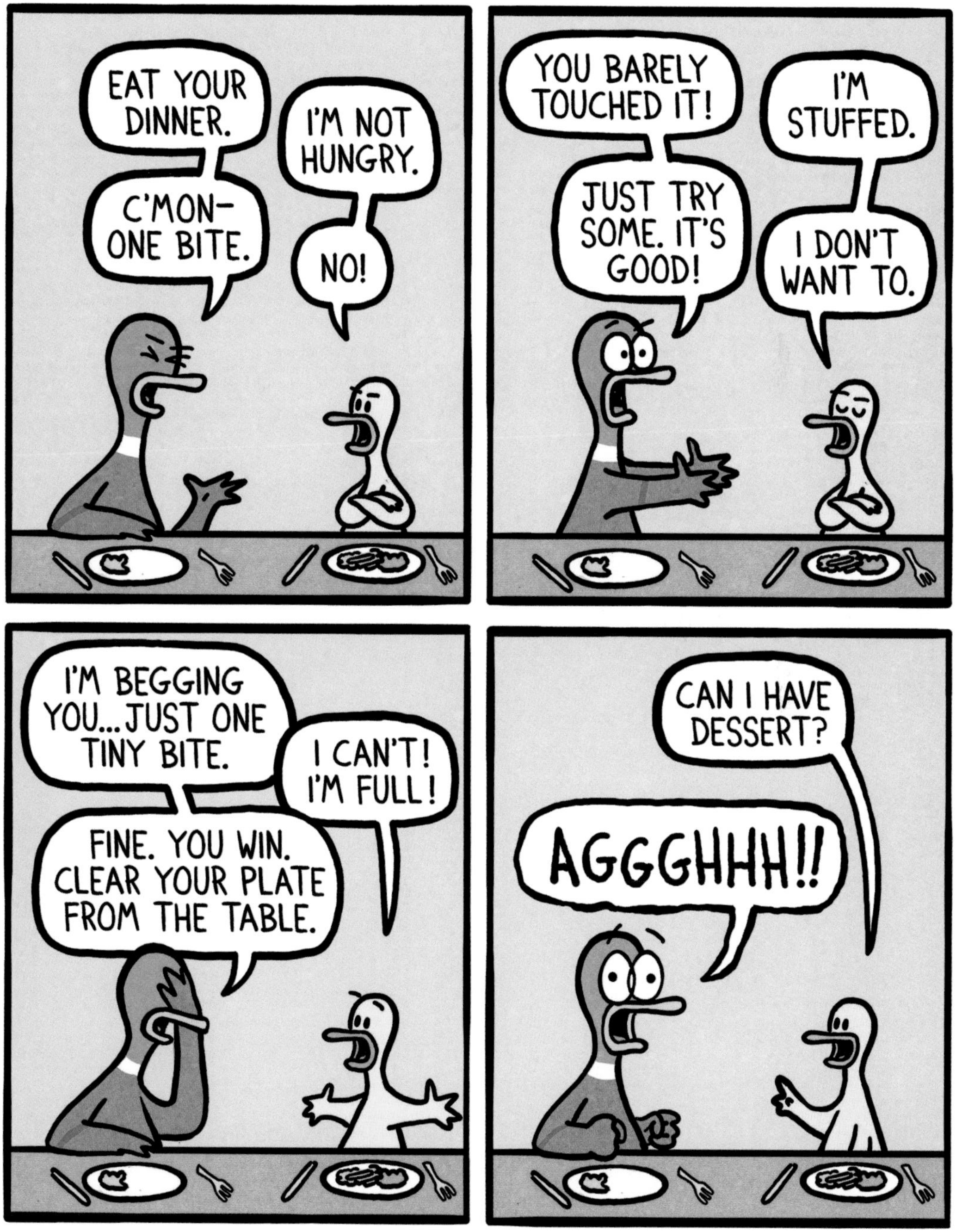
EAT YOUR DINNER.
C'MON— ONE BITE.
I'M NOT HUNGRY.
NO!
YOU BARELY TOUCHED IT!
JUST TRY SOME. IT'S GOOD!
I'M STUFFED.
I DON'T WANT TO.
I'M BEGGING YOU...JUST ONE TINY BITE.
I CAN'T! I'M FULL!
FINE. YOU WIN. CLEAR YOUR PLATE FROM THE TABLE.
CAN I HAVE DESSERT?
AGGGHHH!!

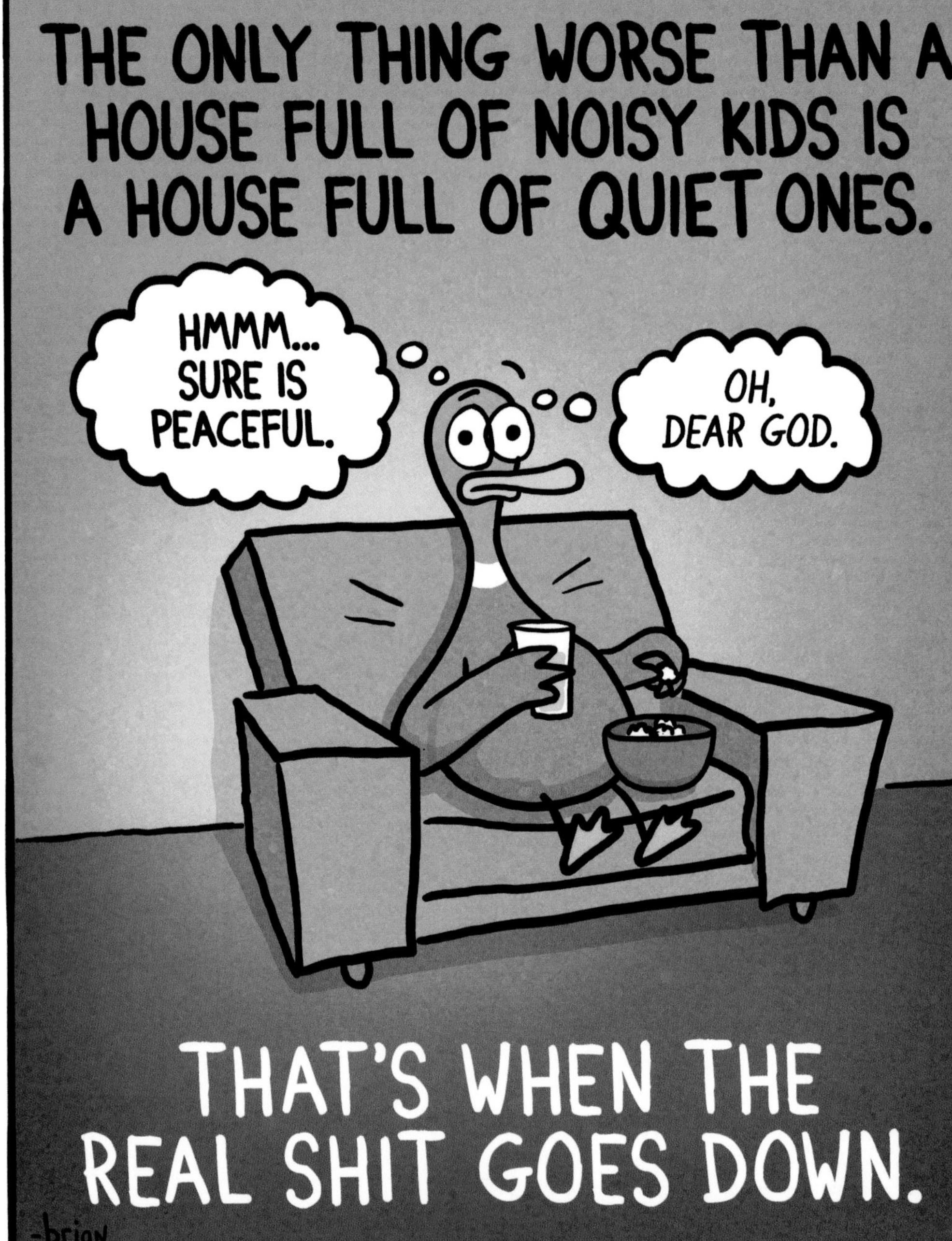
THE ONLY THING WORSE THAN A HOUSE FULL OF NOISY KIDS IS A HOUSE FULL OF QUIET ONES.
HMMM... SURE IS PEACEFUL.
OH, DEAR GOD.
THAT'S WHEN THE REAL SHIT GOES DOWN.
-brian.

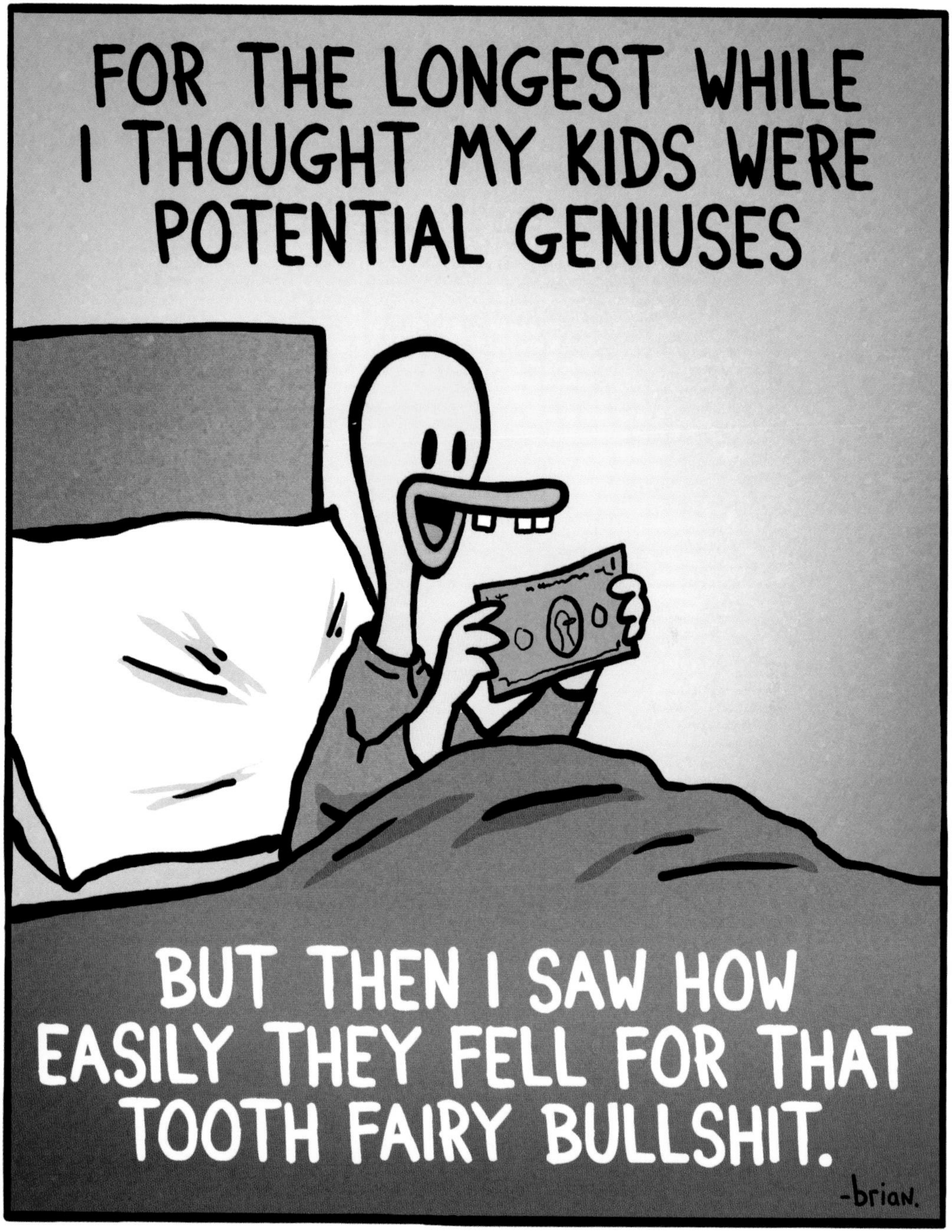
FOR THE LONGEST WHILE I THOUGHT MY KIDS WERE POTENTIAL GENIUSES
BUT THEN I SAW HOW EASILY THEY FELL FOR THAT TOOTH FAIRY BULLSHIT.
-brian.

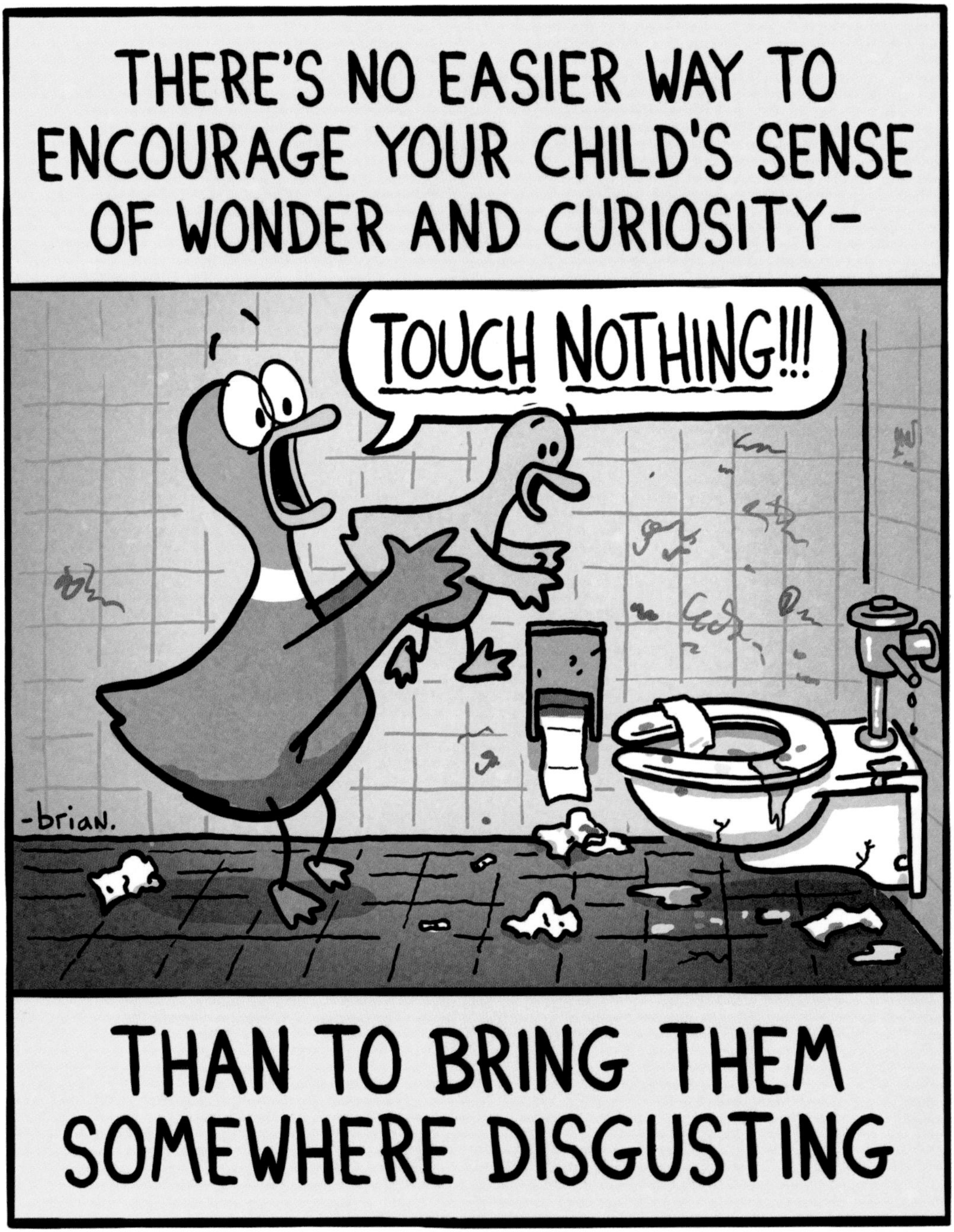
THERE'S NO EASIER WAY TO ENCOURAGE YOUR CHILD'S SENSE OF WONDER AND CURIOSITY-
TOUCH NOTHING!!!
-brian.
THAN TO BRING THEM SOMEWHERE DISGUSTING

THE TWO STAGES OF WINTER

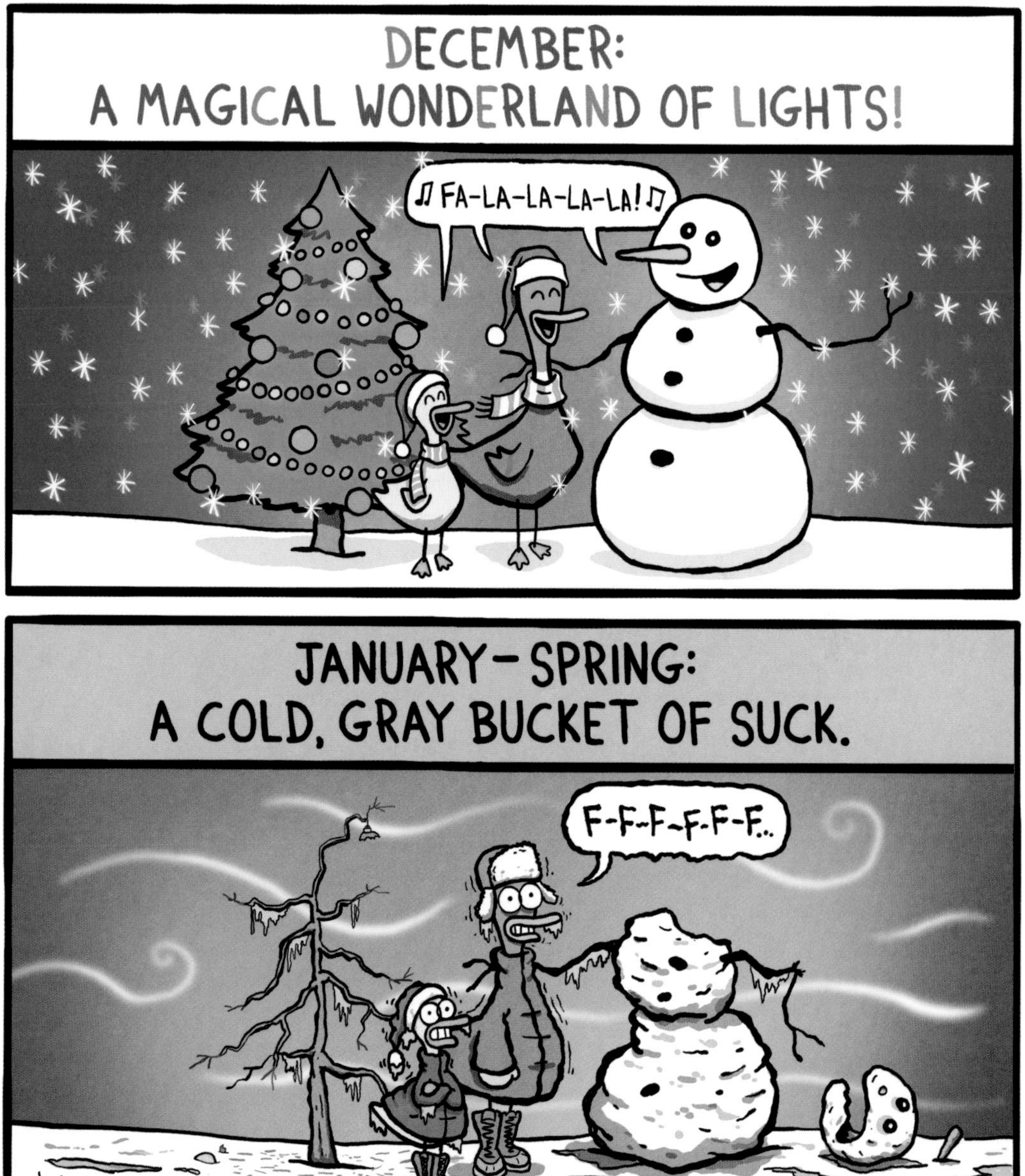
DECEMBER:
A MAGICAL WONDERLAND OF LIGHTS!
♫ FA-LA-LA-LA-LA! ♫
JANUARY-SPRING:
A COLD, GRAY BUCKET OF SUCK.
F-F-F-F-F-F...
-brian.

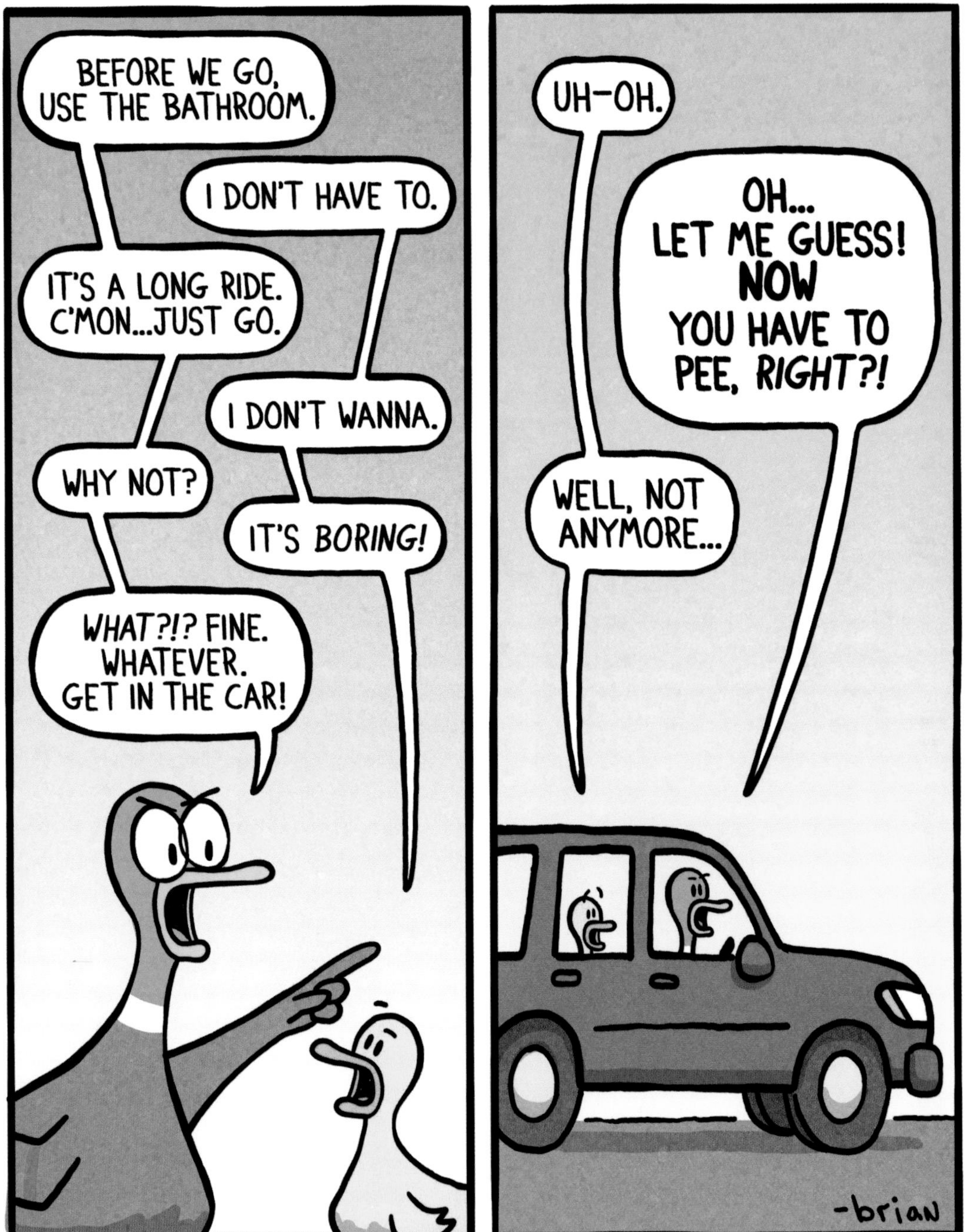
BEFORE WE GO, USE THE BATHROOM.
I DON'T HAVE TO.
IT'S A LONG RIDE. C'MON...JUST GO.
I DON'T WANNA.
WHY NOT?
IT'S *BORING!*
WHAT?!? FINE. WHATEVER. GET IN THE CAR!
UH-OH.
OH... LET ME GUESS! **NOW** YOU HAVE TO PEE, *RIGHT?!*
WELL, NOT ANYMORE...
-brian

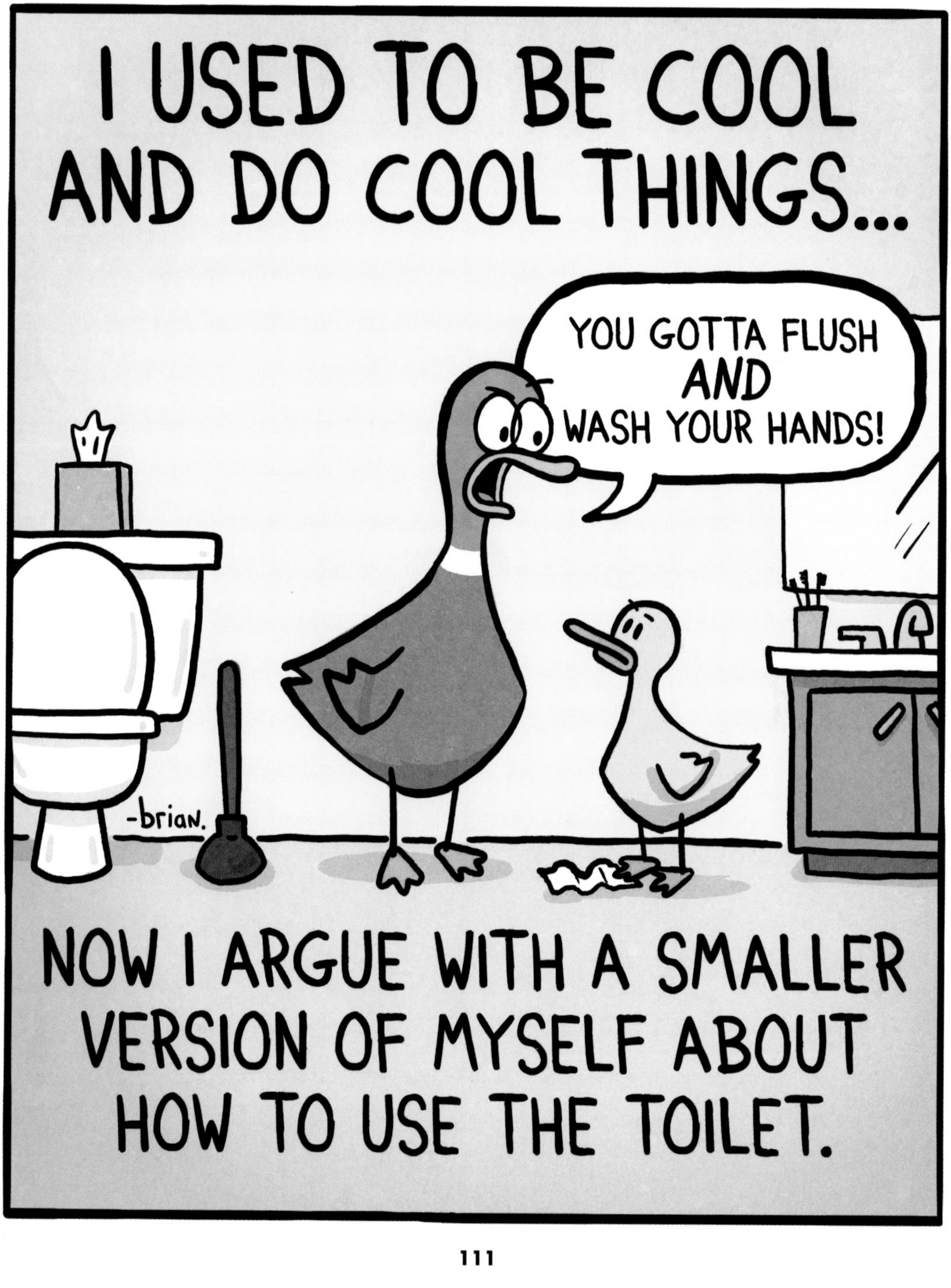
I USED TO BE COOL AND DO COOL THINGS...
YOU GOTTA FLUSH AND WASH YOUR HANDS!
-brian.
NOW I ARGUE WITH A SMALLER VERSION OF MYSELF ABOUT HOW TO USE THE TOILET.

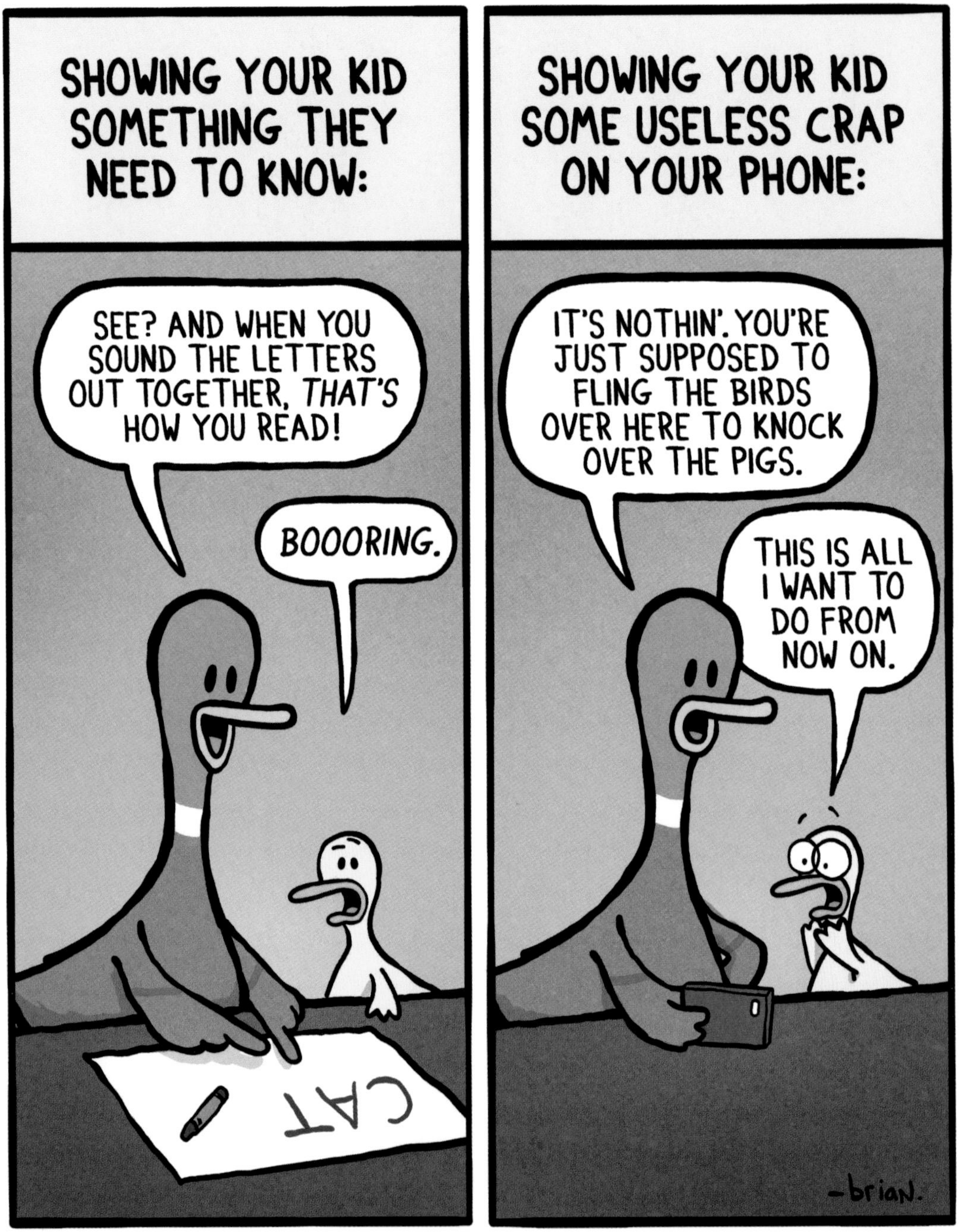
SHOWING YOUR KID SOMETHING THEY NEED TO KNOW:
SEE? AND WHEN YOU SOUND THE LETTERS OUT TOGETHER, *THAT'S* HOW YOU READ!
BOOORING.
CAT
SHOWING YOUR KID SOME USELESS CRAP ON YOUR PHONE:
IT'S NOTHIN'. YOU'RE JUST SUPPOSED TO FLING THE BIRDS OVER HERE TO KNOCK OVER THE PIGS.
THIS IS ALL I WANT TO DO FROM NOW ON.
-brian.

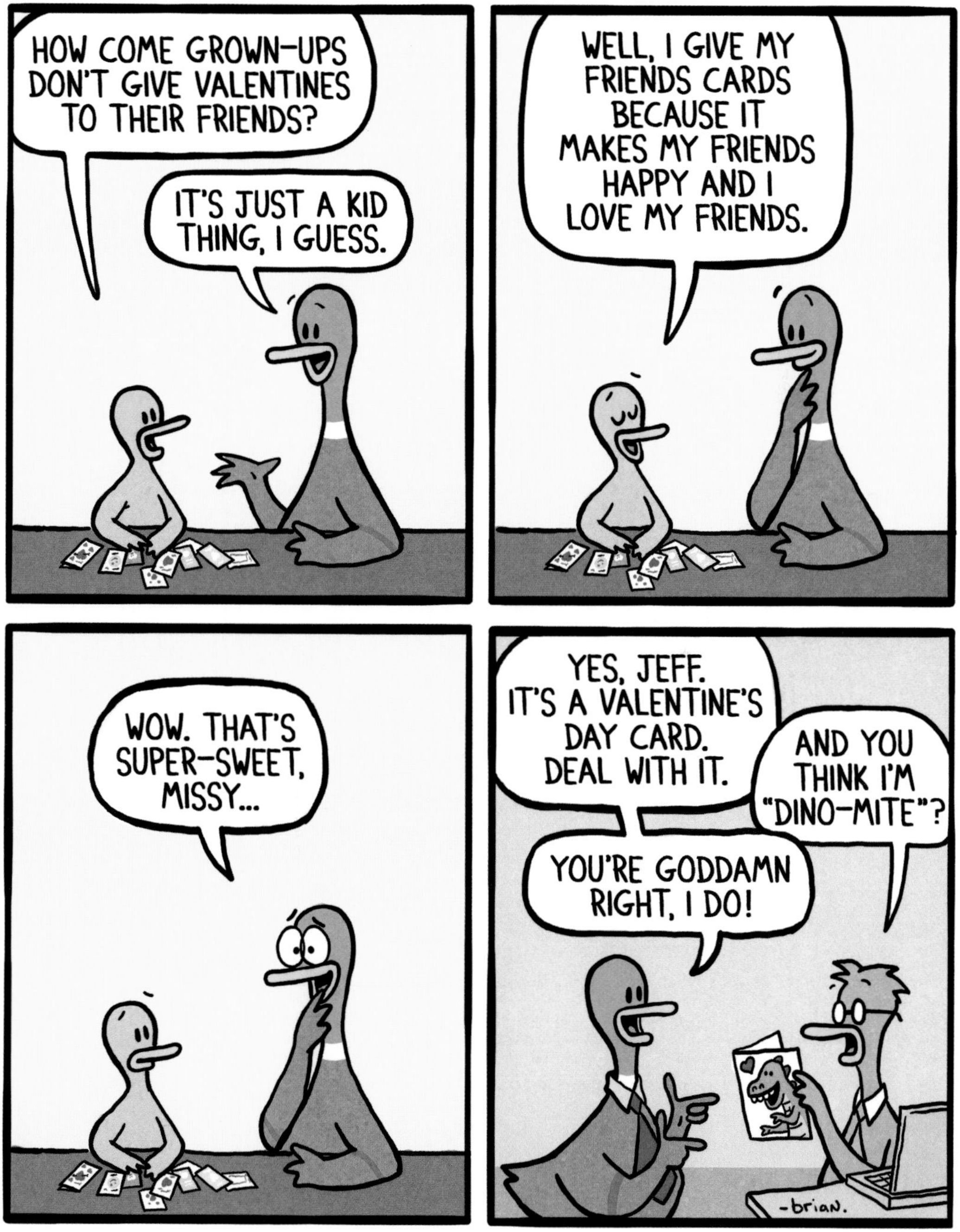
HOW COME GROWN-UPS DON'T GIVE VALENTINES TO THEIR FRIENDS?
IT'S JUST A KID THING, I GUESS.
WELL, I GIVE MY FRIENDS CARDS BECAUSE IT MAKES MY FRIENDS HAPPY AND I LOVE MY FRIENDS.
WOW. THAT'S SUPER-SWEET, MISSY...
AND YOU THINK I'M "DINO-MITE"?
YES, JEFF. IT'S A VALENTINE'S DAY CARD. DEAL WITH IT.
YOU'RE GODDAMN RIGHT, I DO!
-brian.

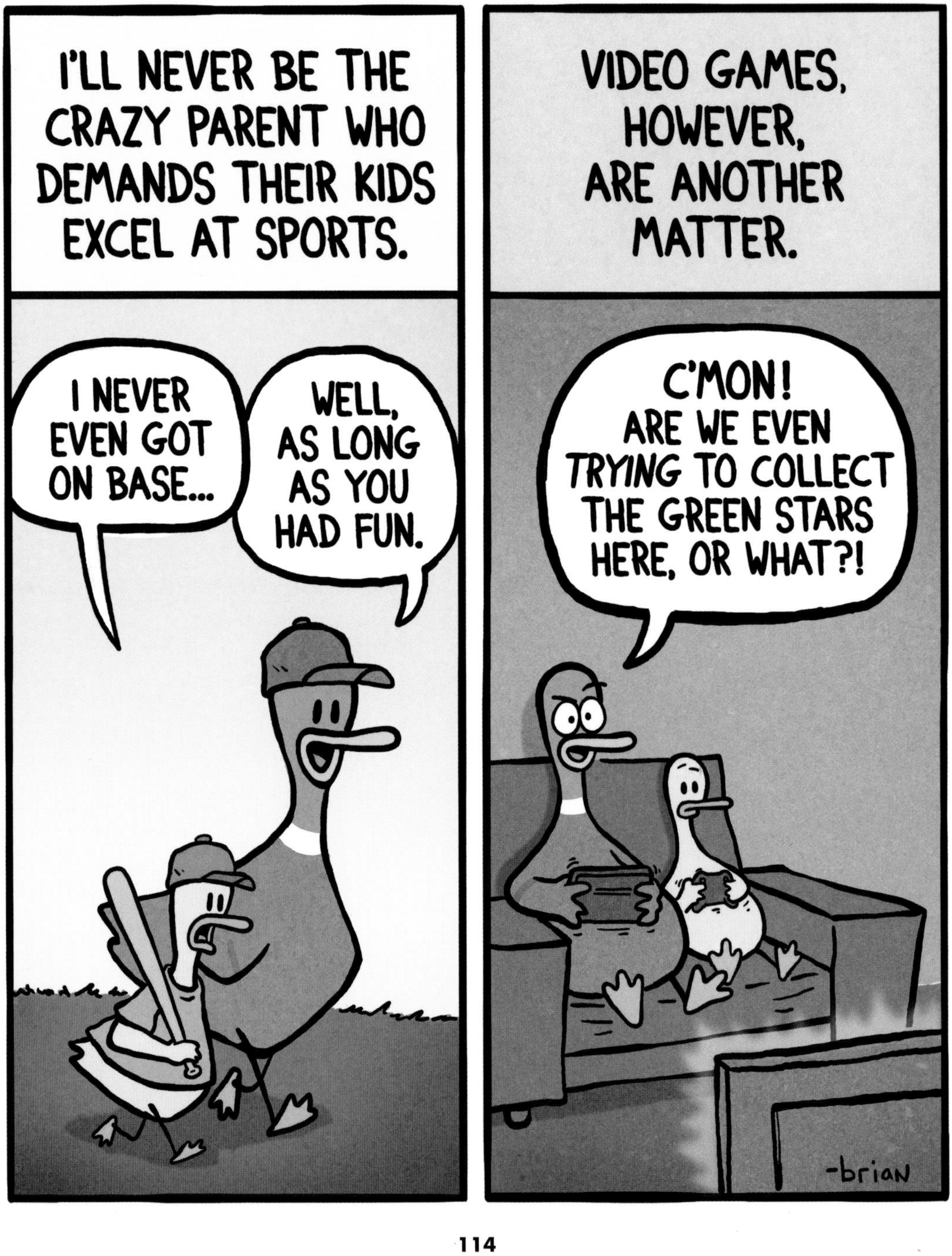
I'LL NEVER BE THE CRAZY PARENT WHO DEMANDS THEIR KIDS EXCEL AT SPORTS.
I NEVER EVEN GOT ON BASE...
WELL, AS LONG AS YOU HAD FUN.
VIDEO GAMES, HOWEVER, ARE ANOTHER MATTER.
C'MON! ARE WE EVEN *TRYING* TO COLLECT THE GREEN STARS HERE, OR WHAT?!
-brian

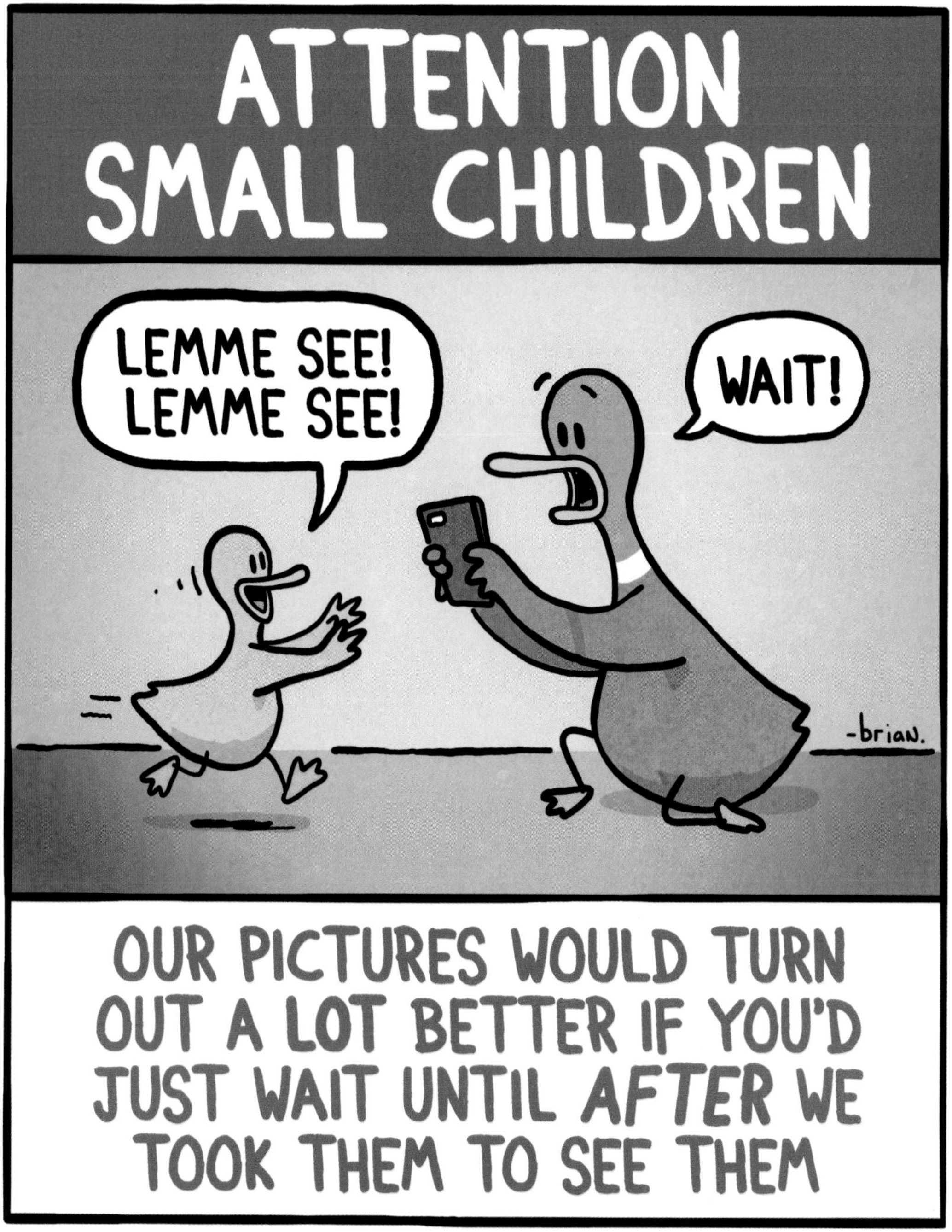
ATTENTION SMALL CHILDREN
LEMME SEE! LEMME SEE!
WAIT!
-brian.
OUR PICTURES WOULD TURN OUT A LOT BETTER IF YOU'D JUST WAIT UNTIL *AFTER* WE TOOK THEM TO SEE THEM

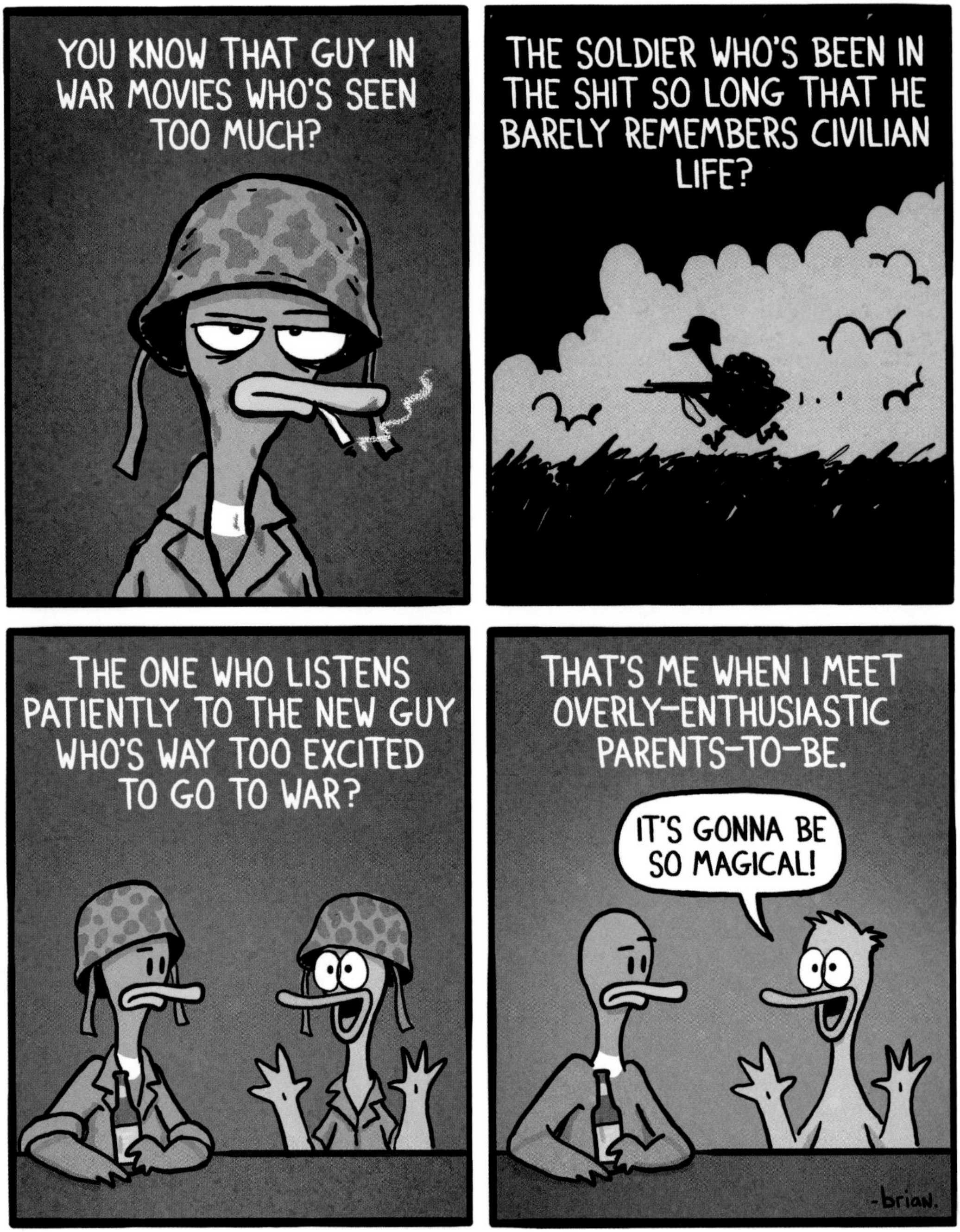
YOU KNOW THAT GUY IN WAR MOVIES WHO'S SEEN TOO MUCH?
THE SOLDIER WHO'S BEEN IN THE SHIT SO LONG THAT HE BARELY REMEMBERS CIVILIAN LIFE?
THE ONE WHO LISTENS PATIENTLY TO THE NEW GUY WHO'S WAY TOO EXCITED TO GO TO WAR?
THAT'S ME WHEN I MEET OVERLY-ENTHUSIASTIC PARENTS-TO-BE.
IT'S GONNA BE SO MAGICAL!
-brian.

WATCHING THE CLOCK

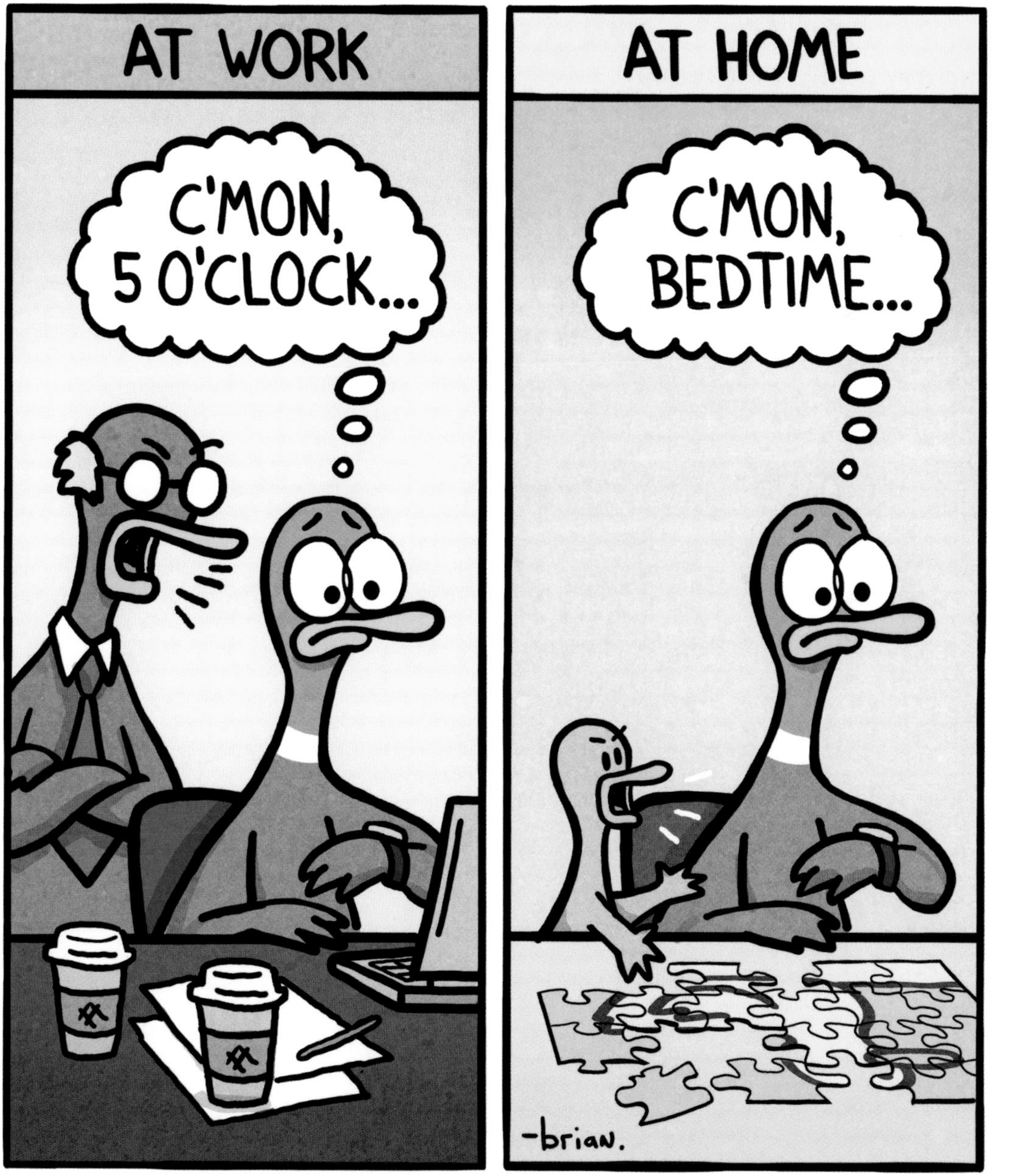
AT WORK
C'MON, 5 O'CLOCK...
AT HOME
C'MON, BEDTIME...
-brian.

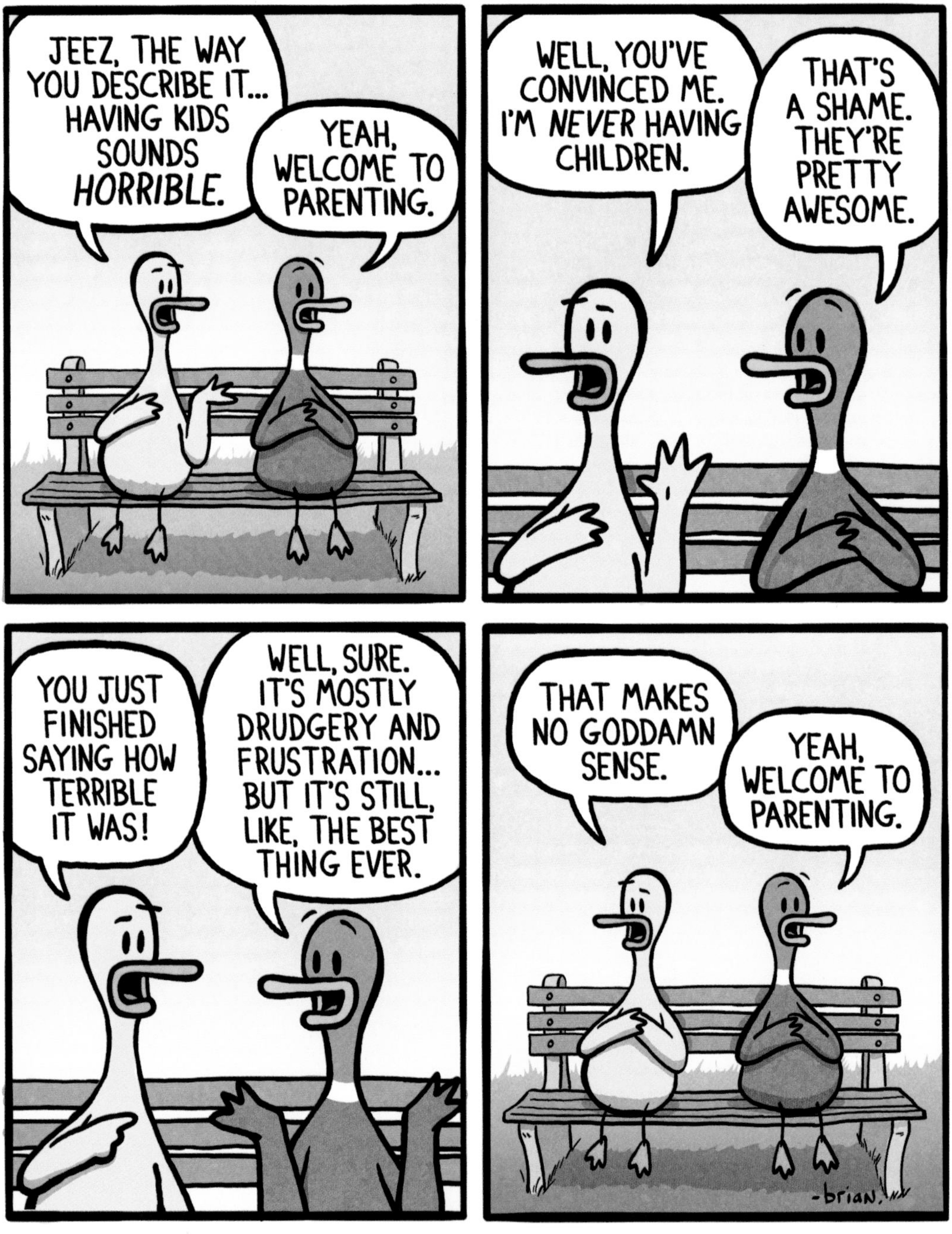
JEEZ, THE WAY YOU DESCRIBE IT... HAVING KIDS SOUNDS *HORRIBLE.*
YEAH, WELCOME TO PARENTING.
WELL, YOU'VE CONVINCED ME. I'M *NEVER* HAVING CHILDREN.
THAT'S A SHAME. THEY'RE PRETTY AWESOME.
YOU JUST FINISHED SAYING HOW TERRIBLE IT WAS!
WELL, SURE. IT'S MOSTLY DRUDGERY AND FRUSTRATION... BUT IT'S STILL, LIKE, THE BEST THING EVER.
THAT MAKES NO GODDAMN SENSE.
YEAH, WELCOME TO PARENTING.
-brian.

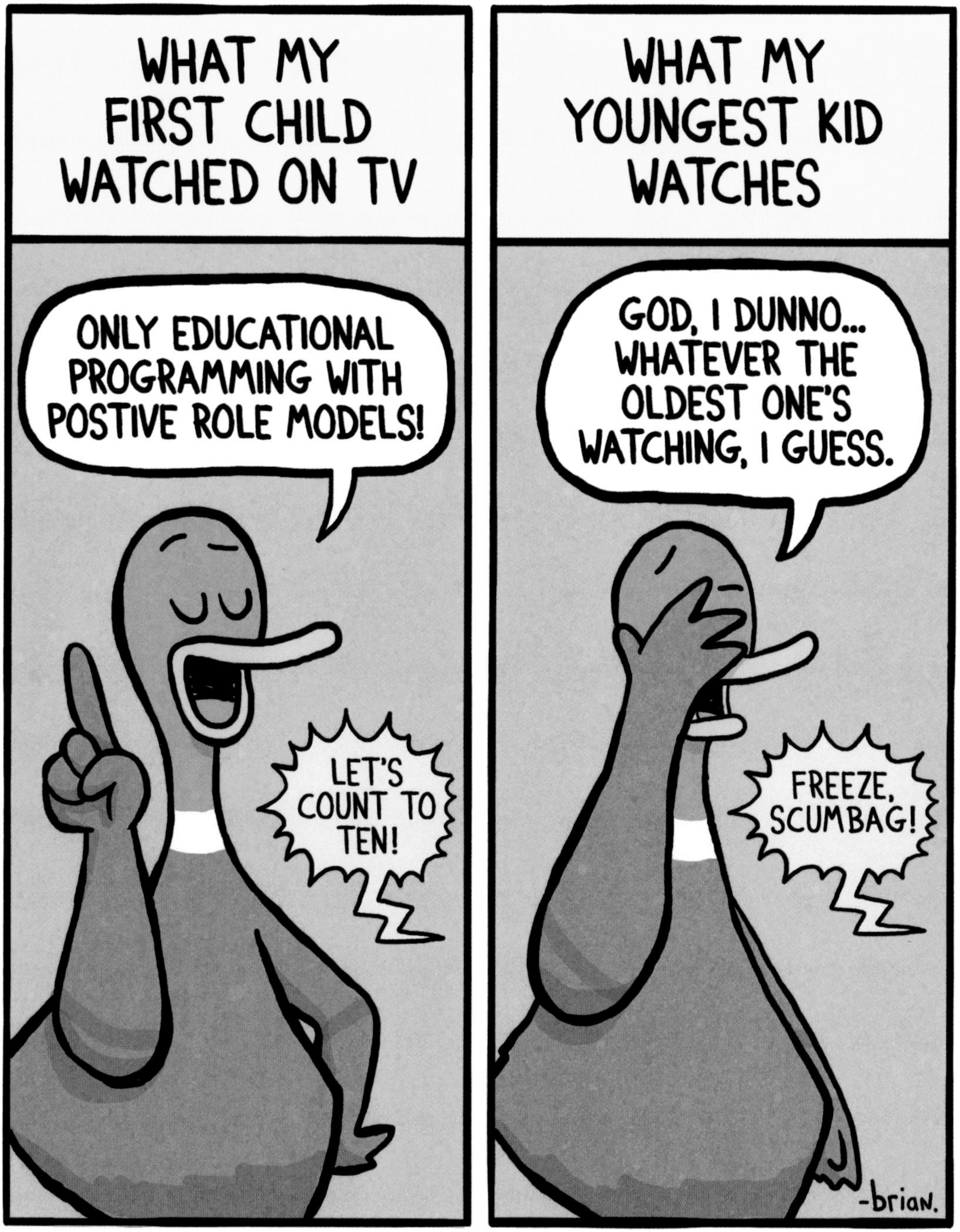
WHAT MY FIRST CHILD WATCHED ON TV
ONLY EDUCATIONAL PROGRAMMING WITH POSTIVE ROLE MODELS!
LET'S COUNT TO TEN!
WHAT MY YOUNGEST KID WATCHES
GOD, I DUNNO... WHATEVER THE OLDEST ONE'S WATCHING, I GUESS.
FREEZE, SCUMBAG!
-brian.

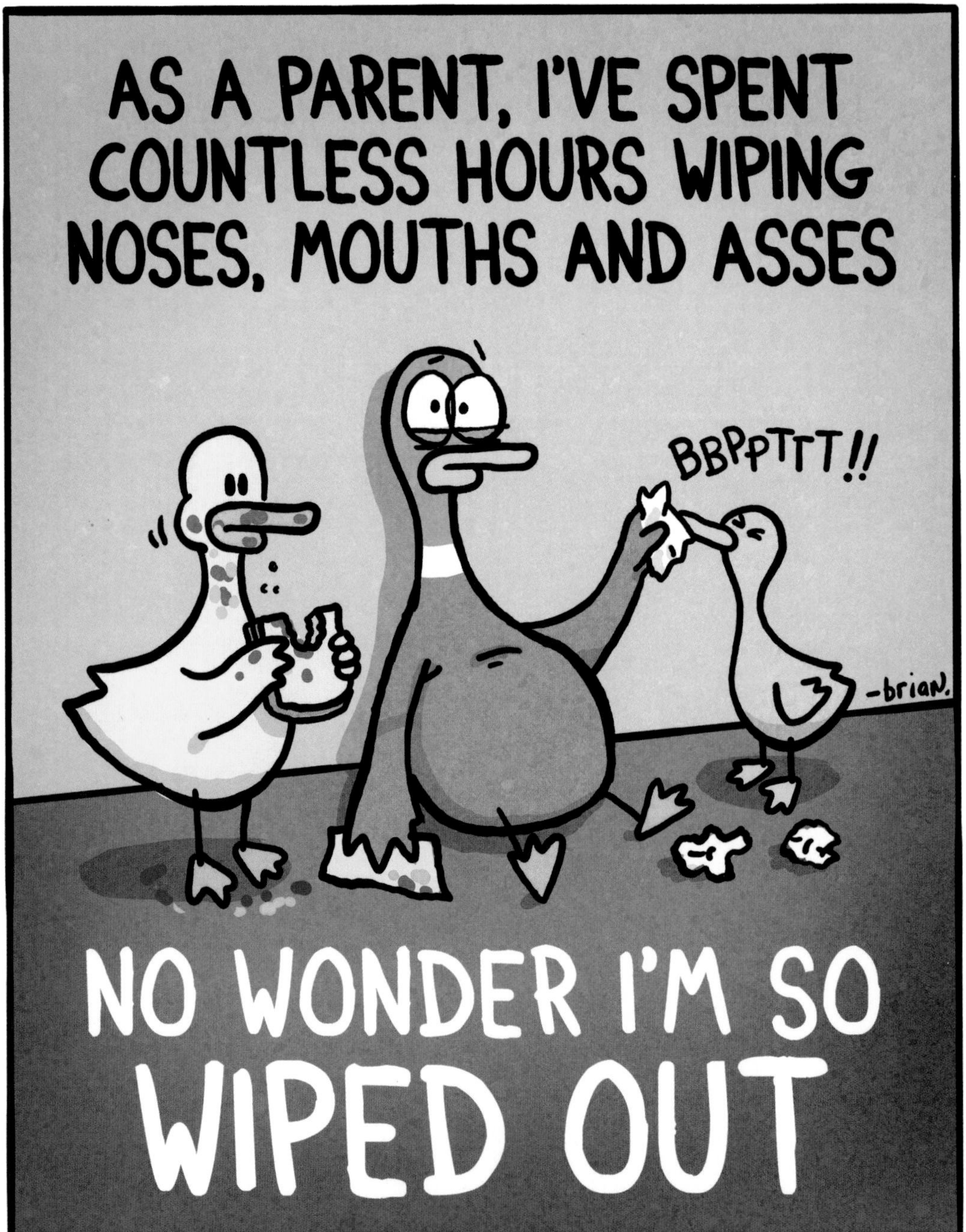
AS A PARENT, I'VE SPENT COUNTLESS HOURS WIPING NOSES, MOUTHS AND ASSES
BBPpTTTT!!
-brian.
NO WONDER I'M SO WIPED OUT

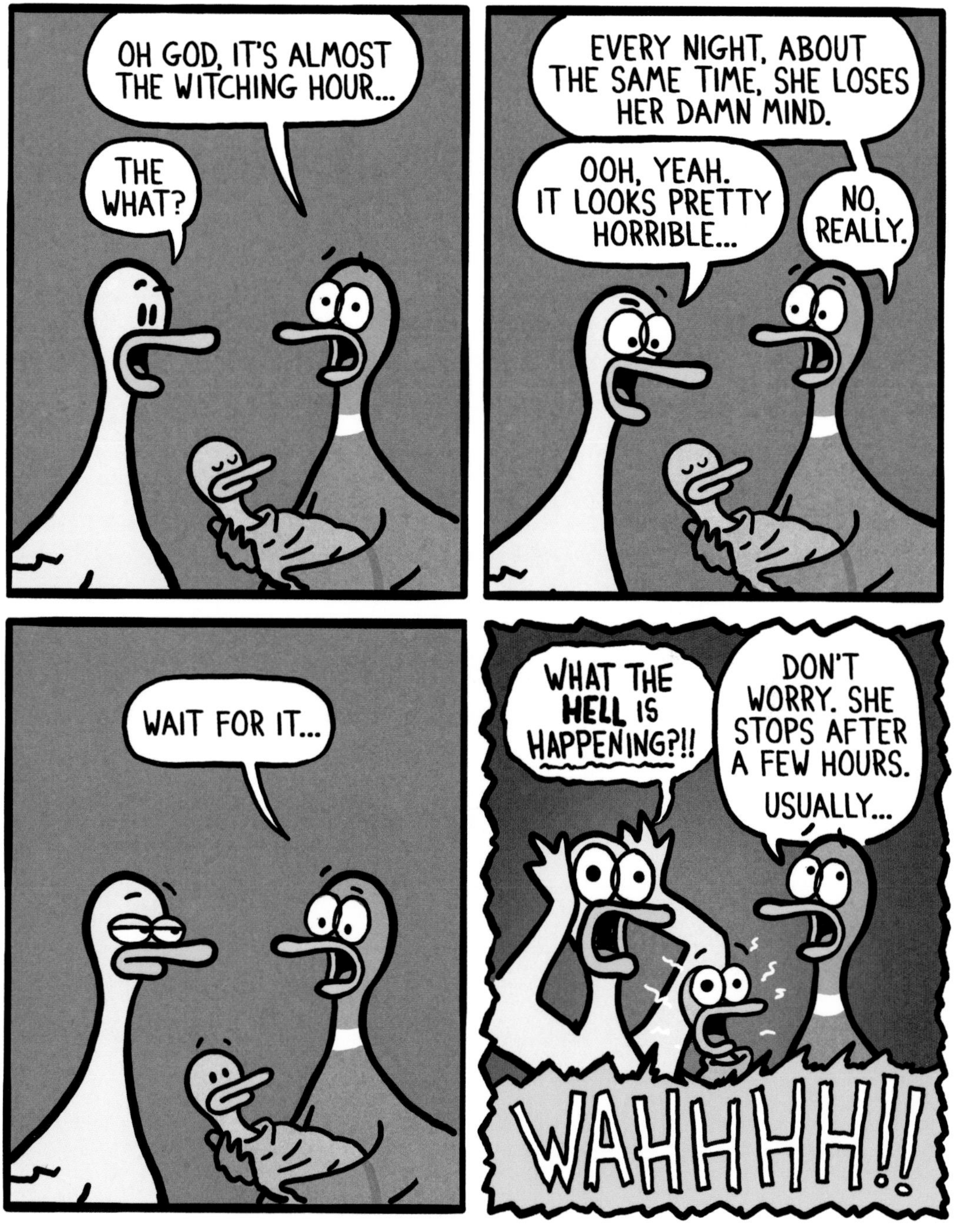
OH GOD, IT'S ALMOST THE WITCHING HOUR...
THE WHAT?
EVERY NIGHT, ABOUT THE SAME TIME, SHE LOSES HER DAMN MIND.
OOH, YEAH. IT LOOKS PRETTY HORRIBLE...
NO, REALLY.
WAIT FOR IT...
WHAT THE **HELL** IS HAPPENING?!!
DON'T WORRY. SHE STOPS AFTER A FEW HOURS.
USUALLY...
WAHHHH!!

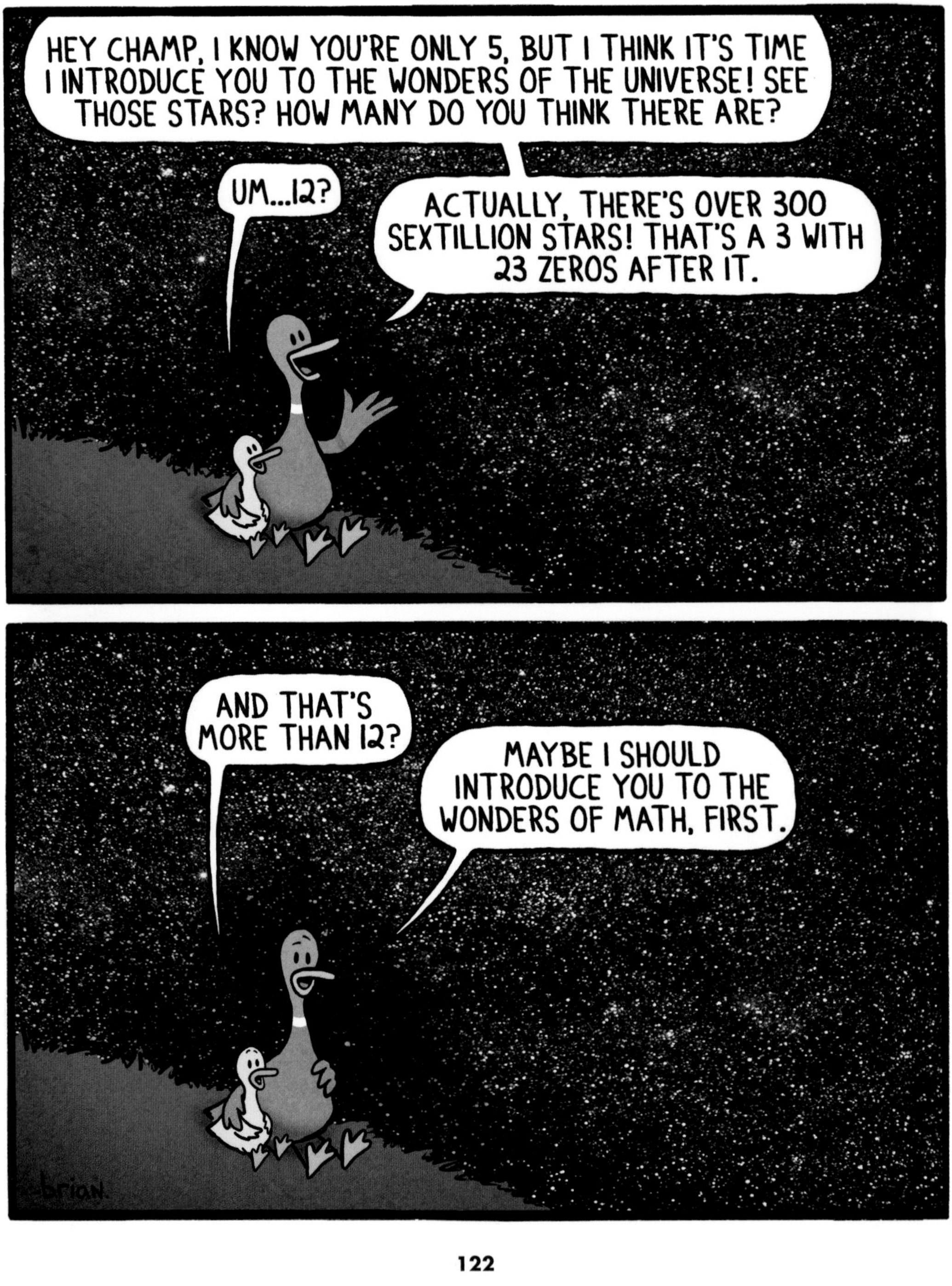
HEY CHAMP, I KNOW YOU'RE ONLY 5, BUT I THINK IT'S TIME I INTRODUCE YOU TO THE WONDERS OF THE UNIVERSE! SEE THOSE STARS? HOW MANY DO YOU THINK THERE ARE?
UM...12?
ACTUALLY, THERE'S OVER 300 SEXTILLION STARS! THAT'S A 3 WITH 23 ZEROS AFTER IT.
AND THAT'S MORE THAN 12?
MAYBE I SHOULD INTRODUCE YOU TO THE WONDERS OF MATH, FIRST.
brian.

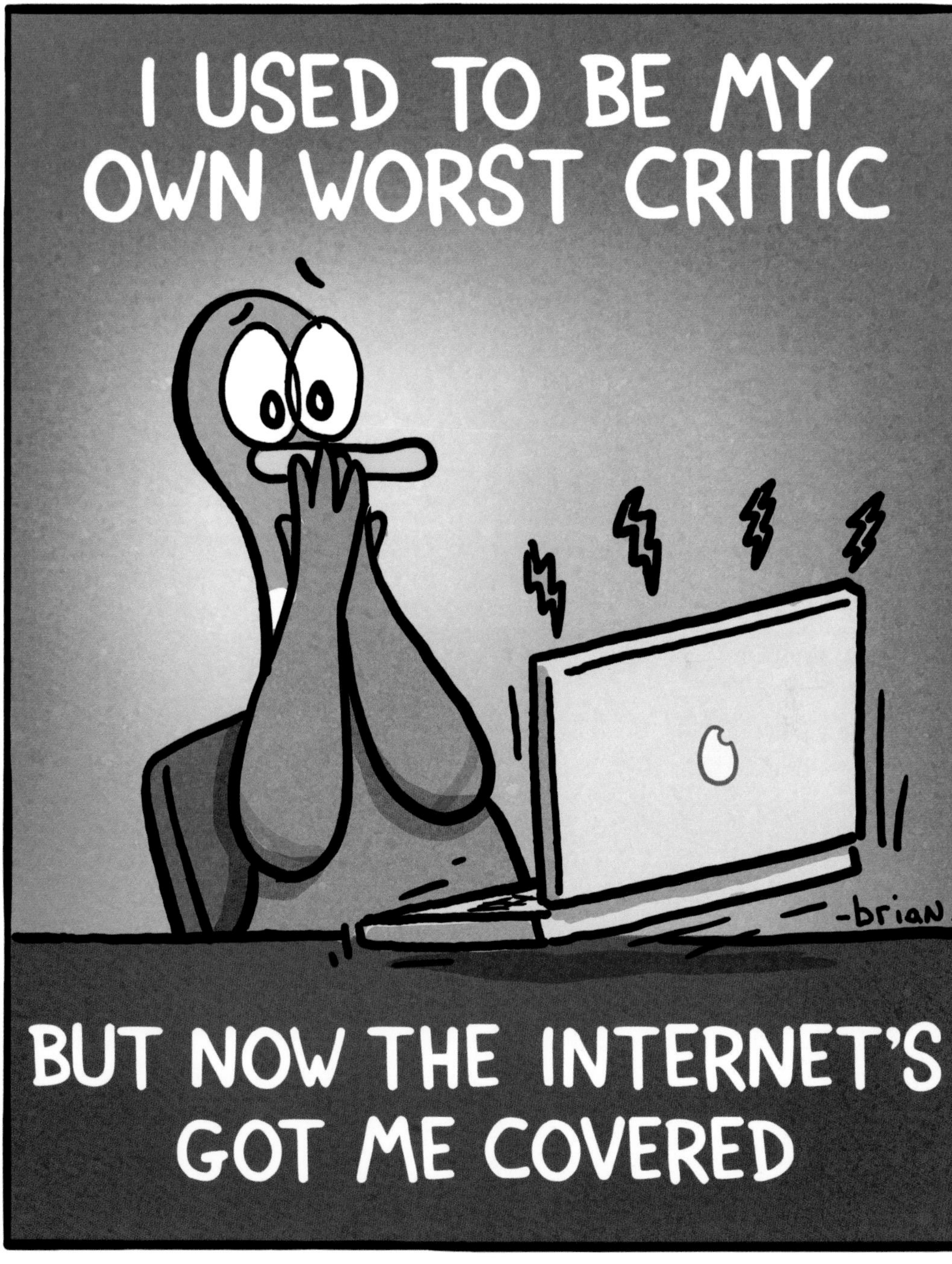
I USED TO BE MY OWN WORST CRITIC
-brian.
BUT NOW THE INTERNET'S GOT ME COVERED

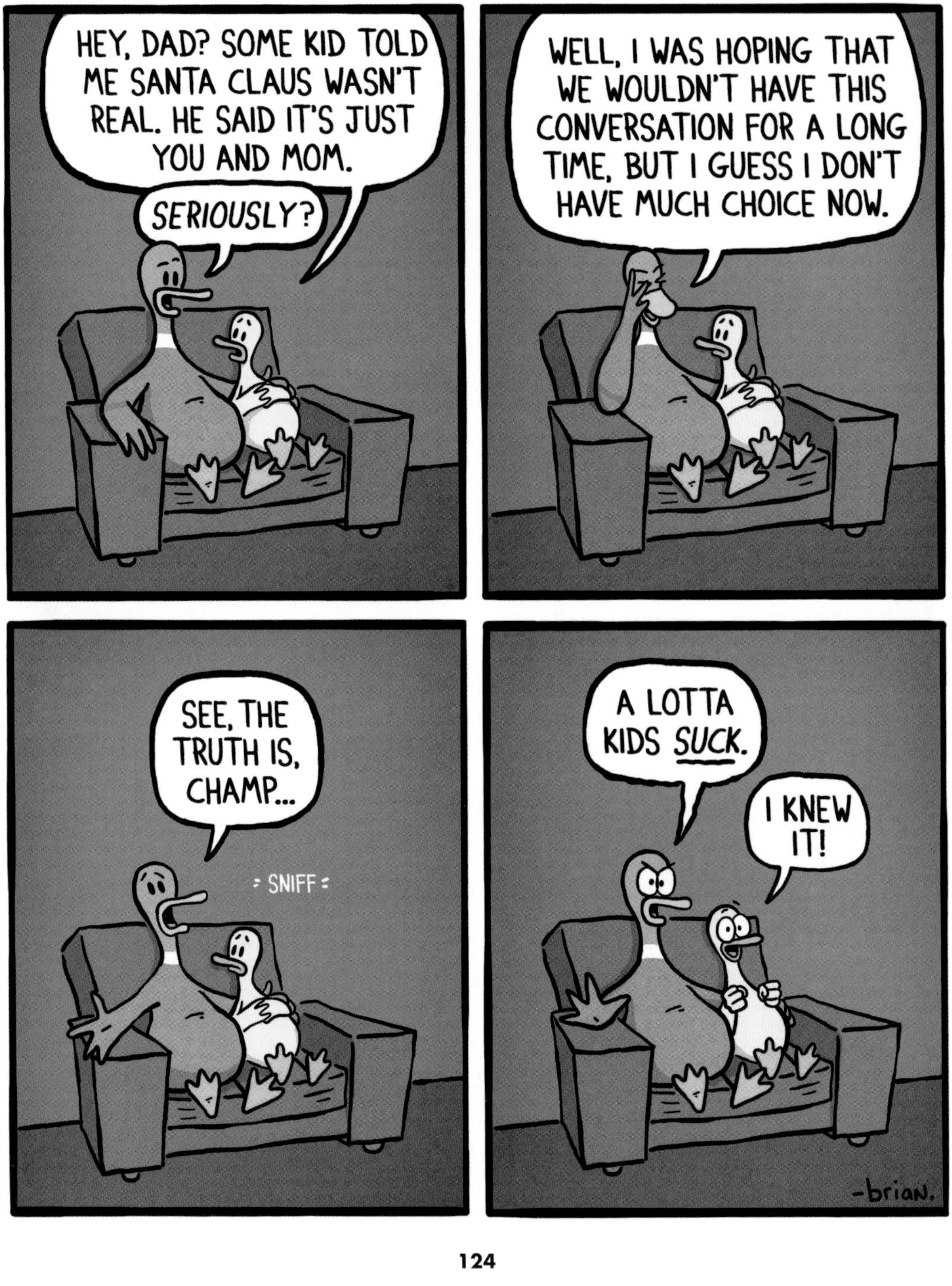
HEY, DAD? SOME KID TOLD ME SANTA CLAUS WASN'T REAL. HE SAID IT'S JUST YOU AND MOM.
SERIOUSLY?
WELL, I WAS HOPING THAT WE WOULDN'T HAVE THIS CONVERSATION FOR A LONG TIME, BUT I GUESS I DON'T HAVE MUCH CHOICE NOW.
SEE, THE TRUTH IS, CHAMP...
SNIFF
A LOTTA KIDS SUCK.
I KNEW IT!
-brian.

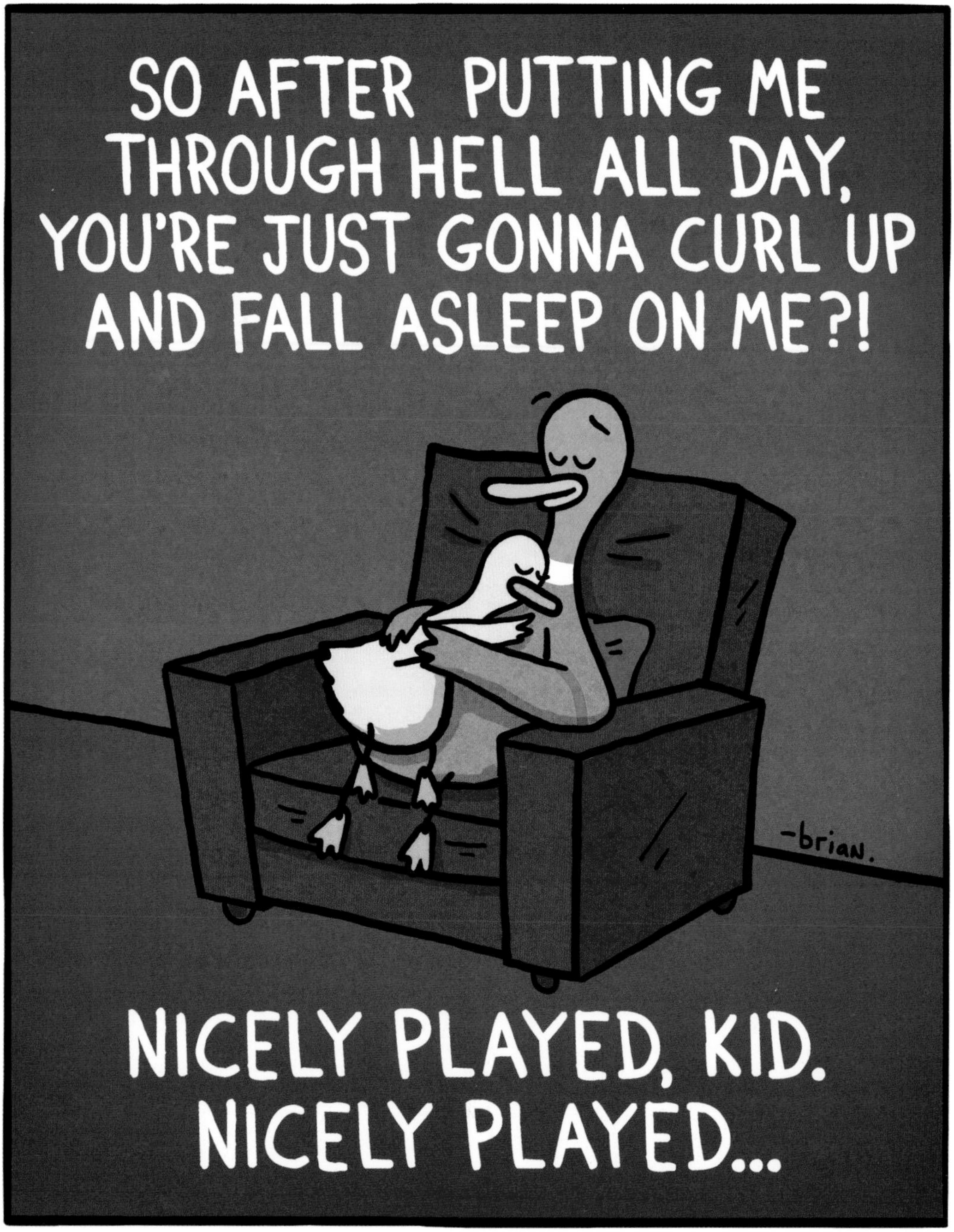
SO AFTER PUTTING ME THROUGH HELL ALL DAY, YOU'RE JUST GONNA CURL UP AND FALL ASLEEP ON ME?!
-brian.
NICELY PLAYED, KID. NICELY PLAYED...

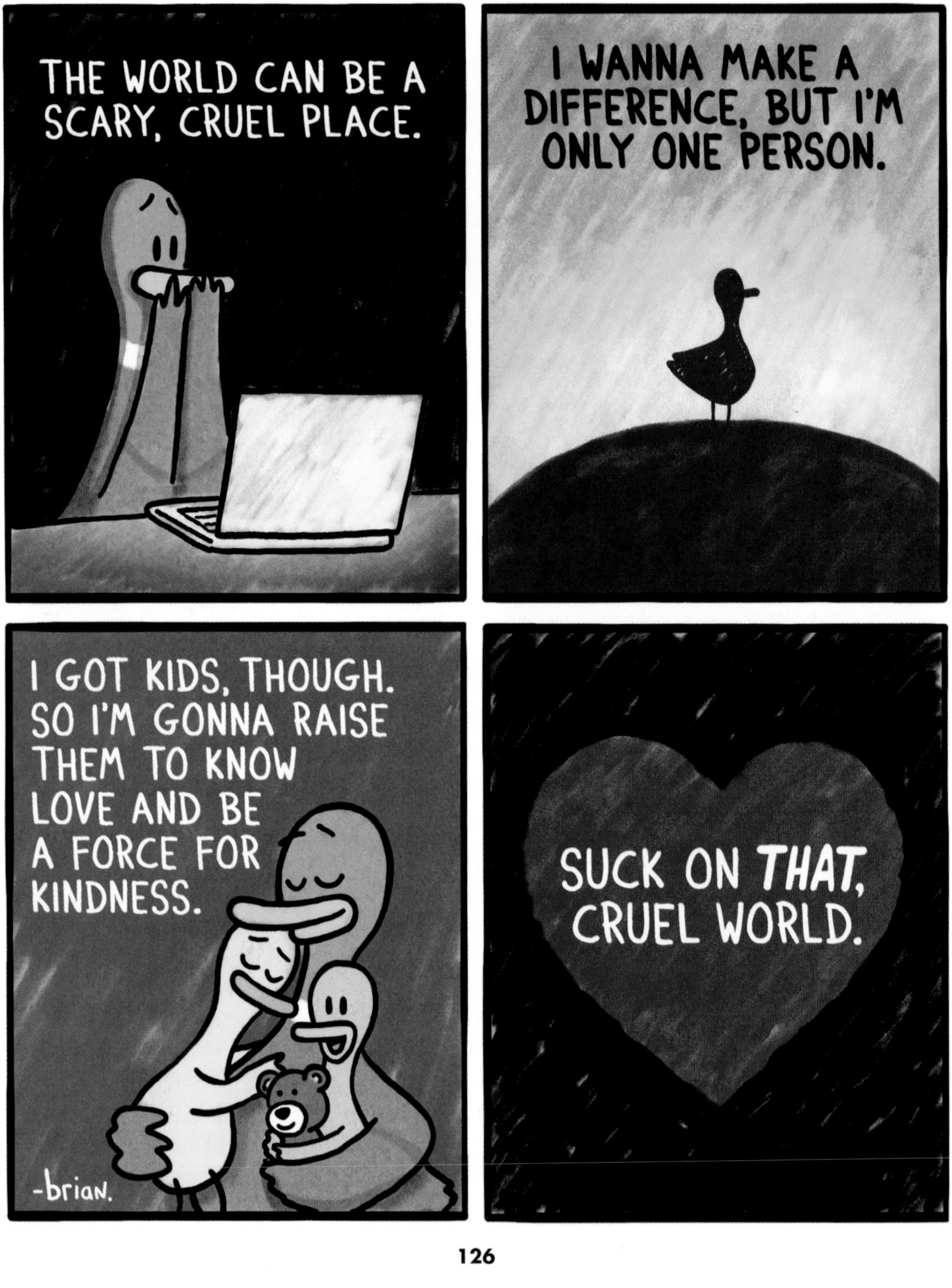
THE WORLD CAN BE A SCARY, CRUEL PLACE.
I WANNA MAKE A DIFFERENCE, BUT I'M ONLY ONE PERSON.
I GOT KIDS, THOUGH. SO I'M GONNA RAISE THEM TO KNOW LOVE AND BE A FORCE FOR KINDNESS.
-brian.
SUCK ON *THAT*, CRUEL WORLD.